D0848483

Speaking of Universities

Speaking of Universities

STEFAN COLLINI

VERSO
London • New York

First published by Verso 2017
© Stefan Collini 2017

1 3 5 7 9 10 8 6 4 2

Verso
UK: 6 Meard Street, London W1F 0EG
US: 20 Jay Street, Suite 1010, Brooklyn, NY 11201
versobooks.com

Verso is the imprint of New Left Books

ISBN-13: 978-1-78663-139-8
ISBN-13: 978-1-78663-140-4 (US EBK)
ISBN-13: 978-1-78663-141-1 (UK EBK)

British Library Cataloguing in Publication Data
A catalogue record for this book is available from the British Library

Library of Congress Cataloging-in-Publication Data
A catalog record for this book is available from the Library of Congress

Typeset in Sabon by MJ&N Gavan, Truro, Cornwall
Printed in Great Britain by CPI Group (UK) Ltd, Croydon CR0 4YY

The invasion of one's mind by ready-made phrases ... can only be prevented if one is constantly on guard against them, and every such phrase anaesthetizes a portion of one's brain.

George Orwell, 'Politics and the English Language' (1946)

If we take the widest and wisest view of a Cause, there is no such thing as a Lost Cause because there is no such thing as a Gained Cause. We fight for lost causes because we know that our defeat and dismay may be the preface to our successors' victory, though that victory itself will be temporary; we fight rather to keep something alive than in the expectation that anything will triumph.

T. S. Eliot, 'Francis Herbert Bradley' (1927)

Contents

Hand-wringing for Beginners

There is a lot of talk about universities these days, not least because there are now a lot of universities to talk about. In recent decades there has been an immense global surge in the numbers both of universities and of students, an expansion that, in purely numerical terms, quite dwarfs anything that has happened in the previous eight centuries or so during which versions of this curious institution have existed. Although this growth has taken place across developed and developing countries alike, the numbers are, as ever, most stunning in China, where it is claimed that over 1,200 universities and colleges have been established in the last twenty years alone. In Britain, the growth of higher education has not quite been on such a dramatic scale, but even so the speed of the changes here should not be underestimated. In 1990 there were forty-six universities in the UK educating approximately 350,000 students. Twenty-six years later, following the upgrading of the former polytechnics and the founding of a whole raft of new universities, often based on an earlier college of higher education, there are now more than 140 universities (or university-level institutions) with over two million students.

However, the changes have not been merely quantitative: the whole ecology of higher education in Britain has been transformed within the past generation. Most of the procedures governing funding, assessment, 'quality control', 'impact' and so on that now occupy the greater part of the working time of academics were unknown before the mid-1980s. Forms of governance have changed no less significantly, even if these changes have been much less noticed: vestiges of academic self-government have largely been removed and replaced by the top-down control of a 'senior management team' implementing the latest government directives. The range of subjects that can now be studied for a degree has hugely increased. New technologies promise to alter the most basic mechanics of the teaching process. Overseas students constitute an ever-higher proportion of the student body (over a third in some institutions). Globalization has been understood to require the setting up of campuses of British universities in other countries or the founding of partnerships with overseas institutions. And all of this is quite apart from the radical reshaping since 2012 of the funding system in England and Wales, though not Scotland, whereby direct public support of teaching in higher education has been replaced by a system of high fees supported by income-contingent loans, along with other market-oriented changes such as the encouragement of 'private providers', including both for-profit and not-for-profit institutions.

But although all of these changes mean that there is lots to talk about, there is widespread uncertainty about the premises and terms of discussion. The pace and scale of change have produced a sense of disorientation, an uneasy feeling that, as a society, we may be losing our once-familiar understanding of the nature and role of universities yet we have not so far replaced it with anything better. The language and categories used in politics and the media when discussing higher education only exacerbate the problem: although such categories may well be appropriate to talking about, say, the economics of an animal-feed processing plant, it is hard to rid ourselves of the suspicion that they may not provide an altogether adequate model for talking about universities. Of course, there are those who will say that it doesn't really matter how we 'talk about' universities, since it's all just talk. Such people can always produce from their pockets a massive solid lump of stuff called 'reality', and they will proudly demonstrate how talk simply bounces off it like raindrops off a bomb-shelter. What matters, they announce with their characteristic mixture of aggression and self-satisfaction, is whether the policies work. All this talk, especially the more high-toned versions of it, is simply waffle.

As false beliefs go, this takes some beating. It would not require any particularly fancy philosophical footwork to establish that our experience of the world is in part constituted by the categories we use. Words are not a kind of decorative wrapping paper in which meaning is delivered, with the implication that they could be stripped away, or others used in their stead, without making any difference to the 'real' content. Concepts colonize our minds and we become used to thinking about ourselves and our world in their terms; our actions are only identifiable as this action rather than that action in terms of the language in which we describe them. In the swirling currents of assertion and assumption that make up our public discourse at any time, there are always a large number of vulgar errors passing themselves off as truisms, but the belief that words are just the decorative wrapping paper round experience is both one of the easiest to refute and one of the hardest to dislodge.

If you really believe that it doesn't matter in the least how we talk about universities, then you probably aren't reading this book in the first place – or, if you are, you will soon give up in irritation. But before you go, I would just like to ask you how you would decide any of the pressing policy questions about universities – what *you* might call undeniable 'real world' issues such as how to pay for them or how many people to admit to them or what to study in them and so on – without using *some* description of what they are like and what they do and what they are for. And if you reply that the answers to those questions are obvious and anyway are practical matters, not requiring any fancy ideas or special vocabulary, then I'd like to ask you where you think the terms in which you would frame your answers come from, because I could quickly show you that they were mostly not the descriptions used even a generation ago, let alone any further back in history. Our concepts and our language have their own histories, and the process by which one pattern of using them comes to be dominant at any given time is something that intellectual historians can chart with considerable precision. There is nothing 'natural' or given about thinking of universities in terms of, say, 'social mobility' or 'wealth-creation' any more than there was about thinking of them in terms of 'character-formation' or 'the propagation of God's word'.

So it most certainly does matter how we talk about these things. It is, of course, easy for any set of critical reflections to be stigmatized as mere 'hand-wringing' – as bemoaning the fallen state of the times or ineffectually lamenting that the world is not a more agreeable place – but on this topic at this time that charge does seem particularly wide of the mark. We need to be able to articulate an understanding of what universities are *for* that is adequate to our time if we are to be able to decide what to do. This does not mean being committed to resisting change or to clinging to how things were done the day before yesterday, still less to denying the fundamental forces in the world that are bound to affect the character and functioning of universities. Quite the contrary, in fact. If things were not changing so quickly, we might manage to hobble along leaving our working assumptions implicit, not needing to be exposed, scrutinized and developed. But we're most emphatically not in that position. We simply have to talk about these general matters because the changes we are experiencing are so extensive and so fundamental that we cannot any longer feel confident that we have any working assumptions that are widely agreed. To adapt the title of a recently successful novel and film: *We Need To Talk About Universities*.

This book is clearly in some sense a continuation of, or sequel to, *What Are Universities For?*, which was published in 2012. Although it will be evident that both books are informed by the same perspective and are campaigning against a sustained nexus of misconceptions, all the pieces re-worked in this book were written after the completion of its predecessor and are thus addressed to somewhat different circumstances; they do not merely repeat the case made there. As the title of this Introduction is intended (with due irony) to suggest, the present book offers a compendium of arguments, expressed in various literary forms, in the hope that readers will find them usable both for clarifying

4

their own minds and for deploying in discussion with others. For these reasons, it has seemed worth trying to preserve at least some of the variety of form that might be pertinent to different kinds of public discussion of this topic, even at the expense of occasional repetition of the main points. Where the date or occasion of a chapter's first appearance is integral to its meaning, I briefly indicate this, and then in the Acknowledgements I provide full details of the occasions for which earlier versions of these chapters were first written. Only the three chapters in Part II (and some parts of the Appendix) have been published before, mostly in somewhat shortened forms; the remaining eight chapters have not previously appeared in print in any form.

Inevitably, some of what I have said in these more recent contributions has been affected by the response to *What Are Universities For?* That the book should have provoked favourable, indeed enthusiastic, reviews, letters and other responses from a substantial number of academics in British universities was perhaps not entirely surprising (and not necessarily attributable to any merits on its part). The book does, after all, attempt to articulate a set of assumptions about universities that are, or were, broadly familiar, as well as addressing a range of anxieties that are widespread in such settings. But I was particularly struck by the positive responses I received from three other groups.

The first were students, both undergraduate and postgraduate. Students, whose direct relation with their university is more short-lived than that of most academics, have many other demands on their attention during that short period and often prefer to ignore these larger questions while they pursue a good degree or a good job or a good time. Even those who do get engaged by questions arising from contemporary higher education policy can sometimes be impatient with the kind of extended reflection that doesn't seem to issue in immediately effective action. But I have been impressed, and encouraged, by the range and vitality of the student responses I have encountered, not least by the often-voiced conviction that our society needs to articulate a more inspiring sense of the larger purpose of education than is represented by graphs of post-degree earnings.

The second group was made up of general readers and members of audiences who were not university teachers or students (and had, it emerged in many cases, not themselves been to university), but who simply cared about the future of these institutions, quite often because they wanted their children to enjoy what they still hoped would be general educational as well as career benefits. I have been struck by how many of these people have an intuitive sense that university policy may have taken a wrong turn in recent years, with the result that something they once valued or esteemed about such institutions, even if from afar, might now be jeopardized.

And the third group were readers from continental Europe, some of them academics or academic administrators, but also including journalists and other commentators. Of all the positive responses, this was the one I had least anticipated, but after a number of visits to speak in various European countries some of the reasons for it became more obvious. Very often my interlocutors and audiences were people who had admired the British university system, but who could see that it was now being treated as the guinea pig in a series of market-fundamentalist experiments. Most northern European countries still maintain a publicly supported system of higher education where, whatever the precise financial arrangements, universities are regarded as a public good, even in some countries as the bearers of civic or republican values. Many European colleagues were clearly worried that business-driven governments might in the future try to impose policies modelled along the new British lines in their own countries; therefore, furnishing themselves with an array of considered arguments against such marketization could seem both prudent and relatively urgent.

Part of what was refreshing about the responses of these three groups was their freedom from two sets of attitudes that are depressingly familiar in Britain. The first is a rather resentful touchiness that damns any confident expression of intellectual seriousness as 'elitist', 'condescending', 'superior', 'lofty' and so on. Complicated forms of reverse snobbery may be at work here. There have been moments when it seemed that the only information people needed to make up their minds about what I must be saying was that I was a 'professor' and I taught at 'Cambridge', two culturally loaded markers from which the patronizing or condescending character of my views could readily be deduced. Online message threads, following an article or review, seem to have licensed the expression of such formulaic resentments in a particularly venomous form.

The second familiar attitude, mentioned earlier, is that of those who pride themselves on their 'realism' and are correspondingly dismissive of 'utopianism' or any alleged failure to understand 'how the world really works'. This attitude is particularly found among some of those who have navigated a career path through quangos and the higher levels of university administration. More than once I have been reminded of Thorstein Veblen's sarcastic little riff, now a century old (I quote it in full in Chapter 3, below), on the types who tended to become university leaders in the United States at the time: 'a plausible speaker with a large gift of assurance, ... some urbane pillar of society, some astute veteran of the scientific *demi-monde* will meet all reasonable requirements'. There are, needless to say, some people of outstanding quality and integrity in such senior positions, attempting to do a difficult job as well as possible in unfavourable circumstances. But looking round the room at any meeting of representatives of universities convened for the purpose of putting a case to ministers and their officials or making up a panel at a policy-oriented event, it is usually impossible not to recognize 'some astute veteran of the scientific *demi-monde*'. The response of such individuals to my book and related writings on universities has essentially consisted of patting me on the head and telling me to run along now: serious matters should be left to the grown-ups.

In addition to reviews, an author is bound to encounter a series of more informal or conversational reactions to what he or she has written (the ready availability of an academic's email address has perhaps increased the volume of such communications). Apart from various kinds of heartening response, I have been struck by two themes in these comments. The first involved people in asserting that although no doubt what I said was true, the fact was that it wouldn't make any difference, that it was just so much spitting into the wind (or some less genteel version of that phrase). The individuals who put some version of that view to me did not, unlike the self-satisfied 'realists' I mentioned earlier, appear to take any pleasure from this fact – indeed, they appeared dejected and resigned. But clearly there are quite a few people, both within British universities and in society more generally, who feel that it is now too late. The changes pushed through in recent years, it is claimed, have a bullish and triumphant political ideology behind them which is now so powerful that nothing can be done to turn back the tide. Obviously, the fact of my having written extended criticisms of these changes indicates that I do not wholly agree with this pessimistic diagnosis, but I have to acknowledge that it has a good deal of empirical evidence on its side, and in my darker moments I don't find it easy to know what any light at the end of the political tunnel would even look like, let alone feel any confidence that I have spotted it.

And the second set of responses – by which I admit I was, perhaps naively, rather shocked – consisted in the interlocutor or correspondent telling me that although they entirely agreed with what I had said or written, they did not feel that they could risk saying these things in this way in their own university. Is this paranoia or some other form of exaggeration on their part, or have things come to such a sad pass in their institutions? I had no way of telling in these particular cases, but such comments have reinforced my conviction that the largely obvious truths which I have attempted to set out need to be repeated – repeated in different settings, repeated in different forms, but repeated sufficiently often that they cease to seem eccentric or purely personal, and that they instead come to take on at least some of that air of familiarity that has been acquired by the officially endorsed commonplaces they seek to challenge.

And then there are the responses that only reach one at third hand or by hearsay – such as the reported embarrassment at having a colleague who seems to be kicking up a fuss, or the anxiety that such polemics risk antagonizing ministers and their officials and thus jeopardizing a future funding settlement. I would be sorry to think that universities, of all places, encouraged such cowed or craven attitudes, but in any case such responses seem to me to exaggerate the amount of attention likely to be accorded any piece of writing by an ordinary academic, as well as, I would like to believe, underestimating the seriousness of purpose and the intellectual openness of the best politicians and civil servants. A related response, which I think is usually expressed in good faith and which I take more seriously, is that, when discussing important public matters, lively engaged writing should be avoided since it can all too easily misfire. In some cases, it is suggested, this may be because any kind of humour or wit risks alienating rather than persuading, especially if it flirts with satire or irony. In other cases, it is argued that very close attention to the language of a policy proposal or other official document runs the danger of seeming both nit-picking and superior, with the critic simply scoring a number of cheap victories at the expense of writing that made no claim to literary polish in the first place. And, more generally, these views are often rolled up into an overarching disapproval of writing that seems to be 'too critical' or 'too adversarial': such writing, it is said (invoking a term favoured by grave persons who are confident of their own judiciousness), is 'not helpful'.

I take this view, or cluster of views, seriously because any reflections on the ways in which particular literary tactics do or do not achieve their ends can be valuable, and authors themselves are notoriously bad judges of where their own writing voice may go astray or even be counter-productive. But after a good deal of reflection I have to say that, in its generalized form, this set of objections seems to me to misunderstand the purposes and demands of the genres at issue. The shortest way to make the point is to say that such writing is not *meant* to be 'helpful' – at least, not in the sense of the limited practical suggestion that is made when a committee round a table is trying to improve a particular measure or proposal. I have spent plenty of time in such settings: I understand how a suggestion needs to be couched if it is to get a serious hearing there, but I also know how limited is the range of considerations that are felt to be 'relevant' or 'constructive' in such circumstances. Criticism, fundamental criticism, is doing something different. Sometimes such criticism may be saying: 'The present terms of the discussion systematically exclude what, from another point of view, would be seen as fundamental.' There are times when criticism needs to be swingeing if such criticism is to be attended to at all: in these situations, trying in the approved way to be 'helpful' will simply allow the existing consensus to deceive itself that it has considered relevant objections and decided against them – this is the lie at the heart of so many exercises in 'consultation'.

But, more pertinently still, none of the writing at issue here has taken the form of a memo or a policy statement to be circulated to members of a committee. We are talking, rather, about forms of journalism or other kinds of writing and speaking addressed to diverse audiences. Such writing needs to attract and hold the interest of its intended readers, and moments of wit or rhetorical invention can, when properly handled, be very valuable for that purpose (whether I have managed to do that successfully or not is another question). A wholly impersonal, impeccably judicious distillation of a position may be admirable from some points of view, but will it have achieved its ends if no one reads it, no one *finishes* it, or indeed if it fails to get published in the first place? Questions of tone and address are, of course, matters of judgement, and any author may get them wrong in particular instances. But we should not be too quick to assume that a certain high-spiritedness is axiomatically out of place in writing about such topics. An 'idea of the university' that can only be expounded in dull prose is failing its topic.

So, much of this book is based on talks, lectures, articles and other interventions that were not always expressed in sober, pin-striped prose. Readers will, as ever, form their own judgement about how interesting or persuasive such writing is. But I hope that they will recognize that some such variety of literary genres and prose voices is both necessary and appropriate where the ambition is to get a wider public to attend to questions which are otherwise in danger of not being attended to or even properly identified. In modern multi-media societies, the received wisdom and its often clichéd forms of expression enjoy huge advantages in public debate. Views and phrases that are so ceaselessly reiterated come to be part of the cultural weather, so 'natural' as almost to escape notice, certainly to escape challenge. This book is intended as a small incitement to focus on what is actually happening and the clichés behind which it hides; an incitement to think again, think more clearly, and then to press for something better.

PART I

ANALYSES

CHAPTER I

What's Happening to Universities?
Historical and Comparative Perspectives

I

Readers will doubtless have noticed how, in the past two or three decades, businesses across the world have been pressured into making themselves look more and more like universities. Companies have been exhorted to abandon commercial competition and to model their behaviour on patterns of scholarly collaboration. Stock-market-listed corporations now have to make returns detailing the intellectual and scholarly value of their products and services. Targets and benchmarks are being replaced by informed judgement; HR divisions are shrinking; and companies are doing less self-advertising and producing fewer glossy brochures. They have also had to adopt a more collegiate and bottom-up form of governance; CEOs are increasingly being replaced by committees drawn from the professoriate, and places on major companies' Boards of Directors have been reserved for experienced Senior Lecturers in Medieval History.

At first sight, it may seem obvious why the changes that are actually taking place are the exact reverse of those I have just fancifully sketched. It has become almost commonplace to observe how universities are now subject to 'incessant hectoring' for their failure to be more like businesses. But it is worth reminding ourselves that capitalism had, in some form, been around a long time before the recent epidemic of business-envy. We should not fall into ahistorical essentializing where either capitalism or universities are concerned – and there is more to be said about the changes over time in both – but in some form they had managed to coexist for a century or more without universities being required to adopt the goals, structures or procedures of corporations, or at least of some business-school model of how corporations should be run. Indeed, for about 150 years after universities started to assume something like their modern form in the early nineteenth century, the fact that they represented in some sense an alternative ethic or antidote to the commercial world was precisely one of the justifications for their existence. This was a view shared even by those who have retrospectively been cited as the champions of applied science, such as T.H. Huxley, who declared in 1894: 'The primary business of universities has to do merely with pure knowledge and pure art – independent of all application to practice; with the advancement of culture and not with the increase of wealth or commodities.' This conception was endorsed by one of the iconic leaders of that commercial world, Joseph Chamberlain, Mayor of Birmingham as well as, later, a cabinet minister, who greeted the establishment in his fiefdom of what was to become the University of Birmingham by saying: 'To place a university in the middle of a great industrial and manufacturing population is to do something to leaven the whole mass with higher aims and higher intellectual ambitions than would otherwise be possible to people engaged entirely in trading and commercial pursuits.' And something similar was reasserted in the most downright terms by Ernest Rutherford, the Nobel-winning 'father of nuclear physics', when he warned the University of Bristol in 1927 that he 'would view as an unmitigated disaster the utilization of university laboratories for research bearing on industry'.

I cite those views precisely because they sound so unimaginably distant from the assumptions about relations between universities and the economy that we increasingly take for granted, though they were a strong, perhaps even the dominant, strain in thinking about universities well into the second half of the twentieth century, especially in Britain and British-influenced parts of the world. But they were never, of course, the only strain even there, for versions of the conflict between those asserting priority for practical concerns and those claiming to represent non-instrumental values have a very long history. The fact is that what societies have wanted from their universities has been historically variable, internally contradictory, and only ever partly attainable. We should certainly begin by recognizing that universities have always in part served practical ends and have always helped to prepare their graduates for employment in later life. Once upon a time their primary role was to teach true religion and provide learned men for the church; once upon another time it was to inculcate virtue or judgement or good manners or any of the other supposed attributes of a gentleman; once upon yet another time it was to select, equip and mould those who were to fill leading positions in state, empire or society; and often it was as much to keep the young out of mischief as to keep alive the flame of learning. What, if anything, therefore, is distinctive about the changes of the last two or three decades? Are critics exaggerating and are the changes just one more mutation in the continuing story of how universities necessarily adapt to serve society's changing needs, or is there something distinctive going on that may do longer-term damage than we currently realize? Perhaps this is where historical and comparative perspectives may help. But first I must warn readers that this chapter contains material of an ethically explicit nature. For, if we confine ourselves to the language of the company report, with its relentlessly upbeat account of productivity, income streams, commercial partnerships and international ventures, then we shall have no way to distinguish the activities of universities from those of the business corporations in whose image they are being remade.

II

From the early nineteenth century onwards, it was the Humboldtian ideal that did most to shape universities over the next 150 years. This emphasized the pursuit and transmission of knowledge and its elaboration into *Wissenschaft*: the professional autonomy of the scholar was essential to this model, and teaching was often conceived as a form of apprenticeship. But alongside various forms of preparation for employment, two further ideals complicated this conception of the university as the protected home of free enquiry. The collegiate ideal focused on close student–teacher relations in a residential setting with character-formation as the aim, whether through inspirational teaching, athletic endeavour or the contagion of one's peers. And the civic ideal prioritized the making of citizens, the inculcation of a shared ethic, whether elite or republican or democratic, that involved developing talents and forms of expertise that were to help define and strengthen the identity of the polity. Most of the universities of continental Europe involved some mixture of the Humboldtian and civic ideals; the English tradition, deriving from Oxbridge, though not the distinctive Scottish tradition, tended to foreground the collegiate ideal, while different types of institution in the US managed to accommodate all three in various proportions.

But at the heart of the implicit contract between university and society in all these places was an acceptance that the distinctive value of the higher learning lay in its cultivation of those forms of scholarship, science and culture whose relation to the instrumental and mundane concerns of practical life was indirect and long term, even at times downright antagonistic. It also entailed granting those who pursued such enquiries a degree of professional autonomy, a convention made to seem natural both by the strictly elite character of higher education until the later decades of the twentieth century and by the persistence of associated forms of cultural and social deference.

The decades after 1945 saw expansion in all systems of higher education, led by the US, but the growth in numbers did not involve fundamental changes to either the conception or the structure of universities. If anything, the reverse was true, as universities that had been founded to pioneer a new model – whether of close engagement with local industry, or of non-departmental forms of interdisciplinarity – increasingly came to resemble the dominant models. In Britain and elsewhere in the English-speaking world they were to a considerable extent self-governing; faculty senates were not merely decorative bodies; the humanities and the pure sciences preponderated and set the intellectual tone; and at undergraduate level (there were still relatively few postgraduates) they were highly selective in entry, residential by design, and usually well equipped with sports facilities. The new universities of the 1960s, in both Britain and elsewhere, may have aspired to draw up 'a new map of learning', but in practice they enabled a larger slice of the children of the middle class, especially the daughters, to attend what were fundamentally quite traditional institutions. It would be an oversimplification, but perhaps a helpful one, to say that in their governance, their intellectual character, and their relations with their host societies, universities in the 1970s were probably closer to those of fifty or even seventy years earlier than to those of thirty or forty years later.

The dramatic changes that have occurred in those last few decades, notably in Britain, have called into question many of the assumptions that had sustained universities over the previous century or more. One of the things most forcibly borne in on me by recent discussions with those involved in debates about higher education in other countries has been the way that many of these people, as I remarked in the Introduction above, have been watching developments in Britain with some mixture of sadness and trepidation: sadness because it was a university system that they once very much admired, and trepidation because they sense that many of the changes that have been imposed on universities in Britain may soon be coming their way, especially in other centralized European systems, but also in more plural and diverse systems elsewhere in the world.

In part, this is because there is an element of copy-catting as some governments or university administrations adopt measures from other countries that they believe would play with advantage in their own circumstances. But when we look more closely we can see that the patterns are sufficiently marked, and sufficiently in synch with similar changes in other areas of society, to suggest that what we are witnessing here is not simply a matter of the policies or politics of a group currently in power in any of these countries, but the working out of certain longer-term social and economic changes. So, largely setting cultural specificity aside, let me simply summarize a story that is now being told, in pretty much these terms, in many of the so-called developed societies of the world. As will be immediately apparent, this story applies most obviously to the experiences of universities in the United States and Britain, but since for much of the relevant period they have been the dominant or leading models that is only to be expected.

So here is the best version of this story about the recent history of universities. *The years from 1945 to the mid-1970s were years of expansion in all developed societies, what the French call* les trente glorieuses, *three decades of recovery and prosperity. As part of this general growth, higher education and research grew at an unprecedented rate. Numbers expanded everywhere, nowhere more so than in the US, partly prompted by the GI Bill in the first instance but fed by the promise of social mobility for millions who were among the first members of their families ever to experience higher education. Moreover, governments everywhere, again led by the US, poured money into scientific research in ways that increased the size and expanded the role of universities in general. During these years, universities retained much of the status and autonomy that they had built up during the century or more when they were much smaller and much more intimately bound up with the dominant elites; from the late nineteenth through to the mid-twentieth centuries, their rather more limited functions had been accorded a broadly consensual respect, but for the most part they had played only a minor role in their societies and economies, usually well out of the public eye. From the 1940s, however, they were increasingly the object both of government policies and of public attention. But although their scale and their visibility changed, their fundamental character changed rather little. Academic faculty still by and large set the tone of their institutions; the humani-*

ties and the pure sciences were still the most prestigious and institutionally dominant disciplines; and society was still respectful of universities as one of the chief homes of a traditionally conceived 'culture', which it was the aspiration of the historically less privileged classes to acquire. Expansion began to subject all these features of universities to pressure, but economic prosperity and a major growth of public funding in Europe, or a mix of federal and foundation funding in the US, meant that hard choices among the various functions of universities could, for now, be glossed over.

But this, so the story goes, *was only ever a temporary and unstable equilibrium. Universities were living on borrowed cultural capital as well as a soon-to-be-reduced flow of actual capital. As developed societies, led by the US, moved from elite to mass higher education, as traditional deference to or regard for elite culture waned, as the demand for professional training and for various vocational and applied sciences increased, and as these societies replaced the ideal of professional autonomy with that of public accountability, so, it was held, universities needed to change. And from the 1980s onwards they did change, despite the protests of academics who had mistaken the contingent good fortune of the decades after 1945 for the timeless essence of universities. In the past thirty years – which critics are prone to think of as* les trente inglorieuses *– universities have begun to modernize. Their primary role as engines of economic growth is coming to be acknowledged, and their activities are becoming more closely aligned with the needs of industry, finance and commerce. Their financing is falling into line with the principles of a market economy, with debt-conscious students seeking value for money and research-users commissioning and paying for research projects. Customer satisfaction is coming to be recognized as the true test of their success in a competitive marketplace. Management has replaced administration, with a senior management team at the apex of an executive structure and all institutions now having a proper business plan. And internally, professional schools and* *vocational and biomedical disciplines are coming to have a preponderant weight commensurate with their position as the chief income-generating programmes.*

These are good and necessary adaptations to the changed world of modern societies competing in a global economy, says the story, *but the changes have not gone far enough. As with all other large retail enterprises, universities have to price their goods differentially according to demand, so there needs to be more variation of price among universities and among courses. Proper key performance indicators need to be used systematically throughout an organization to measure achievement and weed out failure. Commercial corporations need to have a larger say in what is taught, what is researched, and how these services are delivered. Tenure is an obstacle to rational management decisions about labour mobility and needs to be removed. And new technology and more intensive use of time and plant need to be embraced to accelerate throughput and reduce costs. Compared with universities of thirty years ago, many current institutions have changed almost out of recognition; but compared to the benchmark of a rigorous McKinsey organizational assessment, they are badly underperforming, carrying excessive fixed costs and an inflexible labour market, wedded to an outdated collective ethos, poor at marketing their services, and slow to adapt to technological change. More particularly, there are still large elements within universities, especially the tenured academics and especially in the humanities, who resist these changes and cling to some nostalgic ideal of the university which only ever partially suited the social conditions of the day before yesterday. Their criticism of any of these changes in the name of some 'idea of the university' must be exposed, and disregarded, as the self-interested whingeing of a featherbedded elite who simply fail to understand, or want to deny, the nature and pace of social and economic change. In short, what is needed is (in the idiom of debased management-speak that is sweeping all before it) more strategic dynamism.*

So, that's the story – or at least *a* story. It is an influential story at present, and, what's more, one with just enough evidence behind it to make it seem plausible. After all, *some* of what it says about the history of universities in their relations to their host societies since 1945 is true. But it is worth making three immediate observations. The first is that, like all quasi-determinist theories of history, this story is in a tangle about agency. Acknowledging and adapting to the specified social changes is regarded as a freely chosen rational action, but attempting in some way to 'resist' them is represented as self-defeating and ultimately impossible. Second, it assumes that changes in society will simply be reproduced in the same form in universities, rather than recognizing that the relationship will necessarily be more dialectical than that. And third, this story offers no account of what might be distinctive about universities and what they do. A university is regarded as a business like any other and so subject to the same laws which govern change in all businesses.

So, how might those of us who do not find this story totally compelling go about challenging it? Readers will have noticed that as I narrated this brief version of the story I increasingly employed the vocabulary of the business consultants, the vocabulary which has more and more coloured discussion of this and other topics in politics and the media. Clearly, one major step we might take towards telling a more adequate story would be to use a vocabulary appropriate to the activities being discussed. That would, in turn, involve us in some reflection about what it is that distinguishes the university from other social institutions. And, as always, one way to counter bad, selective and tendentious history is to write better, more extended, and more analytical history. This chapter attempts to illustrate, necessarily very briefly, some of the benefits of pursuing all three of these strategies, and it may be that one thing I can do here is to give some sense of how these general issues have played out recently in public debate and policy in Britain. For those in other countries, this will, at the very least, serve the same function as the 'coming attractions' trailers do in the cinema, since these are all issues that will soon be coming to a university near you, albeit with subtitles.

But before I go any further, let me just try to forestall three possible misunderstandings. First, I am not, either here or in my earlier book, proposing some ideal or essence, some way of distinguishing supposedly 'real' universities from institutions that do not deserve the name. I am, rather, reflecting on the very variety of types that have grown up across the world, especially in the past two centuries, and on their relations to their host societies. Secondly, therefore, I am not proposing some story of decline, some claim that there used to be so-called 'real' universities but now they have been debased or destroyed – not at all. I believe, as I have tried to make clear on many occasions, that the expansion of tertiary-level education has been a great democratic gain and it is one that we should continue to support. And thirdly – and I'd like to be very emphatic about this – I'm not saying that universities don't or shouldn't also serve various practical ends. They always have and, I assume, always will. Once upon a time, as I've already suggested, this meant that they principally prepared a small number of men for service in the church, later for service in the state. Once upon a later time they helped put a little polish and a legible social stamp on a gentleman, and later still they helped inculcate Christian morality and build character. They came to provide a home for the 'higher learning', understood as embracing a chiefly curatorial form of scholarship and, increasingly, original work in the natural sciences. By the first half of the twentieth century, their chief roles were to form an elite for leadership positions in society, to cultivate original scholarship and scientific research, and to provide beacons of culture in their local communities. But they were also constantly being loaded with various practical tasks by national and local political leaders, by captains of industry, by churches, by the military, and by any number of other groups in society who were well funded or well meaning, or, just occasionally, both.

Still, however important or worthwhile these successive external tasks have been, they are not the whole story, and one way to begin to think about the distinctiveness of universities is to say that they provide a partly-protected space within which trying to extend and deepen human understanding has priority over any other purposes in a way which it would be madness – or, at the very least, disruptive – for other institutions in society even to countenance. I'm not suggesting (it should be unnecessary to say) that good thinking is only done, or can only be done, in universities. But universities are, I think, the only *institutions* where pursuing such thinking is in principle not subordinate to any other purpose. As a result, there has been, throughout their long history, a constant tension between the practical ends which society thinks it is furthering by founding or supporting universities, and the ineluctable pull towards open-ended enquiry which comes to shape these institutions over time. The very open-endedness of their principal activities threatens to legitimate forms of enquiry that may run counter to the aims of those who founded or supported them. In fact, one begins to wonder whether societies do not make a kind of Faustian pact when they set up universities: they ask them to serve various practical purposes, but if they are to be given the intellectual freedom necessary to serve those purposes properly, they will always tend to exceed or subvert those purposes.

At the same time, there is a deep tension of a related kind necessarily present in the relations between universities and their parent societies. A set of activities whose informing logic requires open-ended enquiry and the exercise of qualitative judgement is always on a kind of collision course with the tendency of all modern societies to require quantitatively measurable forms of accountability and utilitarian outcomes. To put it in deliberately provocative terms we could say that what is most distinctive, and perhaps distinctively valuable, about what universities do is precisely what cannot be captured by the metrics societies increasingly use to measure value.

III

A common element to many of the politically fashionable ways of making universities 'accountable' is that well-meant attempts to demonstrate the 'relevance' of universities to society's needs can end up being counter-productive. The core of the problem lies in trying to move too quickly from the activities carried on in universities to the benefits society can be seen to derive from them. Versions of this mistake are evident in, for example, the discussion about the relations between universities and local businesses, where it has to be recognized that the most fruitful relationships usually arise when university departments concentrate on doing the kinds of research they are good at rather than attempting to second-guess the current (and perhaps temporary) needs of particular businesses and then shaping their research to meet them. And again, it has frequently been pointed out that the leading employers do not necessarily want graduates who have been given some narrow training which is intended to equip them for one particular kind of job: such jobs and their demands change rapidly and such graduates tend to be too narrow in their perspectives and too rigid in their thinking. A graduate who has profited from an intellectually rigorous and culturally extending education will serve many employers' needs far better in the long run. And, as I have argued elsewhere, something similar applies to the misconceived 'impact' criterion in the recent Research Excellence Framework in Britain: while it is essential that a persuasive case should be made for the benefits society receives from scientific and scholarly research, it has to be recognized that these are, necessarily, indirect and long-term. Making it obligatory to pursue certain narrow forms of economic and social impact in the short term ends up damaging the quality of the research and thereby *reducing* its benefit to society. In all these cases, in other words, society actually obtains the greatest benefits from universities by encouraging them to concentrate on doing the things they are particularly good at, and not by trying to turn them into some form of company laboratory or apprenticeship scheme.

But, by the same token, those in academic life should be cautious before claiming for universities all manner of societal benefits. There is a tendency for defenders of universities to want to present them as contributing to every approved moral or social good, including the promotion of equality of respect, social mobility and general niceness. In addition, there is a tendency to present universities as naturally congruent with all approved liberal values. This seems to me a mistake both as a matter of fact and as a matter of tactics. These days the term 'elitist' is used as a conclusive condemnation of any argument or position, but we should, I think, recognize that universities are in some senses inherently elitist in a restricted sense of that term. It's of course true that intellectual enquiry is in one sense irreducibly democratic – the best arguments and the best evidence are decisive, no matter who puts them forward. But in another sense it is unavoidably selective – not everyone is going to be equally good at conducting the enquiry at the appropriate level. And where these values clash, the priority for universities has to be the extension of understanding, not the furthering of desirable collateral values, however uncomfortable a position this may be. I certainly don't think we should put all our eggs in the basket of furthering social mobility, partly because that is itself a confused notion, which often reduces to the effects of long-term prosperity and the replacement of manual labour by white-collar jobs, but also because that would be to justify the activities of universities entirely in terms of the employment patterns of graduates, precisely the kind of reductive and instrumental assessment that we need to contest more generally. In addition, we should surely cast a very sceptical eye over the assumption that three years of residence among a selected group of one's peers is bound in itself to make us all better people. Universities, it may sadden some people to learn, are not collective forms of relationship counselling or extended versions of the kind of weekend in which paint-balling and white-water rafting release the inner buddy in all of us. And finally, we should also acknowledge that, in practice, contemporary universities do not perform some of their distinctive tasks all that well. Not to acknowledge this would be, yet again, to underestimate the intelligence of the public who are well aware that all is not well with many of our over-crowded, over-regulated institutions of higher education.

We should also not let the current market-fundamentalist rhetoric mislead us into idealizing some imagined version of higher education in the United States. All international comparisons are dominated by the leading American research universities whose supposed success has acquired almost mythic status in the aspirational fantasies of those responsible for universities in other countries. Their example is also supposed to provide a powerful argument for private universities and a market free-for-all. There is much to be said here, including, as Howard Hotson conclusively demonstrated recently, that American higher education is overall hugely wasteful and expensive by comparison to many other national systems. But let me make three further brief points.

First, there is no 'system of higher education' in the US: the ecology is diverse and complex, now encompassing almost 4,000 institutions of different types. The fact that the majority of the most highly ranked universities in the US are private means we risk misperceiving the reality of American higher education. It is sobering to remember that 70 per cent of students in the US attend public institutions, and that this is a higher proportion than in some European countries. The stereotypes are misleading here. Only in Scandinavia does the figure for public higher education reach 100 per cent. Confusingly, the OECD classifies British universities as private – 'government-dependent private universities' is its odd term – and this produces some very curious conclusions. For example, their figures show that the proportion of expenditure on higher education that comes from private sources is higher in the UK than almost anywhere, and considerably higher than in the US, surely an implausible conclusion. This is a classic case of where statistics are only as useful and reliable as the definitions on which they are based.

Second, we are often told that 'needs-blind' admission procedures combined with generous bursaries for applicants from less
privileged backgrounds shows that a high fees system is perfectly
compatible with the demands of social justice and the desire for
social mobility. But the reality is that US higher education is at
least as stratified by social class as it is elsewhere, and that the
huge advantages of the children of the well-off include far higher
chances of admission to the most selective universities. Those
who doubt this should consider just one figure: the *average*
(mean) income of the parents of undergraduates at Harvard is
$450,000 per year.

And third, many of the changes currently underway in higher
education systems in Britain and elsewhere are intended to make
them resemble what are *assumed* to be the characteristics of the
most successful US institutions. However, it is a notable feature
of those institutions that the tenured faculty retain, collectively, a
status and power not now accorded to their peers in any British
university outside Oxbridge, and that, when relatively united, the
faculty in major American universities constitute a force that pres-
idents and trustees have to be wary of, as the contrasting cases of
Larry Summers at Harvard and Teresa Sullivan at Virginia illustrate (the faculty played a major role in getting Summers removed
as president in the first case and in getting Sullivan reinstated after
she had been fired by the trustees in the second). Moreover, the
institutional base of the faculty remains the department, which is
a strikingly durable feature of American research universities and
the natural home to those intellectual standards and protocols the
transmission of which from generation to generation is the very
core of scholarly quality. The abolition of departments, or their
supersession by larger units or by interdisciplinary centres and
programmes, which is so fashionable in Britain and Australasia,
essentially weakens academic autonomy and empowers managers. If the record of the most prestigious American universities
is held to be any guide in these matters, then the maintenance
of strong departments would have to be recognized as the key
to the maintenance of academic reputation.

IV

Thus far, I have been suggesting some of the ways in which historical and comparative perspectives can be drawn upon to help to contest the reigning market-fundamentalist orthodoxy where higher education is concerned. But since I am here indirectly urging some of my fellow academics to stick their heads over the parapet, it may also be appropriate to offer one or two reflections on the kinds of missiles they, we, are likely to encounter. Based on my own experience, I would say that part of what provokes hostility is that for an established academic at a leading university to suggest that some contemporary political or administrative measures frustrate rather than promote the true purposes of universities is to court accusations of being 'superior', or of being dismissive of the concerns of ordinary people, or of appearing to brandish an unmerited sense of entitlement. In some quarters there may be a view that academics would, by and large, do well to keep quiet on these matters, or if they do unwisely raise their voices, they should begin with an acknowledgement of their own good fortune, an apology for the failings of universities in the past, and a commitment to work together in the future to push beyond excellence, and similar corporatized versions of Maoist sentiments of self-correction.

In this connection, I want to try to make a point which I know just cries out to be misunderstood or misreported, but I think that, whatever the risks, it is something that needs to be explored. I have, alas, had plenty of opportunity to brood on the hostility likely to be encountered in some quarters by anyone trying to make the case for universities in the appropriate terms. As I've already said, I believe there is in fact an immense reservoir of interest in and good will towards universities among the public at large, and in addressing that public I don't think there is any need to be either apologetic or defensive. But in some quarters, and particularly among those who comment on these matters in political circles or in the media or the blogosphere or other forms of public discussion, there is, without question, a strain of hostility and resentment likely to be encountered by anyone who attempts to characterize and emphasize the value of the intellectual life carried on in universities. Clearly, a wider anti-intellectualism feeds into this, something well charted in the US from at least Richard Hofstadter onwards and brilliantly diagnosed by Thorstein Veblen and others before that.

The narrower version of this response finds it pretty outrageous for academics to criticize or complain about anything to do with universities and their support and regulation by their host society. Along with more understandable and even perhaps justifiable sources of these reactions, we do have to recognize – and here is where I know I am particularly laying myself open to misunderstanding – the force of what Nietzsche termed *ressentiment*. There is a bitterness in these reactions, a combination of anger and sneering, together with a levelling intent, that far exceeds what might seem called for by any actual disagreement about the subject matter. And if I may be allowed to risk a little sally of speculative phenomenology, I think this reaction, for all its hostility and dismissiveness, encodes a twisted acknowledgement that there is something desirable, even enviable, about the role of the scholar or scientist. Part of the reaction, of course, involves a resentment of the supposed security of tenure in a world with very little security of employment; some of it is a sense of how much autonomy, comparatively speaking, academics have in their working lives, how much flexibility in choosing their working hours and so on, in a world where, again, most people enjoy all too little autonomy. But some of it also may be a kind of grudging acknowledgement that the matters that scholars and scientists work on are *in themselves* more interesting, rewarding and perhaps humanly valuable than the matters most people have to devote their energies to in their working lives.

This coexists, it should be said at once, with a parallel conviction that academics are oblivious to or sheltered from the great determining economic necessities of life, and so they are always in need of being given a sharp reminder of the source of their salaries in that hard world of profit and loss that makes everything else possible. So, there is a complex emotional aetiology here. Academics are the objects of, simultaneously, envy and resentment because their roles seem to allow them to deal with intrinsically rewarding matters while being financially supported by the labour of others who are not privileged to work on such matters. This reaction would like to see the chill wind of economic necessity that is the encompassing weather of most people's lives blow a little more searchingly into the too-protected groves of academe. And the idea that, from this privileged and protected position, academics should *then* dare to complain about attempts to make their activities democratically accountable in the only way democracy currently understands that operation – *that* is felt to be simply insupportable. I've no doubt these reactions, in more or less this form, are recognizable to any reader of this book, but I am suggesting that we need also to see that, at the same time, this involves a kind of backhanded acknowledgement of the worth and human desirability of what scholars and scientists do. Part of the baffled rage that is an ingredient in this resentment comes from struggling with an unavowable ambivalence. If academics retained some of their comparatively favourable conditions of employment but in fact spent their working day on the white-collar equivalent of breaking stones, there might still be a feeling from other groups in society that these academics weren't doing too badly, but I suspect there would be less of the resentment-fuelled anger.

Of course, it is in the nature of all phenomenological analyses that they cannot, in the face of a sceptical challenge, establish their truth by appeal to incontrovertible external evidence. Such analyses ask for recognition of a re-description of a particular aspect of human experience, and if there is no shared recognition to build on, then their persuasive power is limited. But perhaps in other areas of our experience there would not be anything particularly surprising about the idea that the vehemence of a negative reaction to an activity might be directly proportional to a muffled recognition that there is something involved which, in another form or in other circumstances, would be found desirable or worthwhile.

Despite these and other risks, I am, predictably, urging my fellow academics to help make the variety of cases that need making to the various relevant publics in the variety of styles that may be called for. For my own part, I have wanted primarily to contest the narrow conception of universities as just institutes for training the workforce and applying discoveries to create economic growth. But in the meantime it would not be difficult to paint a blackly dystopian picture of where universities are headed if current developments continue unchecked, though I should make clear that I do not share the extremer forms of pessimism here. One advantage of having some familiarity with the history of debates about universities over the past century or more is the antidote it provides to ahistorical alarmism and rampant Cassandrism. The fact is that commentators in every generation have thought that it was all going to the dogs, but in that case the dogs must live further away than anyone ever realized. Just as theology will never again be the queen of the sciences or Latin the hallmark of an educated person, so other verities once taken for granted in universities will pass without Armageddon arriving. Still, what would be the gloomiest prediction if the trends I've touched on here were to continue unhindered? That black picture might include the following:

The dominant character of higher education institutions across the world would be as businesses specializing in preparing people to work in business. Beyond that, a substantial number of large-intake institutions will combine the teaching work of an advanced high school with an element of contract research work for outside organizations. A select number of other, mostly small and mostly private, institutions will provide a broad cultural education mainly to the children of the relatively wealthy. And a very small number of historically prestigious, financially well-supported institutions will combine teaching a very select student intake with various forms of scholarship and research across several of the traditional areas of enquiry, though with a huge numerical and financial preponderance in the biomedical and applied sciences and in professional training, especially in business and law. In all of these types of institution, there will be either a shrinking proportion or the complete elimination of tenured academics and a vast increase in a casualized work-force, while the vestiges of academic self-government will disappear entirely. There will be far less face-to-face or small-group teaching, and far more reliance on technology. Students will feel increasingly entitled to the good results they have paid for. The humanities will be marginalized even further and will largely be studied by the children of the well-off.

The more selective universities will feel themselves to be under more and more pressure to provide better facilities: what has been dubbed the 'amenities arms race' will only speed up, and it will become harder to distinguish between universities and various kinds of luxury hotel or spa resort. Universities will become ever more dependent upon overseas student fees, and their selling of themselves in these markets will more and more shape their internal policies. We shall see soaring student debt, which will become more and more socially divisive. Making individual universities responsible for their students' loans will incentivize the production of high-earning graduates who are the best financial risk. The growth of private, and especially for-profit, universities will further reflect and entrench class privileges. The fact that they provide full scholarships for a number of applicants from less wealthy backgrounds cannot disguise the fact that both the commercial logic and the social tone of these institutions is set by the children of the well-off. Companies charging high fees for almost worthless online courses will make larger and larger profits ... I could go on, but I do not believe that this bleak picture is inevitable, though at the moment it looks hideously plausible. Simply setting it out in these bald terms may, I hope, at least help to concentrate the mind.

One conclusion that might be drawn is that the case for universities cannot be made in appropriate terms without at the same time challenging some of the presuppositions of the wider public discourse about economic growth. Let me be clear. I am not suggesting here that we try to change ordinary human motivation about prosperity, still less that we should regress to some pseudo-primitive communalism in which we all make our own sandals and grow our own muesli. But although we nearly all of us live parts of our lives in accordance with beliefs and goals other than those of wealth-maximizing, we have great difficulty articulating the values that inform these common experiences, and we seem to find it nigh on impossible to make those values and their articulated ideals operative in public discussion of social goods. This is one reason why the task seems so daunting. An adequate case for universities cannot be made simply in terms of contribution to economic prosperity, yet to try to change the terms of public discourse more widely can seem both over-ambitious and quixotic.

So, let me end this chapter with one very general reflection. If the language we use to talk about universities represents them as being principally institutions that provide narrowly vocational training for employment and the application of technology to promoting economic growth, and if the language we use about students represents them as being consumers who shop in the educational supermarket purely for what provides the most remunerative future job at the lowest cost, then those are the kinds of universities and the kind of education we shall end up with. It is therefore very important that we should try to articulate a different and more adequate conception of what universities are 'for' because otherwise we risk damaging, or even in some cases destroying, the defining characteristics of universities and what has made them so valuable to humanity in its search for fuller and deeper understanding.

Measuring Up: Universities
and 'Accountability'

I

Much the greater part of public discussion of higher education in Britain in the last few years has been focused on methods of funding, especially the replacement in England and Wales – though not, of course, Scotland – of public funding of teaching by student fees. There has been much less discussion of the kinds of change that have transformed universities internally over the past two or three decades. The lack of public attention to this transformation is not altogether surprising. This is not the kind of single-event change that generates headlines: it takes place by apparently small steps spread over several years and is nearly invisible to the outside eye. But the truth is that the character of British universities, and particularly the experience of being a member of the academic staff of such institutions, has been radically and systematically altered in a remarkably short period of time, yet it has provoked comparatively little analytical attention or wider criticism. The entirely legitimate demand that universities be accountable to society has, in conjunction with certain other features of the contemporary political climate, resulted in the growth of a particular kind of audit culture that is having very damaging unintended consequences. For that reason, this chapter focuses on the consequences of the current interaction between a particular conception of accountability and a particular form of managerialism.

Universities change as societies change, but never as a simple and direct reflection of those changes: the relationship is always more dialectical and indirect. One way to characterize the transformation of much of the developed world in the past three decades is to say that we have moved from having market economies towards being market societies, as more and more domains of life have been reshaped on the model of market competition for profit. This is a large topic and there is no room here to dwell on the different elements in the mix (which have differed in different countries), but it seems to me too simplistic to suggest that this is the straightforward outcome of the imposition of a single ideology, usually called 'neoliberalism'. There have also been several other types of social change happening that are not all attributable to one particular form of political economy, however powerful. The decline of deference, the erosion of trust towards professions, the empowerment of certain kinds of populist relativism – these all have a complex aetiology and have had their own impact on the public discussion of universities. Similarly, it is important to emphasize that some of the application of the principles of so-called New Public Management in public services is actually far more dirigiste than it is the expression of pure free market principles. Nonetheless, it is indisputable that in the past two or three decades governments in Britain and elsewhere have increasingly treated universities as institutions whose 'performance' can primarily be improved by subjecting them to a particular form of market competition, or at least to some simulacrum thereof, and then measuring the results in various ways.

One feature of these changes that is particularly relevant to my theme but is perhaps too little noticed is the way in which the generalization of the consumer model, which is entailed by the metaphor of the market, involves an agnosticism about human ends and a consequent downgrading of reasons as opposed to preferences. This promises to bypass all the difficult judgements about some human activities being more worthwhile than others, and simply allows the mechanism of consumer choice in a market not just to determine outcomes but also to confer legitimacy on them. Its strength, of course, is that no individual or group is seen to be dictating to others what they ought to want. Its weakness is that it makes it harder for public discussion to address the question of whether some purposes may be humanly more valuable than others. Instead of reasons, therefore, all we have are opinions, which are treated, and derogated, as 'merely subjective'. Between them, subjective 'opinions' and objective 'data' are increasingly held to exhaust the acceptable elements of public debate. As Andreas Schleicher, the man behind the controversial PISA tables of school attainment, was quoted as saying recently: 'Without data, you are just another person with an opinion.' The fact that such a statement was allowed to pass without any critical comment indicates, I think, how contemporary public debate tends automatically to relegate anything that is not quantifiable to the status of subjective 'opinion'.

Hence the fetishization of metrics and benchmarks. As the American historian Jerry Muller puts it: 'The quest for numerical metrics of accountability is particularly attractive in cultures marked by low social trust.' There is now an extensive literature on the unintended consequences and even self-defeating characteristics of many of these measures. Several of the examples illustrate two celebrated aphorisms on this topic. First, there is 'Campbell's Law', named after the American social psychologist Donald T. Campbell, which states: 'The more any quantitative social indicator is used for social decision-making, the more subject it will be to corruption pressures and the more apt it will be to distort and corrupt the social processes it is intended to monitor.' There are countless recent examples of this truth, notably the scandal in school systems in the US and elsewhere of teachers falsifying their students' exam results to improve their school's metrics. The other celebrated dictum is the anthropologist Marilyn Strathern's reformulation of a familiar critical point: 'When a measure becomes a target, it ceases to be a good measure.' In other words, initially you set out to measure how much people like doing activity X; then you set a certain figure as the number of times people should aim to be doing that activity, or else there will be penalties; thereafter, that indicator only tells you that people are now doing what they have been more or less forced or induced to do. 'The result is goal displacement, where the metric means come to replace the ultimate ends that those means ought to serve.' Muller has assembled many illustrations of these truths, the most chilling of which concerns the introduction of surgical report cards in some states in the US in the early 1990s as a way of rating individual surgeons' efficiency and hence their salaries. This created a pressure to operate only on categories of patient with high survival rates and to neglect the, possibly needier, others. As Muller drily summarizes the outcome: 'More patients died, but the metrics improved.'

The extension in the course of the 1990s and 2000s of New Public Management techniques to all forms of provision led to what has been termed 'the reporting imperative', defined as 'the perceived need to constantly generate information, even when nothing significant is going on'. These procedures inevitably engendered numerous externalities in excess of the goals aimed at. One has been the sheer scale of the machinery and cost involved in devising ways to collect evidence of efficiency. Another has been the increased availability of and reliance upon quantifiable data: those who work in management studies are familiar with the maxim: 'If you can't measure it, you can't manage it.' But another, less noticed, change has been entailed by the shift of attention from specifying aims to measuring outcomes. This shift has, in many areas of life, given rise to an enhanced emphasis upon the perceived satisfaction of those who are meant to be the beneficiaries of a given service. This in turn adds significantly to the burden of data-gathering, as Helen Small has argued with reference to universities, but it also entails finding a way to replace judgements of worthwhileness with the quantitative measurement of end-user satisfaction. All citizens undergo compulsory role-reassignment and emerge from the process as consumers. Surveys and polls obsessively record what percentage of a target population are 'very satisfied', 'satisfied', 'not satisfied' or 'don't give a monkey's'. This is what accountability now largely means in relation to any form of public provision, but it is, I think, particularly problematic when applied to universities, and attempts to give effect to this requirement where matters of intellectual quality are concerned involve a significant shift away from the implicit acceptance of the relevant degree of professional autonomy upon which universities had previously relied.

Asking users of, say, a given rail service whether they are 'satisfied' with the punctuality or cleanliness of the trains may yield information that can be both quantified and moderately useful. Asking 'users' of a higher education system if they are 'satisfied' with the quality of education they have received is likely to produce either responses that are quantifiable but of little use, or responses that may be relevant to the activity but are not quantifiable – and anyway, it is not clear that the category of 'users' applies in such a case. Are the parents of students 'users'? Are employers? Are those bodies who compete for young citizens' votes, or those concerned about the level of public debate or cultural provision? All of society is in some way or another potentially an interested party here. But, more fundamentally still, is 'user satisfaction' a relevant way of assessing how effectively the purposes of education have been achieved? User *dis*satisfaction may sometimes be an important sign that genuine education is happening.

And, taking up the most contentious aspect of the question, how should this version of 'accountability' be made to work in the case of those intellectual activities we currently classify as 'research'? Universities are pressed to show that society is getting 'value for money' by investing millions in the research activities of its academics. But how to argue for this expenditure in the face of the allegedly quantified benefits of spending those millions instead on building roads or hospitals or aircraft carriers? We here start to enter territory where there is always likely to be some tension between the short, easily intelligible and often quantifiable case required for public debate in a market democracy, and the more extended and indirect case that may be needed in order to give an adequate characterization of the central purposes of universities.

It should go without saying that it is entirely proper for those societies that invest considerable sums of public money in universities to want to be provided with some reasoned justification for this expenditure. In what I say here or elsewhere, I am not assuming that academics should be exempt from that wholly legitimate expectation – I am certainly not, as one particularly abusive commentator put it, taking 'the Stefan Collini line that the liberal academy is owed a living by the world'. But – it ought to be equally obvious – that reasoned case must be couched in terms that actually capture what is distinctive and valuable about what universities do.

However, the terms and temper of contemporary public debate make it difficult to articulate that justification in ways that those who largely shape attitudes in the media and policy-making worlds assume will be acceptable to most of their audiences and electorates. (Whether their assumptions are too pessimistic is a question I take up elsewhere.) In a public culture that is so sensitive to the prejudices of the right-wing popular press, there is a very great and easily mobilized hostility to anything that can be represented as professional-class welfare-sponging. No matter that the corporate and financial elite creams off unimaginably greater proportions of what should in some senses be seen as public wealth, any group which can be represented as combining direct receipt of public funds, historic cultural capital, and some form of professional autonomy is going to come in for a good kicking, whether they be academics, directors of national theatres and museums, BBC producers or MPs. This popular interpretation of 'accountability' means, therefore, not just democratic answerability or demonstration of proper stewardship of public funds. Insidiously, it comes to mean – though this is never made explicit, of course – that the working conditions within these professions should be made to correspond more closely to those recognizable to the majority of the working population in society at large, regardless of whether those are the conditions favourable to high-quality work in those fields.

The issue of the *quality* of intellectual work is bound to be a vexed one in a culture of accountability because it necessarily

involves the exercise of informed judgement in place of pur-
portedly objective measurement. Our society's solution to this
problem can be expressed in a single word, a word that is in
danger of becoming so naturalized as part of our discourse that
we no longer even notice its fatuity. In practically every official
statement or document issued by practically every university
explaining its aims or its 'mission', you will encounter that
institution's 'commitment to excellence'. I shan't now dwell on
'commitment', though I would just remark the way business-
speak depends on harnessing but devitalizing the language of
the emotions: no candidate now for a job in any walk of life is
merely 'interested' in something – they are always 'passionately
committed' to the activity in question. Job descriptions in turn
embed the same hyperbole: I recently saw a vacancy advertised
that declared to prospective applicants: 'you will be passionate
about stock-flow control'. It is hard not to feel that any sensible
appointments committee should regard such an applicant as suf-
fering from a curious emotional derangement. But as part of the
same almost meaningless corporate-speak, 'excellence' is now
the ubiquitous term for what we in universities are, of course,
passionately committed to. The late Bill Readings pointed to the
growth of this usage in the United States some years ago, but I
want to press the analysis a little further.

It is worth pondering both the derivation and the semantic
range of 'excellence'. Roget's thesaurus rightly gives two clusters
of near-synonyms: the first refers to those terms that indicate
that something is 'good of its kind', and the second to those
that suggest it is 'better than the others'. Excellence connotes
both fulfilling the telos of something (it is, for example, sometimes given as a translation of the ancient Greek term *areté*),
but also excelling, rising above, being outstanding. In all ordinal
scales of evaluation, we ascend through 'satisfactory' to 'good'
to 'very good' and on to 'excellent' – the best. So 'excellence'
totters unsteadily between being part of an Aristotelian tautol-
ogy – to attempt to fulfil any purpose is to attempt to exhibit the
excellence appropriate to that activity – while also smuggling

in the notion that it involves coming out top in some form of competition.

No determinant meaning can be ascribed to the claim that a university is 'committed to excellence'. Every institution presumably thinks that ideally it should be trying to do whatever it does as well it can. Of course it is 'committed to excellence': what else could it be committed to? Imagine the alternative statement: 'Only a university committed to mediocrity in both teaching and research can attract the losers of tomorrow. Only universities vigilant about constantly lowering standards can hope to flourish in the global competition to do rather badly.' But though strictly meaningless, the use of 'excellence' and similar bits of patter does have a function: it signals that the university accepts the sovereignty of the current cant, especially the dominion of audit populism. Its public-relations people and the corporate world's public-relations people are, in another favoured cliché of our time, 'singing from the same hymn sheet'. And it not only signals acceptance of the coercive fiction of competition – we try to excel, to beat the others, to win – but, implicitly, it also signals acceptance of the conventional forms of the measurement of achievement. This is the great unspoken about 'excellence': since it is entirely devoid of content in itself, its presence can only be vouchsafed by some quantitative evidence recognized by outsiders. To be 'committed to excellence' serves to announce that your institution will act as though there were some genuine value in being ranked in, say, 'the world's 100 top universities' or ranked in the 'top 10' in the REF and so on. Yes, says a university – or at least its 'senior management team' speaking on behalf of the university, says – we believe in excellence, and so we will with conviction submit ourselves to these exercises and strive to do well, to excel, by their criteria. We are 'team players'; we are 'serious about making a contribution to society'; we understand the 'need to be accountable', we accept the need for 'objective performance indicators' – all this, I suggest, hovers around the ubiquitous discourse of 'excellence', numbing us into not noticing how far we are from a modest and accurate account of the defining activities of a university.

II

This cluster of issues also illustrates what I would call the 'paradox of management' within universities. The more dirigiste forms of university administration are bound to be endlessly frustrating for the administrators themselves, since they cannot compel or otherwise bring about the production of the thing that matters most – intellectual quality, whether in teaching or scholarship or research. They are therefore encouraged by society to expend their considerable energies on schemes which they can control – forms of surveillance and assessment which have the appearance of ensuring that the objects of a university are being properly pursued, but which are in reality simply external indicators of their lack of effectiveness in the one thing needful.

Lest I be accused of calling only partisan witnesses, let me cite Adam Smith, not always my most obvious ally. Smith long ago remarked that external overseers (his age was not yet blessed with the concept of 'quality assurance professionals') could only force a university teacher to 'attend upon his pupils a certain number of hours'; they had no means of making him provide good teaching. Smith went on:

> An extraneous jurisdiction of this kind, besides, is liable to be exercised both ignorantly and capriciously. In its nature, it is arbitrary and discretionary, and the persons who exercise it, neither attending upon the lectures of the teacher themselves, nor perhaps understanding the sciences which it is his business to teach, are seldom capable of exercising it with judgement ... The person subject to such jurisdiction is necessarily degraded by it, and instead of being one of the most respectable, is rendered one of the meanest and most contemptible persons in the society.

Perhaps even the normally careful Smith gets a little carried away in that last sentence, but in general terms this is still a surprisingly good brief epitome of the failings of so many current attempts to measure intellectual or educational productivity. Society demands accountability, but from the more mechanical expressions of this demand all it gets is the external show of accountability, and this highlights a broader distinction between administration and management. A good administrator helps to put in place the conditions in which academics can teach and think well in ways they judge best. A poor manager exacts compliance from academics in procedures which are proxies for the real business of teaching and thinking well. Good administration, good financial management, good maintenance of buildings, and much else are all vital to the good functioning of universities, but the inescapable (if potentially unpopular) fact is that the academic staff are the ones whose primary activities are constitutive of what is *distinctive* about these peculiar institutions. Consequently, the most lavishly funded and most efficiently run university which has largely fourth-rate academics will remain a fourth-rate university.

There is an uncomfortable truth here, uncomfortable for academics as well as everyone else. Uncomfortable in part because intellectual quality and creativity cannot be programmed, but uncomfortable also because the ultimate standing of even the best-run institution depends on factors that are partly not under its control. After all, good intellectual work is not the product of one university or even one generation alone. It depends upon, among other things, those intangible ideas and standards that clever graduate students absorb almost by osmosis from the publications and conversations of their seniors and peers in disciplines that spread across institutions, across countries, and across generations. A new or up-and-coming university can try to hire a few of the best people in a given field if it has the resources and can promise productive conditions of work, but it cannot, *by itself*, make the field an exciting one, or make the star recruits continue to do good work, or produce their successors. In addition to being part of, and dependent upon, wider intellectual worlds and disciplinary traditions, strong universities are those that, having established over an extended period of time a reputation for high intellectual quality in the main academic disciplines, actively sustain an ethos that supports creativity and autonomy, thereby continuing to attract the best academics and students. In all of this, those clever graduate students I mentioned know, intuitively, what matters. I'm willing to bet that no intellectually ambitious would-be graduate student ever applied to study at a particular university because he or she had heard that the institution boasted an outstandingly good Quality Assurance Division.

This is where the category of managerialism becomes particularly relevant. All enterprises and institutions have, of course, to be run and run as effectively as possible. We talk of 'managerial-*ism*' when the procedures, values and interests of those charged with running an institution take priority over the purposes for which it is supposedly being run. Moreover, managerialism requires, not long familiarity with the knotty particularity of a single institution or group of people, but rather with the processes that can be applied across all such institutions as managers move from post to post, and metrics are the indispensable means of making different activities in different universities uniformly manageable. Developments within universities over the past couple of decades have clearly pushed them quite a long way in this direction. In most British universities (Oxford and Cambridge may, as so often, be partial exceptions), there has been a cumulative reduction in the autonomy, status and influence of academics – in governance, in research and in teaching. In some respects, academics themselves have colluded with these changes in that the overwhelming priority now given to research achievement in career progression means that it is increasingly difficult to find senior academics willing to take a turn in the higher administrative offices of their university and then returning to a career of teaching and research. As we know, over the past two or three decades there has been a dramatic downgrading or even elimination of anything like academic self-government: faculty senates have been abolished or bypassed, and we have seen a vast expansion in a cadre of professional managers who come over time to have their own aspirations and career paths. In addition, the greatly increased casualization of the teaching force in universities not only saves money but it also reduces the institutional voice of the established academics and increases the power of the manageriat. And so, indirectly, does the current regime of research assessment. It should be obvious but it may be worth underlining that everything that tends towards greater 'performance-management' increases the power of the managers.

Managerialism operates through various mechanisms, not just by means of direct command. Thus, both externally and internally a pattern of providing long-term funding in ways that are most conducive to good intellectual work has been largely replaced by a system of artificially contrived short-term competition for the necessary resources. Stable and adequate, if limited, funding is derided as extravagant feather-bedding inimical to innovation. Systemic underfunding plus competition and punitive performance-management is seen as lean efficiency and proper accountability. A recent report showed that academic staff in many British universities are now set annual targets for the amount of money they *must* bring in from external grant applications. No matter that much research, especially in the humanities, does not require lavish expenditure on equipment and postdocs; no matter that the rate of success in some grant competitions is currently running at 12 per cent and so the great majority of applications are wasted effort; no matter that constantly inventing and then managing large research projects may be more likely to obstruct than advance a scholar's capacity to do interesting work – despite these and many other telling objections, the manic search for quantifiable measures of intellectual quality, turns, in accordance with prevailing economistic prejudices, to money as the most reliable metric and proxy. This results in careers, and even in some cases continuing employment itself, being determined by the mechanical application of such targets.

And then there is the fallacy of 'continuous improvement'. If the only publicly acceptable way to attend to questions of quality is by means of annual measurement against a quantitative benchmark, the imperative to so-called continuous improvement becomes both self-fulfilling and self-contradictory. The logical conclusion of such a process is obviously a situation in which 100 per cent of students get top firsts, 100 per cent of staff get maximum external grants, and 100 per cent of departments get 4* research ratings and so on. Clearly, when that farcical moment is reached it will be time, as one particularly fatuous university advertisement put it recently, to go 'beyond excellence'.

A related development that has attracted far too little comment has been the systematic downgrading of academic departments. This may sound to be a boringly dry issue of university structure, but it again illuminates the clash between intellectual and managerial values. In recent years there have been moves away from departments in two apparently contradictory directions. On the one hand there is the fashion to dissolve them into larger units, usually called schools or colleges. In these cases a determined managerial attempt is often made to stamp out the vestiges of a departmental culture, and the reorganization not infrequently involves bringing in an external head of the new larger unit. The other change is to set up programmes and centres that are defined in terms of a particular theme or contemporary issue. These are usually smaller units than departments, but are 'problem-centred' and 'interdisciplinary' – these incantatory terms now have the power of magic spells – and they are also often the beneficiaries of a separate funding stream. The net result in both these apparently divergent but actually complementary changes is to increase managerial power at the expense of the relevant collectivity of scholars who are the only people capable of creating and maintaining intellectual value in a particular discipline from generation to generation. As Marginson and Considine say in their discussion of recent changes of this kind in Australian universities, from the point of view of the new managerialism 'the traditional academic disciplines, with their self-organizing and republican traditions, define themselves as problematic'.

We also get a small but revealing insight into the character of these changes by considering the revalorization that has taken place of the contrasting terms 'collaboration' and 'cooperation'. Collaboration is now prized because it goes, as the cant phrase has it, 'outside the silo' – it involves working with a group or body defined as external, perhaps to the discipline, perhaps to the institution, perhaps to the country. It is an institutionally defined and financially consequential set of recorded transactions with a predetermined outcome. Cooperation, by contrast, is scanted because this tends to be informal and a matter of ethos. It is usually an aspect of relations among scholars as individuals, its effects are impossible to quantify, and it has no direct financial consequences. (We may pass over for now the fact that cooperation may be the very life-blood of scholarly activity.) We can put the contrast most pithily by saying that collaboration is about being entrepreneurial, while cooperation is about being scholarly. So no contest there.

III

I now turn to what are perhaps the two most familiar examples of the marriage between the demand for accountability and the drive towards forms of supposedly objective measurement. In Britain, the felt need to identify a demonstrable justification for public investment in research has issued in the requirement that university departments provide evidence of the non-academic social and economic 'impact' of their research. I have written about the characteristics of this exercise before, but I want to return to it briefly here precisely because it is such a telling illustration of the tension between the current interpretation of the imperative to accountability and the actual character and value of scholarly and scientific enquiry.

The Higher Education Funding Council's notion of 'impact' looks, at first sight, intuitively appealing: this, it suggests, will demonstrate where academic research goes beyond the narrow circle of fellow specialists to directly benefit the wider public. But in fact, given the way 'impact' is defined, what the exercise does, following a very expensive bureaucratic process and a huge expenditure of uncosted academic labour, is to assemble a great deal of detailed evidence of what are, in many cases, incidental by-products or side-effects of such research. Remember, 'impact' is defined in such a way as to distinguish it not only from any shaping influence on other scholars or on students, but also from 'public engagement' – that is, academics explaining to wider audiences the interest and significance of their work. Such engagement seems to me clearly desirable and to be encouraged, though no one, presumably, would think it could function as a criterion of the quality of the research itself. But impact involves something else and something that is *extrinsic* to the defining purpose of the research itself. I speak with feeling here, having been in charge of preparing my department's submission for the 2014 Research Excellence Framework. Many readers may be familiar with the demands of this exercise, but let me briefly offer an actual example – an example which, for obvious reasons, has to be anonymized. One of my colleagues is a leading scholar of the work an English poet upon whom he has written some major studies. Partly as a result of a chance personal connection, in recent years he helped choose the exhibits, write the captions, and make other contributions for a display at a small museum devoted to this writer's life and work. I spent no small amount of time in 2011 and 2012 chivvying the poor staff at this museum. Could they supply visitor numbers? Sorry, could they please document those numbers in a publicly verifiable form? Did they have evidence of what visitors to the exhibition made of the experience? Did they ask them to fill in questionnaires, did they have a comments book? Sorry, could they provide extracts in a duly authenticated form? What was the evidence of the benefit the visitors derived from their visit? Sorry, I mean evidence of what the exercise calls 'change in their behaviours'? And so on.

Not only did this exercise consume large amounts of academic time and labour – remember it had to be repeated for all case studies from all departments in all universities in the UK – but it also put a considerable burden on all those institutions and members of the general public who were thought likely to be able to provide the looked-for evidence. When the results were finally made public in December 2014, it was entirely predictable that the government and the Higher Education Funding Council would claim that the exercise had been a resounding success. We were told that the great range of the impact of academic research on the wider society had been documented for the first time and that this would enable a much stronger case to be made for future public funding.

But is that really the case? These instances of effects or spin-offs that are in many cases incidental to the main aims of the prior scholarly or scientific research cannot provide the justification for the social value of *that research itself*. Moreover, they are presented as a significant element in the judgement of research quality, and departments are funded accordingly. But in reality these kinds of effects, even if desirable in themselves, as no doubt many of them are, do not testify to the *quality of the research* at all. My colleague's scholarship on this poet would still have been of the same high quality whether or not he had happened to be involved with this museum, let alone whether we could demonstrate beyond doubt that a thirteen-year-old visiting with a school party had written in the comments book that the exhibits were 'ace'.

'Impact', as this exercise defines it, is a proxy for the public value of the research, but it is not in reality a good proxy. It is not actually a measure of that value, but a measure of something else, something that is secondary, and in many cases contingent or incidental to the activity of doing good research, something the required evidence for which is bound to be unevenly and somewhat arbitrarily distributed among a given population of scholars. A department where the research has, often for purely accidental reasons, generated such by-products is judged to be superior in terms of the *quality of research* to one which has not, and this is surely the fundamental conceptual confusion in the exercise. The attempt to measure quality, when combined with the prevailing interpretation of 'accountability', results in measuring something that is not quality.

Indeed, one can see how over time the exercise will lead (has already led?) some departments to focus on securing this kind of 'impact' *at the expense* of primary scholarly quality. After all, these impact cases are all graded, and they contribute significantly to the 'score' each department is given which in turn translates into a place in a national league table as well as determining the award of public funding. The result is that something that may initially have been an incidental by-product of research becomes a 'target' to be aimed at since such significant financial and reputational goods depend on doing well – and it is here that the two fallacies I mentioned at the start come into play. Many of the activities the exercise records may be admirable in themselves, but, to repeat, they are not a measure of the value of that research to society, and hence they *cannot* in fact provide a justification for public support of that research.

What this exercise (and the larger research assessment process of which it is a part) does do, of course, is provide data, and this allows for far more extensive and intrusive performance-management of academics by administrators and external bodies. The attempt to impose an easily measurable form of productivity can be represented as a minimal requirement of public accountability, though in practice it has far-reaching effects on the kinds of research undertaken or the shape of academic careers and so on. Research assessment of this kind is a textbook example of the way in which the current notion of 'accountability' ends up reshaping the character of the activity it is ostensibly designed merely to monitor.

When I say that my next example concerns global rankings of universities, I anticipate that a flicker of impatience or even boredom may pass across the face even of the most well-disposed reader. The fact is that most people think they know that these rankings are flawed or limited in various ways, but they also think they know that such rankings nonetheless tell us something that is useful – and anyway, they're here to stay. But the current fashion for such league tables is particularly revealing of the difficulties contemporary public debate has in coping with questions of intellectual quality, and so is germane to my larger argument. By way of introducing my remarks, let me ask three short questions about these global rankings: 1) What do they actually provide reliable information about? 2) Whose interest is served by them? 3) Why do they persist even in the face of quite devastating criticism? In practice, it is not so easy to answer these questions, but even simply to ask them is to reveal something important about the current relationship between universities and society.

The first point, not seriously denied by anyone familiar with these league tables, is that the attempt to provide quantitative measurements of quality, and then arrange them as an ordinal ranking, has to use a series of proxies for what it purports to be measuring. For example, the number and level of higher degrees possessed by the academic faculty of an institution has sometimes been used as one proxy for educational quality. In this case there may well be some correlation between the proxy and what it stands for: it can say something about the recruitment of faculty in lower-level or teaching-only institutions, though it tells us little about differences among the more highly regarded research universities where doctorates are now pretty much universal. But faculty salaries, another proxy sometimes suggested for this purpose, do not even exhibit this minimal correlation with quality of teaching or research. One could even facetiously suggest that there is more of an *inverse* correlation: younger and less well-paid faculty may tend to put more into their teaching than older and better-paid colleagues, but that only shows that this is a defective proxy. In any case, national variations in pay and standard of living make this an unviable proxy in international comparisons, and within national systems it is difficult to make adequate allowance for the different salary scales of public and private institutions, proportions of highly paid medical and legal faculty and so on. Where such a proxy is relied upon (different ranking systems use different proxies), it represents the transposition of a pure piece of market ideology which maintains that higher prices are generally an indication of higher quality, but there is no good reason to accept that dogma.

A second defect that is more damaging than is commonly recognized is the use in some rankings of one or another form of 'reputation'. Here the undeniable fact is that no one respondent can ever have first-hand knowledge of the work in their own discipline of more than a tiny handful of departments among the many hundreds of universities being ranked. This does not mean that there can be no comparative judgements of any kind. It is possible that an experienced senior professor of early modern Swedish history may have a reasonable idea about the general level of the quality of work in the few institutions in his or her country which sustain this field. But even if there were agreement that that professor was sufficiently informed and sufficiently judicious, there would still be no reliable way to convert those judgements into a numerical scale, and no basis whatever for making reliable judgements about other aspects of those departments' work in other areas of the discipline, let alone the work in different fields in history departments in other countries and so on. On this scale, no judgement about quality can be both reliable and comprehensive, and even the somewhat reliable and severely limited local judgements cannot usefully be given quantitative expression. What the reliance on this proxy does is create a circularity whereby respondents rank institutions in part on the basis of impressions acquired from reading accounts of previous rankings.

Thirdly, and this really is fatal, all attempts to produce a single ordinal ranking have to make decisions about the relative *weighting* to be assigned to the different proxies measured. Do you make 'student satisfaction' (itself a clumsy proxy for educational quality) 15 per cent of the overall total or, say, 20 per cent? As careful statistical critiques have shown, small variations in such weightings produce dramatically different results, catapulting into the 'top ten' institutions not previously included in the 'top fifty' and so on. There is no neutral or agreed way to weight the different components. Every decision – and the various global league tables embody many such decisions – necessarily favours one type of institution or one national tradition over others. It is bad enough that the attempt to rank a single factor such as the quality of teaching or research across all types of institution is hopelessly flawed, especially since these institutions reflect various social conditions and cultural traditions. But the attempt to convert the already flawed ranking of widely disparate and incommensurable factors into a *single* numerical sequence when there is no agreed way to determine the proportion each factor represents is – to employ an underused critical term – surely bonkers. Moreover, the idea that the qualities supposedly being measured may change significantly on an annual basis (as is required to enable each year's tables to grab the headlines) further indicates the deep disconnect between the measurement system and what it purports to be measuring.

And finally, rankings are a further form of zero-sum game; one institution cannot go up without another going down. This encourages the same irrational gambler's attitude as the lottery. Every player in the lottery has to believe not just that they will be luckier than their fellow players, but also that their own chief incentive to play is predicated on others' misfortune. Only if enough people lose their bets will there be a huge prize for the winner. Few things do more to poison what ought to be the cooperative and collegial relations among universities, either in the same system or internationally.

But even when all this is said and demonstrated far more conclusively than I have room for here, an intelligent and reflective and broadly sympathetic reader is still likely to take away the impression that I am exaggerating. Surely, you may say, these league tables do, despite all their defects, tell us at least something worth having. After all, they do consistently show us that Harvard and Stanford and Oxford and Cambridge are among the world's top half-dozen universities, so they are broadly right about that. But we can only think they are 'right' about that because we think that is something that we *already know*. And because we think, on that circular basis, that they are right about the ones at the top, we are willing to assume that they are roughly right about the difference between the university ranked, say, 39th and the one ranked 51st, though there is no rational basis for that conclusion. For the most part, the rankings give us pseudo-statistical tabulation of incommensurable proxies, inflected by impressionistic judgements which have been shaped in part by previous rankings.

There is more, much more, that could be said, but let me return to my three questions.

1) What do they actually provide reliable information about? They provide reliable information about those individual indicators which can be meaningfully represented in quantitative form. They provide reliable information, for example, about how much different universities spend on research. That tells us something, especially about big science, even if not always what commentators assume it tells us. But they do not provide reliable information about whether one type of institution in country A is, in some meaningful comprehensive sense, 'better' than a different type of institution in country B.

2) Whose interest is served by them? This is not easy to answer. Obviously, in the first instance, those who make money out of them, including the sponsoring publications – sales of whose special issues are boosted, and who thus have an incentive to tinker with the weighting system to produce newsworthy shifts in ranking positions each year. Those universities that think they can turn the results to their advantage are very willing to cooperate, and they then confer a further legitimacy on such rankings by making selective use of the results when it suits them. And everyone enjoys league tables: they are easily assimilable and provide some of the vicarious interest that the statistical tabulation of all sports does. But, ultimately, they serve the interests of those who want their fellow citizens to assume that these institutions can be ranked as accurately as sports teams so as to encourage the belief that outsiders can measure their quality in

the same way they can measure the quality of the providers of any service.

3) Why is the principle of these obviously flawed rankings impervious to criticism? This touches on some very deep questions about a market democracy's distrust of reasons and judgements, as well as its superstitious belief that numbers somehow escape the perils of bias and subjectivity. The devastating criticisms that have been levelled at these rankings are, where not simply ignored, regarded merely as a stimulus to tinker with the metrics, whereas what such criticisms are really telling us is that the very project of producing a single global league table is fatally flawed. But recognition of that truth might depend on wider acknowledgement of the fact that we cannot have a single ordinal ranking of most of the things that really matter in life, and there is little in contemporary public discourse that makes such acknowledgement likely any time soon.

What the examples I have been discussing so far have in common is the currently favoured, but actually doomed, endeavour to translate informed judgements of quality into calculable measurements of quantity, and then to further reduce those quantitative proxies to a single ordinal ranking. But, we shall be told, surely anything that matters can, in the end, be measured – or, as the bullish slogan has it, 'what counts can be counted'. But is that really true? How much love should a parent give a child? Scientific tests show that the minimum requirement is 561 full body-hugs per annum. That translates as, depending on the units of measurement, 48 ice-creams, 28.6 smiley emoticons, or one electric train set. Yes, it's easy for me to make fun of it, but there is a serious point here. Until we free ourselves from the current fetishized form of quantification we shall find it impossible to have an adequate discussion of the nature of intellectual activity, and until we can have such a discussion we cannot say whether universities are doing what they should be doing and doing it well. That may be a lot to ask for, and a lot more than those who concern themselves with universities can bring about. But in the meantime, we should surely have the self-respect to acknowledge publicly that 'impact' rankings and league tables and similar devices do not in fact measure what they claim to measure. They are all examples of what, almost a century ago in talking about American universities, Thorstein Veblen described as 'obsequious concessions to worldly wisdom'.

IV

As I've tried to indicate very briefly, there are forces at work in shaping contemporary universities that are more powerful and more pervasive even than the question of replacing direct funding with a system of fees plus income-contingent loans. Part of what we should have learned from the experience of the past few decades is that just as relative stability of funding is at least as important as the actual level, so the mechanism of funding can be as important as the source. The value of the so-called 'arm's length principle' lay in a recognition that the providers of the funding were not competent to create the conditions most favourable to good intellectual work. The premise of the currently fashionable form of accountability, at once panicky and dirigiste, is that the funding and assessment framework can be used to make universities contribute more directly to the prevailing conception of national needs.

It is often said that these arrangements are necessary and appropriate now that we are approaching a mass system of higher education, and that critics merely reveal their nostalgic longing for the days when the shared values of a social elite and the relatively small size of higher education permitted universities much greater autonomy. So let me, once again, make emphatically clear that I do not share any such nostalgic view and I certainly do not believe in some past golden age of universities. But I am concerned that we should not short-change or cheat either the new generations of students or the wider public by reshaping universities in ways that *reduce* rather than increase their value to society. Universities have to be partly-protected spaces in which the extension and deepening of human understanding has priority over any more immediate practical purpose, no matter how politically or economically desirable such practical purposes may be. That is not an old-fashioned or elitist conception of their role and it is one that is perfectly compatible, as it has been throughout the history of universities over the past couple of centuries, with the task of providing students with the kind of education that will help them to flourish in later employment.

I do not pretend to have any simple answers to the problems I have briefly identified, but I do think that those of us who are academics need to do a better job of helping to make available a vocabulary and set of arguments that are more adequate to the task of characterizing the value of what universities do. We need to remember our wider obligations, but also that those obligations extend beyond the present. There is an understandable tendency for hard-pressed scholars and scientists – and of course there is no other kind – to assume that forms of university funding, governance and assessment may come and go, but that as long as we are at least *partially* free to do the work we feel is important in the library or the lab, and as long as we can strike the spark of intellectual curiosity and disciplined enquiry in at least *some* of our students, then we do better to concentrate on these primary tasks and leave the larger structural and financial issues to others. But that assumption may now be false.

It is already the case, at least in Britain, that ill-considered changes to funding, governance and assessment, and their sometimes quite unintended effects, have fundamentally altered not just the conditions in universities but the very sense of identity and relation to one's work. There is an insidious process by which we become what the categories we use every day tell us we are. It has, for example, surely become more difficult for academics in research universities, especially perhaps for those under forty, not to think that one defining indicator of how good they are at their job is their track record of obtaining external funding. I suspect there are few teachers in university systems that charge high undergraduate fees who do not come to feel, at least on some days, that another defining indicator of how good they are at their job is the number of students who record that they 'like' their courses and get good marks for them. Perhaps soon there will be few scholars and scientists working under funding regimes that require evidence of a particular form of 'impact' who do not come to think that a third defining indicator of how good they are at their job is the number of instances of 'take-up' of their research by 'external users' that could bolster their department's 'impact statement'. These things matter not just for the harm and misdirection of effort they involve, but also because they exemplify a damaging loss of confidence in the central activities of universities on the part of those who are uniquely charged with carrying them out. I am not an optimist about short-term political change, but I do think that as academics we need to do a better job of explaining to wider audiences – audiences beyond universities but beyond narrow policy-making circles also – what universities are really for and why their true long-term value to society is increasingly jeopardized by the kinds of development I have discussed in this chapter.

CHAPTER 3

Reading the Ruins: Criticism and 'the Idea of the University'

I

In the past century and a half there have been numerous books and essays addressing, in different guises, 'the idea of the university', and a recurrent pattern is discernible across these otherwise widely varying publications. Broadly speaking, these statements all see themselves as protesting against the current subordination of universities to economic or other utilitarian purposes. Implicitly if not always explicitly, this literature takes the form of a call to arms: universities' role as centres of open-ended enquiry, transmitting a belief in the value of the life of the mind, is imperilled by ill-conceived measures aimed at training students for immediate employment and applying technology in ways that directly benefit the economy. Given the repetitiveness of this literature, we may think it surprising that the alarm is never sounded in the contrary direction. We never, it seems, meet the claims that the proper vocational, applied and technocratic identity of the university has already been badly eroded, and that now it is on the point of being overwhelmed completely by the engulfing tide of pure scholarship and classical *Bildung*. After all, if what we might, as shorthand, call the 'ideal' and the 'instrumental' have been the two main rival understandings of universities over at least the past couple of centuries, we would expect that each would have its champions and each would have its periods of flourishing or even dominance as well as its periods of being recessive or on the defensive. But, to judge by the various statements of 'the idea of the university', it hasn't been like this at all. The idea being articulated in this literature is *always* in some sense on the defensive, while the contrary utilitarian conception is *always* depicted as being in the ascendant. And that is partly so because the latter is treated as being not just supported by, but expressive of, the constitutive logic of modern societies – what one of the contributors to this literature representatively described in somewhat reductive terms as 'the blind drive onward of material and mechanical development'. At bottom, the literature on 'the idea of the university' is defined by the felt need to articulate, to *re*-articulate, the way in which universities, by their very nature, obey a different logic.

Once we become aware of just how repetitive this pattern has been, several questions propose themselves. First, why is it that all the celebrated statements seem to be on just one side of this divide? Has no deathless prose been written about the aims of servicing the economy or training the workforce, and is that because the forces of social and economic change are seen as their own vindication, not in need of any such rhetorical assistance? Or is the very idea of an instrumental or utilitarian position in fact just a straw man, the self-serving creation of those who wish to represent themselves as upholding some higher or nobler ideal? Closer inspection suggests that the alien measures which each generation of champions of 'the idea of the university' complain about are usually introduced by statements from politicians or administrators that at least pay lip-service to a diluted version of the day before yesterday's 'idea of the university' literature. So the asymmetry is deceptively deep: not only is all the imperishable prose on the 'ideal' side of the conflict, but its authors have written many of their opponents' lines for them as well. Then there is the question of just why this pattern *is* so repetitive. Not only does one 'side' never seem to win a decisive and enduring victory, but similar terms of debate and similar argumentative moves recur in each generation. If new circumstances have given rise to a particular staging of this clash, why are the arguments so manifestly not new? If the case was powerfully and unforgettably stated by a writer in the past, what need to attempt to restate it now and so on? These reflections suggest that there may be some advantage in shifting our focus from the content to the medium, considering 'idea of the university' writing as a literary genre in its own right.

It is not difficult to state the hostile case against this literature. When some time ago I told a friend I was reading works on 'the idea of the university', he wrinkled his nose and declared that surely it was an inherently arid and pointless form of writing. More generally, it tends to be damned for its lack of realism, its preference for mellifluous generalities over useful practical suggestions, and its allegedly conservative or nostalgic character. Such writing tends to be stimulated by the threat or actuality of new measures made necessary by social change, to which its response, it is argued, is to invoke some idealized notion of how universities used to be in the very different social circumstances of the past. Since such writing is often produced by people in universities unhappy about the direction of change, especially where such change represents expansion in both numbers and range of subjects as part of the adaptation to a more modern and democratic society, surely the truth is, say its critics, that literature on 'the idea of the university' is just a polysyllabic way of keening for the privileges of yesterday's elite.

Apart from its other failings, this hostile characterization fails to address one obvious fact about this literature, namely its durability. The institutional arrangements being presupposed by such writing may long since have disappeared, the measures being protested against may have long been forgotten (or simply accepted), but the piece of writing itself lives on, re-read and sometimes re-edited in subsequent generations. The most conspicuous example of this is, of course, Newman's *The Idea of a University* which, as I have argued elsewhere, was, even when it was published in the mid–nineteenth century, presuming certain features that had already passed away with early nineteenth-century Oxford. And yet, the book itself remained the most frequently invoked work across the debates of the twentieth century and their entirely different realities of higher education. Although Newman's book is in a class of its own in these respects, it is nonetheless true that several other contributions to this literature enjoyed when they were published, and in some cases have continued to enjoy long after, a prominence that may now seem puzzling given their datedness and their lack of any directly useful proposals.

Let me at this point mention a few examples of this genre, confining the selection to works published in English in the twentieth century. A classic starting point, in this case American, might be Thorstein Veblen's *The Higher Learning in America*, published in 1918, followed by Abraham Flexner's *Universities: American, English, German*, published in 1930. In Britain the 1940s saw several notable examples, including Bruce Truscot's *Redbrick University* and F.R. Leavis's *Education and the University*, both of 1943, followed by Walter Moberly's *The Crisis in the University* in 1949. As we move to more recent times, there is an abundance of candidates, though their durability is not yet attested, but here I will just mention Jaroslav Pelikan, *The Idea of a University: A Re-examination* (1992), Bill Readings, *The University in Ruins* (1996), Duke Maskell and Ian Robinson, *The New Idea of a University* (2001), and Gordon Graham, *Universities: The Recovery of an Idea* (2002). Two related genres that I shall ignore here, though much might be said about them, are, first, the subset of writings on the nature of the humanities, including R.S. Crane's *The Idea of the Humanities* (1935) and the 1963 collection edited by J.H. Plumb on *Crisis in the Humanities*, as well as more recent examples such as Martha Nussbaum's *Not For Profit* and Helen Small's *The Value of the Humanities*; and, second, those official reports that aspired to state some enduring truths and exercised considerable influence, such as the 1945 Harvard report on 'general education' or the 'Robbins Report' of 1963. Such publications clearly belong to a different genre or sub-genre, even though their thinking was sometimes closely bound up with that of 'the idea of the university' tradition. The books in this tradition that I have mentioned, and the others that might be put alongside them, differ among themselves in various ways, and they were, of course, addressing different historical circumstances and represented more than one national pattern. I shall say something in a moment about the individual or local characteristics of some of them, but my main emphasis throughout will be on features that they share, and, more ambitiously still, on what I shall try to identify as the function of this kind of writing.

II

It may seem surprising to say that if you want some insight into the brave new world into which British universities are now moving, you should turn to a book first published in another country a century ago, but Veblen's *The Higher Learning in America* remains a brilliant indictment of misapplied commercialism. As a brief illustration, we have only to consider his description of the way the dominant business ethos believes it must be possible to reduce all learning to 'standard units of time and volume, and so control and enforce it by a system of accountancy and surveillance; the methods of control, accountancy and coercion that so come to be worked out have all that convincing appearance of tangible efficiency that belongs to any mechanically defined and statistically accountable routine'. Ah yes, 'that convincing appearance of tangible efficiency': how on earth would we fill our days if we did not have to keep up that appearance? Those not familiar with the nature of scholarly work believe it can be measured and quantified like more familiar commercial activities, and universities cowed by the dominant business ethos fall over themselves to comply. Similarly recognizable is his withering specification (partly quoted in the Introduction, above) of what is required to fill the role of the American college president: 'As to the requirements of scholarly or scientific competency, a plausible speaker with a large gift of assurance, a business-like "educator" or clergyman, some urbane pillar of society, some astute veteran of the scientific *demi-monde* will meet all reasonable requirements.' Ah yes, 'a plausible speaker with a large gift of assurance' – the 'head-hunter' firms that help fill senior managerial posts in universities keep up-to-date lists of such types. Examining the public statements of such worthies, Veblen concludes that their overriding aim is not to offend: 'Hence the peculiarly, not to say exuberantly, inane character of this brand of oratory, coupled with an indefatigable optimism and good nature.' Ah yes, few things in the contemporary university make the flesh crawl more than the kind of unctuous corporate uplift which is clearly intended to placate the powers of the non-academic world.

Part of what gives Veblen's critique its continuing vitality is the sharpness of his perception of the clash between fashionable economic models and the true nature of untrammelled enquiry. He may at first seem high-handed when he writes 'No scholar or scientist can become an employee in respect of his scholarly or scientific work', but actually he is pointing to an enduring tension inherent in the role of the salaried searcher after truth. He acutely identifies how the market model leads to an over-emphasis on making a university 'competitive', with everything devoted to acquiring prestige, expanding numbers, keeping up positive appearances. This concern with the management of appearances results in 'statistical display, spectacular stage properties, vainglorious make-believe, and obsequious concessions to worldly wisdom'. Veblen is unwavering in his conviction that scholarly and scientific enquiry is the true heart of the university; other functions have accumulated around that, but they tend, as he said of professional schools, 'to create more of a bias hostile to scholarly and scientific work in the academic body'. Even much of undergraduate education is in this sense a secondary or derivative function: a college that operates just as a glorified high school is not, in his view, a university.

Veblen's baroque sarcasms are clearly a vehicle for the classic tropes of cultural criticism: misconceived machinery threatens to throttle the true nature of open-ended enquiry; an alien language colonizes the minds of those who should be the defenders of such enquiry; and, particularly striking, but perhaps not uncharacteristic of this literature, is Veblen's confidence that popular sentiment supports the true idea of the university rather than the fashionable commercial distortions of that idea – 'this massive hedge of slow but indefeasible popular sentiment that stands in the way of making the seats of learning over into something definitively foreign to the purpose which they are popularly believed to serve'. It is not just that, like any cultural critic, Veblen writes as though, however powerful may be the forces of darkness, his implied readers will be able to recognize the truth of his message; it is also that he believes there are deep-seated intuitions among the wider public that uphold the true idea of the nature of universities. Perhaps some version of this hope still haunts much writing about universities even today, and perhaps it is not wholly misplaced.

Although Veblen was a radical social theorist and Abraham Flexner was principally an academic administrator, their apparently dissimilar books turn out, on closer inspection, to be animated by some very similar ideas. For all its comparative empirical focus, Flexner's book is squarely in the 'idea of the university' tradition. In his opening chapter, 'The Idea of a Modern University', he says he will 'not discuss universities, but the idea of a university'. He went on to identify what he saw as the four 'major concerns' of universities: 'the conservation of knowledge and ideas; the interpretation of knowledge and ideas; the search for truth; the training of students who will practise and "carry on"'. In practice, he makes research and the passing on of research to advanced students the defining core of a university's activity; some undergraduate education might fall within this purpose, but much of it is really just a continuation of the work of the high school. Similarly, he is willing to allow that law and medicine may properly be studied within a university, being 'learned professions' with significant intellectual content, but most applied and vocational matters, he insists, should be assigned to other types of institution. The main part of the book is then an unsparing indictment of the low standards, the vulgar commercialism and the general loss of intellectual direction exhibited by American universities. British universities come off somewhat better, though Oxford and Cambridge are in his view still too absorbed by undergraduate teaching, but clearly it is German universities of the late nineteenth and early twentieth centuries that come nearest to his ideal of what a university should be.

The rhythm of Flexner's writing is shaped by the classic confrontation of high ideals with low realities. 'The graduate school ... is by far the most meritorious part of the American university', he observes at one point, finding in it signs of an intellectual seriousness almost wholly lacking in undergraduate education. But some pages later he can declare with typical downrightness: 'Fifty years ago, the degree of PhD had a meaning in the United States; today it has practically no significance', and so on. As with so much of this literature, if the ideals were not so demandingly high, the realities might not seem to be so unrelentingly low. He can refer, almost in passing and as a truth scarcely needing to be argued for, to 'the scholars and scientists who *are* the university', a common theme in this literature, but then later follow this up with the acknowledgement: 'The truth is that, with exceptions, of course, the American professoriate is a proletariat, lacking the amenities and dignities they are entitled to enjoy' – 'entitled', that is, by Flexner's conception of their high calling. He rightly observes that amenities for the students in most American universities are much more extensive and luxurious than for their teachers.

It is surely striking how much the persuasiveness of critiques such as Flexner's depend upon an appeal to the self-evident. He describes the way universities use their name to market extra-mural classes that have no relation to the true business of a university as simply 'scandalous', one of many examples where he appeals to what he takes to be a widely shared intuitive understanding of the proper role of universities. He appears to believe that, as he puts it, before long 'the "money-changers" will be driven – or laughed – out of the university temple', though given the abundant evidence he cites of such misconceived commercial priorities it is hard to see what the basis for his optimism is unless it be that mere exposure of the facts will mobilize a widely shared but latent conviction of the true purposes of universities. The *reductio* of such argument comes when he cites various activities smiled upon by the Harvard Business School and simply concludes: 'And this at Harvard!' His use of an exclamation mark here and elsewhere is a small stylistic indicator of the implicit appeal to self-evident truths. One notices an enduring confidence in this literature that the true purposes of universities are, at bottom, understood by at least some sections of the population and that exposing the absurdities of particular practices will therefore serve as a corrective. He does this again when, for example, he writes: 'It pays better to be an athletic coach than to be a university professor!' Again, the exclamation mark proclaims the self-evident absurdity. Well, yes, that must, by his austere conception of the true purposes of a university, be so. The fact that in many large American universities the football coach is now paid a salary many times higher than that of the *president* of the university, let alone that of mere professors, may suggest Flexner's confidence in the corrective power of such widespread intuitions was not altogether well founded.

Part of what he admires about the German system at its best is the rigour of its scholarship and high intellectual standards generally, going back to the *Gymnasium*, but he particularly emphasizes the German professor's freedom to choose his teaching and research topics. 'Neither the faculty nor the ministry supervises him: he has the dignity that surrounds a man who, holding an intellectual post, is under no-one's orders.' Even the power of the ministry in the German system and the notorious vulnerability of the *Privatdocent* does not shake Flexner's admiration: 'as a well thought-out institution for the doing of certain definite and difficult things, the German university ... was a better piece of mechanism than any other nation has as yet created' – his use of the past tense expressing his ambivalence towards the changes that had taken place since 1914, including the impact of 'democracy' on universities. His ideal is of a fiercely selective elite system. In view of later developments, one can ask whether Flexner did not underestimate the capacity of universities to perform multiple tasks without thereby necessarily lessening the intellectual level of their core scholarly and scientific activities, but this underestimation may also be representative of the genre. Flexner's is a very different book from Veblen's, much more a well-informed empirical survey, much less a sustained exercise in sarcasm. But both books share this sense that merely to identify many of the features of the contemporary American university is to display their fatuity.

Turning to two mid-twentieth-century British examples, we find some of the same themes recurring, but given a distinctive inflexion by their different national setting. The title page of *Redbrick University*, published in 1943, declared it to be by 'Bruce Truscot', and that is how its author was thereafter referred to. But this was in fact a pseudonym for someone who certainly knew these universities at first-hand, Edgar Allison Peers, who was professor of Spanish at Liverpool. In choosing to publish pseudonymously, Peers was avoiding giving various kinds of offence by seeming to criticize his own institution, but he also hoped that it would help his more scathing or sardonic comments not to be disregarded or explained away in purely personal or local terms. His book generated an extraordinary level of attention, and continued to be frequently referred to in subsequent decades. The educational historian Harold Silver reckons that it was the twentieth century's 'first book about English higher education to have a popular appeal'. The concrete detail and witty writing gave it a force and readability that more abstract ruminations on the subject have lacked. The book is still recognizably a piece of cultural criticism in the 'idea' tradition even though it dealt with just one group of institutions within English higher education (principally the early civic universities such as Manchester, Birmingham, Bristol, Leeds, Sheffield and Liverpool).

Truscot surveyed the damaging contrast that existed between high-status Oxbridge and the lower-status (and less well resourced) civic universities, and his book was in part a plea that this divide should be reduced. But it is, above all, a plea to the Redbricks themselves to live up to the true idea of a university, which at present they are not always doing. He makes plain that 'the search after knowledge is the essential function of the university'. 'We must lose no opportunity of stressing the double aim of the university – research and teaching – and of putting research first.' (I will just observe in passing the curious fact that almost all the best-known works in the 'idea' tradition take the opposite view to Newman, who did not regard research as a proper function of a university.) Truscot's leading indictment of contemporary civic universities was precisely that not enough of their staff gave this priority to research – indeed, that many of them did not pursue research at all. As far as students were concerned, he identified two main problems: the honours degrees are over-specialized, and these universities are largely non-residential. In other words, as with all 'idea' literature, *Redbrick University* contends that contemporary universities are falling short of the 'proper' performance of their function. Though only focused on a section of British universities, Truscot's book conforms to the logic of the genre throughout. In particular, he emphasizes that universities are the homes of that kind of disinterested enquiry which then has some prestige in the outside world precisely because it is not driven by partisan or utilitarian purposes from the start. In a revealing declaration of faith, he celebrates

> the virtues of the scholar – those same sterling moral qualities as are brought out by the scholar's characteristic activity, research – and when these, which make their appeal to the highest that is in us, are once recognized, they cannot fail to touch all but the unthinking or the perverse. Even the fools, who come at first to scoff, will remain to pray.

Both his emphasis on the ethical qualities cultivated by scholarship and his belief in their infectious power are striking. A similar faith implicitly underwrites the enterprise of his book itself. He assumes considerable agreement that the qualities evinced in and encouraged by intellectual enquiry simply are 'the highest that is in us', and he likewise assumes that 'once recognized, they cannot fail to touch all but the unthinking or the perverse'. So, again, the pathology that is the state of the contemporary university will correct itself when it is identified and its distance from the shared ideal of institutional health is called to the surface. In practical terms, he recognizes that the Redbricks have been starved of resources, and he assumes that the greater part of the money will, in the post-war world, come from the state. He is not principally making the case for such funding or even for expanding the university system and contributing more to the post-war economy. Instead, he is anatomizing a group of institutions he knows well and itemizing how they fall short of an ideal which is not simply that of Oxbridge, but is that of the university as the home of unfettered intellectual enquiry by the academic staff and of all-round development of mind and personality by the students. Though the conditions of the post-war world were very different (and Peers died in 1952, without fully taking their measure), what he called for was certainly the direction in which civic universities moved in the post-war decades and could also be seen as congruent with the informing ideals of the new 'plate-glass' universities of the 1960s.

By the time he published *The Crisis in the University* in 1949, Sir Walter Moberly had become the consummate Establishment figure. An Oxford-educated philosopher, he had been principal of University College Exeter before moving on in 1926 to be vice-chancellor of Manchester University and from 1935 (until 1949) the chairman of the University Grants Committee. Moberly was also a committed Christian, very active in a variety of lay Christian bodies, notably the Christian Frontier Council and the Student Christian Movement; it was under the auspices of the latter, and as a result of collective discussion by its leading members, that his book was published. Hardly surprisingly, therefore, the 'crisis' of his title is, fundamentally, a spiritual crisis – the loss of agreed beliefs and values. His overriding preoccupation is the need for students to be led to address the fundamental problems of existence and develop their own philosophy of life. Along the way, both his Christianity and his insiderishness can now seem distractingly intrusive. For example, it may seem a little disconcerting to have a chairman of the UGC declaring that 'In the fulfilment of God's will for the world a special mission may be assigned to Great Britain.' Or, as an instance of the clubby assumptions Moberly felt able to take for granted, consider his comment, in discussing how governments need to respect the autonomy of universities in all academic matters: government, he wrote, 'should no more think of dictating these things than of dictating the rules of the Athenaeum or the MCC'. No doubt it is of a piece with these assumptions that he does not translate his quotations from Greek and Latin.

But for all its dated or estranging features, Moberly's book rehearses a very familiar case. He focuses chiefly on the civic universities, where he repeats many of 'Bruce Truscot's' strictures. Specialization has been taken too far, universities have become simply a collection of non-communicating departments, and we have lost sight of what knowledge is for. The fact that most modern universities are largely non-residential means the loss of those larger benefits of social interaction and informal social contacts between teachers and taught which are essential in shaping the whole person. Students are too purely focused on getting a good degree as a route to a good job. He also makes a lot of perennially relevant observations, as, for instance, when he writes: 'There is always the danger that the layman, employing criteria which he can understand and seeking to satisfy the felt need of the moment, will impair or destroy the university's most precious, but intangible, assets.' And at one point in discussing teaching methods he almost becomes witty, though I fear it is inadvertent: 'Whatever the quality of lectures,' he declares, 'the crying evil is that the bulk of students attend far too many of them.' Though he focuses less on scholarly or scientific enquiry as the defining activity of universities than Veblen, Flexner and Truscot had done, he makes clear that, as he puts it at one point, 'the university should be a place of resolute and untiring pursuit of truth in matters of the highest significance', and that anything else represents what, using more than once the phrase made popular by the translation of Benda's *La Trahison des clercs*, he calls 'the treason of the intellectuals'.

Unlike many recent contributors to the literature on universities, Moberly is not circling the wagons as a defence against external attacks, however defined. It is, rather, that he fears that the expansion of universities, which he claims to welcome, will not be accompanied by sufficient rethinking of what the university ought to mean or can mean in a technological and democratic age. His book is, at bottom, a call to Christians to get involved. The book received a great deal of attention and continued to be a dominant presence in discussion of universities for some time. As Robert Anderson remarked in 1983 of the books by Truscot and Moberly, 'for a long time they were where you turned if you were looking for ideas about university education'.

From the several more recent contributions to this genre, let me focus on Bill Readings's widely cited 1996 book, *The University in Ruins*. Readings's book might most economically be characterized as an attempt to rethink the modern university through the categories of late twentieth-century literary theory. He does this with much acuity and brio, though his form of analysis and its constant recourse to the highest levels of abstraction means that his account, while stimulating as a critique, ends up being rather simplistic as history. In Readings's view, the modern university is initially theorized by Kant, Humboldt and the early nineteenth-century German Idealists, and it is based on the union of Reason and Culture, or in educational terms of *Wissenschaft* and *Bildung*. Readings gives this a particular twist, which owes something to this German focus, in seeing the university as by its very nature committed to furthering the project of the nation-state, as forming through its teaching of an agreed syllabus what he calls 'the national subject'. This premise informs the whole argument of the book – and constitutes, in my view, one of its chief limitations. Readings was a literary scholar and he makes much of the importance of the teaching of the national literature to the project of the nineteenth and early twentieth-century university, though in reality this formed a very small part of the curriculum in most European and even American universities.

Nonetheless there is considerable value, I think, in the central trope of Readings's book: that of the modern university as now 'an institution in ruins'. It has, he contends, lost whatever informing 'idea' it may once have possessed, and he has some sharp pages on how the empty category of 'excellence' now expresses this situation. The university is an administered set of activities united by no more than the fact they derive from an earlier more restricted set of activities that were carried on in institutions of this name, though there is now no agreement on what the range of these activities should be nor whether they have a determinate content. And it is an institution without any transparent social function that intelligibly links these activities to the presumed needs of society. Again, he seems to me to con-centrate too much on the humanities and to neglect the way that a vast array of applied scientific and social scientific enterprises flourish within the modern university without lacking any intel-ligibility or rationale. But he is surely acute about the situation of the humanities, especially perhaps in the elective system that is almost universal in the American 'liberal arts' model, where, he argues, they function as a supplement to the tourist industry, with partly interested, partly bored, trippers traipsing round the sites to which our predecessor cultures attached value.

It is much harder to say what Readings recommends we should now do. We should, it seems, inhabit the ruins with some sense of postmodern irony while also pragmatically using them to explore the limits of what can be thought. We should see what we still call 'the university' as a site or occasion for the practice of dissensus, a dissensus not redeemed by any belief in an ultimate agreement, not even the agreement to differ. As with all states of methodological self-consciousness, one of the problems with this re-description in terms of literary theory's systematic collapsing of every category is that it makes it hard to see how we decide to do anything in particular. Taken to its limit, Readings's argument would seem to suggest that the whole university will become a kind of continuous seminar mixing philosophy and cultural studies, endlessly questioning the status of any proposed object of study. Readings certainly wishes to resist the pure consumerism of student choice, but he does not seem to provide any rationale for any one object of study rather than another, so sheer consumer choice seems likely, by default, to end up dictating the pattern of his 'post-historical university'. He invokes the centrality of Thought with a capital T, but the harsh truth is that, without a series of established disciplinary enquiries through which such thinking is to be done and in its turn questioned, 'Thought' risks becoming as empty and, as he puts it, 'de-referentialized' a term as 'excellence'.

Nonetheless, for all its 1990s high-theoretical invocation of Derrida, Lyotard et al., this is recognizably a contribution to the literature on 'the idea of the university'. It is, for instance, about the university in general, not about any actual university or any one type of university or even about just one country (his constant reference to the US is partly offset by his own location as an Englishman teaching in a French-speaking university in Montreal, and anyway, as I have already indicated, he does not neglect European intellectual and institutional history). Even though he disclaims any nostalgia for what he calls 'the university of Culture', his perspective is that of the cultural critic alerting his public to the fact that something has gone badly wrong. And although he also disowns any notion of the university as society's organ of consciousness, he clearly still believes that it is a uniquely favourable location for certain sorts of analytical thinking, as his reference to an almost exclusively academic range of writing confirms. It would be reductive and a little unfair to say that Readings's book allows the most radical critical theorists to retain their intellectual self-respect without feeling obliged to give up their jobs, but his book was certainly a restatement for the age of the so-called 'culture wars' within and around the North American university in the closing decades of the twentieth century. Yet, for all the 1990s hipness of Readings's articulation of these ideas, there is something oddly familiar at work here. The university still does seem to rest on our old friend open-ended enquiry, given a post-structuralist twist. Even if there is no shared ideal of *Bildung* to appeal to, there is still *Wissenschaft*, provided we gloss that as accepting there is no such thing as objective truth. Like so much of the 'idea' literature, Readings's book is more compelling as critique than as blueprint. It is acute on the university conceived as 'the administration of excellence', but it is oddly limp about what the theoretically alert denizens of the ruins should actually do with their time.

III

Although I am for the moment treating these various writings as a single genre, it hardly needs saying that each example was intimately bound up with a set of particular historical circumstances, and one thing we can do – a task that falls particularly to intellectual historians – is attempt to unravel the specificities of each text by reconnecting it to the practices and ideas it was engaging with. It might be interesting, for example, to see how far the actual history of universities in any period corresponded with the pictures painted in these texts; contemporary practice in those institutions may already have been far removed from the ideal being restated. 'Idea' writing is always suggesting that something is wrong with current practice or at least with what threatens to become current practice – hence the occasion for writing – and so it might also be revealing to see how far those fears were realized and whether the resulting pattern turned out to be as fatal to the life of universities as was prophesied, and if not why not. I shall not pursue these questions here, but I shall instead focus on the recurrent rhetorical structure of these debates.

One way to address the issue of repetition is to note that all these classic works claim to be merely *re*stating some familiar truths. 'Idea' literature has above all involved reinterpreting, in the idiom of the time, the ideal of free enquiry which has been at the heart of the conception of the modern university since at least the end of the eighteenth century. This is a regulative ideal, one its proponents are prone to feel is constantly neglected or overridden in practice; hence the need for it to be correctively restated so often. At the same time, from the perspective of the proponents of 'social needs', there is an equally constant oppo-site process of 'academic drift', whereby the practical purposes of universities are being neglected by the internal imperatives of academic professionalism (or self-interest), and so they must constantly be recalled to their social purpose. Thus, where 'idea' literature is constantly seeking to crystallize what is entailed by the logic of open-ended enquiry, 'needs of society' statements are constantly attempting to rein in the consequences of an exces-sive attachment to that ideal as it has allegedly shaped actual academic practices.

Clearly, 'idea' literature has been one, indirect, way of articu-lating a conception of society which registers some dissonance or lack of fit between its determining economic practices and the life of the mind. Seeing how powerfully and effectively the impera-tives of the commercial world remake society in their own image generates an unease or, if you like, a surplus, a sense of the 'more' to human life – more than getting a job or making money – that we cannot shake ourselves free from yet also cannot easily inte-grate into our everyday arrangements. Museums and libraries or theatres and galleries are among the other types of institution that generate this sense, but they are more specialized and not primarily involved in education, whereas universities can seem to embrace both more unspecialized or unlimited aspiration *and* more practical and measurable social goals. Universities are in this way doomed to be homes both to instrumentality on a large scale and to the critique of that instrumentality in a tension or conflict that cannot be wholly resolved. Hence, in part, the repetitiveness of the literature.

For obvious reasons, I have never much cared for that old incantation that alleges: 'Those who can, do; those who can't, teach; those who can't teach, teach teachers.' But let me offer a relevant adaptation of the rhythm. 'If you want to make money, go into business. If you want to learn how to make money, go to business school. If you want to learn what money is and how it has functioned and what might be the point of making a lot of it, go to university.' This has the defects of most such brisk and knowing apophthegms, but it does gesture towards one aspect of what has traditionally been taken to distinguish teaching and studying at universities from more immediately practical activities. Second-order questions of that latter kind – what money is and how it has functioned and what might be the point of making a lot of it – always have the tendency to relativize the primary activities which are questioned in this way, to make them seem in some way more contingent or limited or just questionable, and hence such reflection and scrutiny imports some notion of critique. I do not share the view, propounded by some radically inclined theorists, that the university is *defined* by its commitment to critique or even oppositionality. That seems to me culpably to oversimplify and over-romanticize the role of universities. But I think it is true, as I've tried to explain before, that the very open-endedness of enquiry that is required if fresh understanding is to happen and be communicated has a tendency to generate these second-order questions, which in turn start to challenge the implicit premises of the practical purposes for which such enquiry was instituted in the first place. The paradox of universities in their modern form is that in this way they are bound to be simultaneously subservient to *and* distant from – even, at the limit, implicitly critical of – the dominant economic processes of society.

This also helps to explain, if explanation be needed, why there is no such distinguished tradition of literature on, say, 'the idea of the insurance company' or 'the idea of a refuse collection service'. The point may seem to be too obvious, perhaps even too cheap, to need to be made, but it is a reminder that there are large hopes of a nebulous kind invested in the idea of the university, hopes that can never be met simply by improving operational efficiency as could be the case with those more instrumental enterprises and services. That 'surplus of meaningfulness' that I mentioned earlier simply doesn't exist in these latter cases. And this thought may also bear on the asymmetry I pointed to: the tradition of literature on 'the idea of the university' cannot be genuinely paralleled by a comparable body of writing that asserts the priority of the instrumental needs society constantly wants universities to meet. These claims tend to be made, instead, in ways that are more practical, more patchy and more embedded in one kind or other of official document. Where 'the idea of the university' literature, mostly taking the form of the stylish book or at least sequence of extended critical essays, has usually been written by intellectual figures who stand in some intimate relation to universities, the 'needs of society' case brings together statements by politicians, journalists, officials and businessmen, statements which may take the form of White Papers, reports of commissions or committees of enquiry, leading articles, public lectures, letters to the press and so on.

But if they do not have a common form, these latter statements certainly have a small number of recurrent themes. They typically tend to convict universities of being too introverted, too sluggish, too prone to the vices of scholasticism, too unresponsive to the needs of the economy and so on – what we might designate as 'the ivory tower indictment', except that that may seem to confer legitimacy on that tired and empty cliché. From the campaign against the alleged failings of Oxford by the *Edinburgh Review* in the early nineteenth century up to whatever is the latest reiteration of essentially the same case by the representatives of business organizations in the present, the spokespersons for the needs of society rail against the self-perpetuating character of academic life, its unjustifiable privileges and its divorce from something called 'reality', about which these spokespersons are, apparently, experts by definition. One might mischievously suggest that these pronouncers are, contrary to their intentions, testifying to the uncontrollable dynamic of intellectual enquiry, because they see that this is what constantly drags universities away from the more immediate instrumental aims that have only recently been laid down. They also see that the kind of autonomy that academics claim as the essential precondition of fruitful intellectual work is constantly open to abuse. The conditions of work that favour genuine originality of thought also appear to favour shirking and loafing. Rather as with periodic battles over welfare policy, one side sees the systemic benefits of adequate provision, the other concentrates on such a system's vulnerability to exploitation by the lazy or the unscrupulous.

We may not wish to go quite as far as the Liberal cabinet minister, Lord Haldane, writing in 1911, who declared resoundingly that 'it is in universities that ... the soul of a people mirrors itself', but however hard-headed we try to be, we cannot altogether discount the fact that universities always seem to be endowed with a surplus of meaningfulness. This does not appear to happen with technical colleges, institutes of manufacturing, or cookery schools. Apprenticeship schemes have not thrown up their Newman; institutes of chartered accountants have not been lambasted by their Veblens for falling away from the high ideals they should embody. The very antiquity, or at least apparent antiquity, of a few universities may partly be in play here, while as a category universities clearly still benefit from a wider cultural prestige. It is, after all, a striking fact that whereas several other types of institution have, over the decades, converted themselves into, or at least rebranded themselves as, universities, there is no such flow in the other direction. This cannot simply be because of an increasingly vestigial association with the elites of earlier periods. Just as some of the aporias of the literature on intellectuals can be seen as a kind of back-handed acknowledgement that the category involves or conjures up something desirable – something about the place we would, in some moods at least, like to see intellect and reflection occupying in public life – so, similarly, at least some of the contradictory attitudes that cluster around the idea of the university signal that, even now, the institution is seen as providing the setting, in some cases the unique or necessary setting, for the realization of cherished cultural values.

The recurrent rhetorical patterns discernible in the literature on 'the idea of the university' can also be exhibited by considering what literary theorists would call the 'implied addressee' of such writing. For example, both Veblen and Flexner are sweepingly critical of higher education in the United States and see its failings as having deep roots in the dominant commercial character of American society. But if that character is so dominant, then it is not immediately clear where readers sympathetic to their critical messages might be found. Yet it is a recurrent feature of such writing, as of the larger category of cultural criticism more generally, that the appeal to self-evidence is one of its central argumentative moves. The structure of their prose assumes that merely to describe some of the activities of contemporary American universities is sufficient for their readers to join in dismissing them out of hand. If all cultural criticism has what might be called (in a technical sense) a 'utopian' element, an horizon of hope, then it has to assume that this will be in some way recognizable to its readers. If there were no such ideal that could be appealed to, however implicitly, then there would be no vantage point from which current practices could be condemned.

Cultural criticism tends to proceed by exposing to view the inadequacy of some set of practices or particular uses of language rather than by trying to specify the appealed-to ideal with any concreteness. Such criticism is usually at its most memorable and powerful when engaged in the dissection of various examples of contemporary insensibility, and in the case of the literature on the university the critique of various forms of official and dominant discourse is particularly fertile ground. Just as canonical cultural critics such as, say, Carlyle or Ruskin or Arnold were not usually proposing specific alternative practical policies in the political or economic spheres, so most of this literature is at its best when gesturing towards barely expressible deep truths about the nature of education or scholarship rather than in composing an alternative White Paper.

But the cultural critic is not just a licensed gadfly or court jester, who can be indulged and whose mockery can be tolerated because, fundamentally, it doesn't actually affect anything important. Perhaps what Arnold had to say about the damage done by the policy of 'payment by results' had more influence in the long run than any measures enacted by Robert Lowe, the minister responsible for that policy. Similarly, it may be that 'Bruce Truscot's' *Redbrick University* is most readable when in satirical or jeremiad mode, but it was also a serious attempt to understand a particular form of university life, and its strictures on the lack of community in most such universities may have had considerable influence on the move to build residences for students and better facilities for staff at those universities in the late 1940s and 1950s. Criticism in the name of what some may see as impractical idealism is not always without its practical consequences.

IV

One unsurprising truth we may learn from considering the long literature on the idea of the university is that each generation fails to envision not just the path of future change but also how universities may adapt to this change without ceasing to be recognizable as universities. Some changes may indeed signal the end of the world as we know it, as the doomsayers predict, but a world that we don't know and cannot foresee which arises in its stead may still turn out to be a tolerably good place. The rise of industrialism did not mean that only subjects directly related to industrial production came to be studied in universities. The same may now be true of the financialization of the world. The rise of credit default swaps does not signal the inevitable end of the study of English literature any more than the rise of the Bessemer Convertor announced the demise of classics. On the other hand, classics occupies a vastly smaller place in the university now than 150 years ago and there are intelligible social reasons for this change. It would be foolish to think that social and economic developments now under way may not bring correspondingly significant changes to universities of the future, so let me, in conclusion, briefly turn to the question of whether the long tradition of writing reflecting on the nature of the university helps us to resist the more apocalyptic current predictions.

Those who are confident that the unprecedented pace of change in the present makes past experience largely irrelevant are fond of pointing to what they see as the two great transforming powers of the contemporary world: first, the processes summed up as 'globalization', and, second, the revolutionary power of new technology. If universities are imagined as the direct expression of the age of global capital, then, it is argued, there is no reason for them to be funded by a particular state. They simply become one means for players in a market to seek advantage, and those players can come from anywhere. Therefore the relation should be that of customer to provider, not of citizen to state. And the new technology reinforces this: there is no need to be physically in one place rather than another. The only connection between a student and a university that is essential is the ability to click on a PayPal account. Indeed, even the language of 'promoting national economic needs' is, fundamentally, at odds with this truly global picture, as the masters of global capital realize all too well. HSBC is not concerned with Britain's 'national needs' any more than is the 'British' hedge fund which, for tax purposes, has its offices in a Swiss canton. As far as such commercial enterprises are concerned, 'countries' simply figure as sets of trading conditions: one has a 'more flexible labour market' (that is, flexible about sacking people), another has a 'supportive fiscal regime' (that is, supportive of making and retaining large profits). Similarly, if it proves a better return on investment to get your training in Singapore, to start building future networks at MIT, to pick up a useful dollop of cultural capital at Cambridge and so on, then those are the decisions global consumers will make – all the relevant goods can be priced into the market. Those who want to see British universities largely funded by the British taxpayer, and perhaps even imagine them largely filled with British students, can be portrayed as survivals from the era of the nation-state, or even as the educational equivalent of UKIP.

Techno-futurologists go further still and ask whether, if everything that has previously been done face to face can now be done online, location matters at all. If a university is a brand, why should it not sell in all available markets? If a library is in effect just a website and a lecture is in effect just an internet clip, and if an exam is a machine-graded multiple answer quiz, why not just enrol everybody who applies, wherever they are? What were once brand-name doctrines only obtainable from a particular source have now become over-the-counter commodities obtainable anywhere. Or, garbling another cultural referent, the study of almost any discipline has now become a *jeu sans frontières*: couched in a sophisticated version of 'Globish', universally available introductory packages constitute the 'canon' of the internet age, just as online reviews turn literary criticism into a variant of TripAdvisor. The metaphor of 'inside the walls' has long survived the functional demise of such architectural structures themselves; now the only relevant kind of wall is a paywall.

The exaggeration built into such doom-mongering tends to undermine its case, and notoriously the record of correctly anticipating and estimating the worth of such changes as have been forecast in the past is not good. But one prediction I would make is that in fifty or a hundred years' time there will be fresh examples of 'idea of the university' literature. The drive by capital and its markets to mould human existence to its will is hardly going to lessen, and so neither will the flickering and uncertain recognition that universities are one major expression of a still-valuable ideal of the open-ended search after fuller understanding that is not wholly governed by that economic logic. Such writing constantly reminds us of the slippage between what is humanly valuable and what is merely unnoticed or accepted or fashionable. The ceaseless rhythm of the waves of everyday life causes a deposit of insensibility to build up that clogs our perceptions and dulls our responsiveness. Procedures established for a series of transient and ad hoc reasons acquire that patina of inevitability with which economic logic needs to coat its operations if we are not to rebel against its unconscionable exactions. Alien language first invades our territory; then it settles and reproduces; and finally, in a familiar imperialist twist, it colonizes our minds and leads us to treat its barbarous, exploitative categories as a true description of our necessary state. The literature on 'the idea of the university' constitutes a series of attempts to chip off some of the limescale that corrodes the pipes of our thinking, allowing us to see the inappropriateness or even absurdity of terms and procedures that we were otherwise in danger of treating as our own.

So, yes, this literature is repetitive, but in the way that the application of any solvent has to be repeated if it is to be at all effective in combatting an unrelenting pressure. Yes, this literature is idealistic, but in the sense in which anything that calls us back to reflection about what makes life worth living can seem idealistic: its function is not to propose detailed alternative procedures, but to jolt us into recognizing how far our present procedures now are from serving the true ends of universities. Yes, this literature can seem nostalgic at times because it is protesting against the forms taken by the most recent build-up of ideological sediment, and so it is bound to seem to be hankering after a time when these forms were as yet unknown, though that does not actually entail mourning for a lost paradise, as earlier critiques of the abuses of *that* time made plain. And yes, it must always mix restatement of general principle with detailed criticism of recent idiocies, partly because it is the accumulated build-up of such misguided practices and distorting language which has stirred the critic to this restatement in the first place, but partly also because the process of persuasion requires the recognition of particulars. And, finally, yes, examples of this literature continue to be read and re-read long after the conditions they addressed have become historical curiosities because the energy released by the collision between, on the one hand, the immovable mass of decayed half-truths and rotting clichés and, on the other, the irresistible force of genuine ethical insight functions like a prose version of the Large Hadron Collider. Sentences in which the pulse of thought has been accelerated by insight and indignation can simply shatter an inert list of bullet-points, revealing their basic structure to be no more than a random collocation of managerial anti-matter.

We do not have to admire everything about the great cultural critics of the past, or even agree with any of their particular views, to feel that the force of their writing remains generative of fertile thought for us now in our very different circumstances. If we stop writing and reading (and re-reading) the literature on 'the idea of the university', it will mean that we have suppressed, or perhaps just lost, the ability to identify the ways in which our current arrangements traduce and betray our understanding of what is distinctive – certainly what has been and, arguably, should be distinctive – about the university, that odd institutional-conceptual amalgam that we have inherited from the contingencies of history and which we reinvent in each generation. In reiterating that idea, we are not just banging our heads against a brick wall. We are enabling ourselves to see that the supposed wall is merely a piece of stage drapery, yet another of ideology's insidious *trompe l'oeil* effects.

It is because universities are so intimately bound up with the place which the extension of understanding has in human life, individually and collectively, that we cannot simply bracket off fundamental questions about worth and purpose in the way it is sensible to do with a variety of more limited and more purely instrumental enterprises, no matter how essential these enterprises may be to the maintenance and reproduction of existence. Questioning whether our present arrangements do genuinely serve that purpose of extending and deepening human understanding is not 'elitist' or 'conservative' or 'unrealistic' or any of the other dismissive labels that busy important people find to hand in the corporately maintained cliché-pool that passes for the conventional wisdom. Such reflexive questioning is an ineliminable part of the functions that universities serve. So, if you feel something is not quite right when you are told by your line manager that robust and transparent procedures are necessary if our deliverables are to be quantified in a way that makes us competitive in the global market, then you are already taking the first step in a process of reflection that eventually culminates in reading, or perhaps even writing, a book about the true purposes of universities. Of course, you may feel that there is nothing at all wrong with the sentence I have just ventriloquized, but in that case I suspect you need an altogether different kind of professional help.

PART II

CRITIQUES

CHAPTER 4

From Robbins to McKinsey:
The Changing Policy Framework

I

One of the most fascinating yet elusive aspects of cultural change is the way certain ideals and arguments acquire an almost self-evident power at particular periods, just as other arguments, which once possessed this power, come to seem irrelevant or antiquated and largely disappear from public debate.[1] In the middle of the eighteenth century, to describe a measure as 'displaying the respect that is due to rank' was a commonplace commendation; in the middle of the nineteenth, affirming that a proposal contributed to 'the building of character' could be an almost unnoticed part of the mood music of public discourse; in the middle of the twentieth, 'a decent standard of life' was the goal of all parties and almost all policies. As with the wider processes of language change, readers and listeners become inured to what were once jarring neologisms or solecisms, while phrases that were once so common as to escape notice become in time unusable.

It will be a long time before historians can adequately chart, let alone explain, the changes in public discourse in Britain in the past half century, but when that task is attempted, official publications will have a special evidential value. They tend not to bear the marks of an individual sensibility, but rather to deploy idioms and arguments that are thought to command the widest acceptance, even when, perhaps especially when, the actual policy proposals they contain are novel and controversial. The relation between the legitimating phrases and the policies is neither that

---

1 A shorter version of this chapter was published in the *London Review of Books* in August 2011.

of strict entailment nor of complete randomness. Widely varying policies can all claim to be furthering some approved general goal, though conventional assumptions about the character of that goal will limit the range of policies that can do this persuasively.

'Markets are a mechanism through which buyers and sellers interact in the trade of goods and services. The boundaries of markets are not easily defined, but may be thought of in terms of the choices that customers are able to make about substituting between products or the choices of suppliers in switching production.' No, not a passage from the opening chapter of a textbook in economic theory, but a pair of sentences buried on pages 101–2 of 'Supporting analysis for the Higher Education White Paper' (BIS Economics Paper no. 14). According to its own self-description, this dense and hefty document 'provides the economic analysis underpinning the Government's Higher Education White Paper. This has been fundamental to policy design in striking the right balance between private and public funding, competition and regulation, and growth and social mobility.' The author of these words from the Foreword (though presumably the document as a whole is to some extent a collective compilation) is identified as Tera Allas, 'Director-General, Economics, Strategy & Better Regulation, Department for Business, Innovation & Skills', an economist who previously worked for ten years as a management consultant with McKinsey & Company 'with a primary focus on corporate and business unit strategy'. Away from the headlines, we are here getting close to the way in which, deep in the heart of its big steel and glass box in Westminster, BIS develops the policies that will turn Britain's (or, at least, England's – more on that later) universities into corporate suppliers that will, as it promises, 'ensure that all aspects of the organisation are supporting the reputation and brand that they have developed – right from the way they innovate to deliver the services to the organisational design to support delivery'.

Wherever one turns in this document, there is matter to nourish the soul. For example:

Economic theory suggests that individuals will invest in higher education up to the point where the private marginal benefit (PMB) equals the marginal cost (MC). However, there are additional benefits to society (SMB) which are not considered by the individual when making their [*sic*] decision to invest in HE. As a result the optimal level of investment from society's perspective may exceed that which individuals would make, causing lower investment in HE than would be socially optimal.

These are the terms on which the case is made for 'government intervention in the HE market'. In other words, the 'supporting analysis' provided by this document reasons from the theoretical assumption that higher education functions as a perfect market, and then suggests a role for government intervention where, for one reason or another, it identifies 'market failure'. That, after all, is what economists do, or at least that is an aspect of what some theoretical economists do as a preliminary to exploring whether any bit of the world actually works like that. And such reasoning is at the heart of BIS's overall strategy. When Ms Allas was appointed to her present position, a spokesman for the department announced: 'Encouraging sustainable economic growth is the key priority for BIS in 2011. Tera and her new group will be at the very centre of delivering that; making sure that we coordinate all the different strands of work and are all pulling together.' Universities are one of these strands of work: economic growth is the goal, markets are the method.

Since perhaps the 1970s and certainly the 1980s, official discourse has become increasingly colonized by an economistic idiom, one that is not strictly derived from the language of economic theory proper, but rather from the language of management schools, business consultants and financial journalism. British society has been subject to a deliberate campaign, initiated in the free market think-tanks in the 1960s and 1970s and pushed strongly by business leaders and right-wing commentators ever since, to elevate the status of business and commerce and to install 'contributing to economic growth' as the overriding goal of a whole swathe of social, cultural and intellectual activities which had previously been understood and valued in other terms. Such a campaign would not have been successful, of course, had it not been working with the grain of other changes in British society and the wider world. Very broadly speaking, the extension of democratic and egalitarian social attitudes has been accompanied by the growth of a kind of consumerist relativism. The claim that one activity is inherently of greater value or importance than another comes to be pilloried as 'elitism'. Arguments are downgraded into 'opinions': all opinions are equally valuable (or valueless), and so the only agreed criterion can be what people say they think they want, and the only value that has any indefeasible standing is 'value for money'. Any substantial government document dating from the last couple of decades is immediately identifiable by the presence of the acknowledged buzz-phrases of the time – 'it is essential to sustain economic growth and maintain Britain's global competitiveness', 'consumers must have a choice of services', 'competition will drive up quality' and so on.

Higher education policy has been something of a barometer of the growing dominance of the view of the world these phrases express. The frequent shuffling of responsibility for universities around government departments in recent decades graphically illustrates the way the weather has changed. For several decades following its establishment in 1919, the University Grants Committee, largely composed of senior academic figures, served as a valuable buffer organization, making the case to the Treasury for the size of grant needed by universities and then distributing that sum among institutions. Until 1964 the UGC dealt directly with the Treasury, but then the new Labour government set up the Department of Education and Science (DES) which oversaw the UGC until the latter's abolition in 1989. The establishment in that year of the Universities Funding Council, complete with members drawn from the world of business, was a deliberate attempt to make the funding of universities more directly responsive to government priorities. With the abolition of the distinction between universities and polytechnics in 1992 a new body was set up to oversee higher education funding as a whole, the Higher Education Funding Council for England (with cognate bodies in the other parts of the UK). In 1995 its parent ministry, the DES, was dissolved and a new ministry set up, the Department for Education and Employment. In 2001 a re-shuffle of responsibilities led to this being superseded by the new Department for Education and Skills, which itself was then broken up in 2007 and replaced by another new ministry, the Department for Innovation, Universities and Skills, and then, in yet another reorganization in 2009, responsibility for higher education passed to the new Department for Business, Innovation and Skills.

By this point the picture had long been further complicated by the existence of research councils, such as (initially) the Medical Research Council, which were variously the responsibility of the Cabinet Office or the science branch of the DES. In 1992 the Office of Science and Technology was set up, at one point answerable to the Cabinet Office, but from 1995 under the aegis, tellingly, of the Department of Trade and Industry. In early 2006, this body was renamed the Office of Science and Innovation, and was absorbed into the Department for Innovation, Universities and Skills in the summer of 2007, when the Department for Education and Skills was split in two. I realize the detail of these changes may be less than riveting to some readers, but what it signals about the reshaping of official attitudes towards higher education is surely very striking. Universities and research have come more and more under the aegis of bodies whose primary concerns are business, trade and employment. The terms in which the activities of universities are now discussed are those that have been honed in shaping other kinds of 'corporate and business unit strategy'.

Back in 1963, one of the most interesting and, in its way, radical suggestions of the Robbins Committee was the proposal that a new ministry should be created to give universities more direct representation within government. Arguing against the then fashionable idea that universities and schools should be brought together in a new Ministry of Education (which is what happened in the following year), Robbins maintained that the connections between universities and schools were less close than those between universities and 'other forms of organised research' which also operated on a version of the arm's length principle: the research councils, the Arts Council, the Committee on Museums and Galleries and so on. His committee proposed the setting up of a Ministry of Arts and Sciences with overall responsibility for this range of institutions. Such a ministry, the report insisted, 'would recognise the importance to the spiritual health of the community of a proper organization of state support for learning and the arts'. There can clearly be different views about the potential benefits of these various structures, including the question of whether a particular area of policy benefits more from being part of one of the big battalions, which can argue the larger funding case effectively in Cabinet and with the Treasury, or whether this invariably leads to that area's real needs being subordinated to the priorities of the larger departmental strategy. Nonetheless, compared to the present arrangement, Robbins's suggestion still has much to recommend it, including the emphasis it puts on the comparable long-term cultural and intellectual role of universities alongside museums, galleries and arts councils. There can be no question but that classing higher education as just one part of the remit of a department of business encourages the treatment of universities primarily as contributors to economic growth.

As the recent history of the ministerial game of pass the parcel should indicate, the subordination of universities to this supposed policy priority is something that has been furthered by both Conservative and Labour governments. Much of the language of the 2011 White Paper is to be found almost verbatim in *Higher Ambitions: The Future of Universities in a Knowledge Economy*, produced by BIS in 2009 when Peter Mandelson was the presiding minister. It also has to be remembered that it was a Labour government that first introduced 'top-up fees' (in 1998) and then 'variable fees' (in 2006). Variable fees turned out, of course, not to be variable, as all universities very soon charged the top rate. The frustration felt in the policy-making world at this fresh demonstration of universities' unwillingness to operate according to good market principles was not the least of the impulses that had to be accommodated by the independent committee, set up in 2009 with cross-party agreement, to review the effect of the 2006 fees and to come up with a sustainable form of future funding for higher education.

Lord Browne, a businessman with no particular experience of teaching or working in a university, was chosen to chair the seven-person committee, whose members included the head of McKinsey's Global Education Practice, a former Treasury economist who is a member of the UK Competition Commission, and a banker; one of the two vice-chancellors on the committee had also worked in the engineering industry. The committee was due to report in the summer of 2010, after the election. But while it was still deliberating, the new coalition government was drawing up the attack on public services that is known as the Comprehensive Spending Review, and when the report did appear its radical solution was to cut almost all public funding of teaching, leaving universities to replace the lost income by charging students much higher fees. (We shall have to wait until historians can inspect official records from the summer of 2010 to document exactly how it was that Lord Browne's 'independent' review happened, as though by chance, to come up with a proposal that fitted exactly onto the coalition's not-yet-announced spending plans.) The Browne Report was a shoddy, ill-argued and under-researched document which rightly attracted a firestorm of criticism, but the coalition immediately announced that it would 'accept' its main recommendations. (In practice, it has had progressively to abandon several aspects of Browne's proposals, partly because of political pressure, especially from the Liberal Democrats, partly because the cost implications became frightening, especially to the Conservatives, and partly because they came to seem, when looked at more closely, unworkable.)

One reason why the Commons' vote on 9 December 2010 to remove public funding from teaching and to triple undergraduate fees was a scandal was because such a measure had not been a manifesto commitment of any party – indeed, the *abolition* of fees had been a manifesto commitment of the junior party in the coalition whose MPs were now being forced into the division lobby – and had not been subject to any proper democratic scrutiny. But another reason was the flagrant disregard of what used to be normal government practice whereby a measure is first spelled out in some detail in a White Paper, then subject to criticism and consultation, and then later turned into draft legislation to be debated and voted upon in parliament. But on this occasion we were told that the White Paper would follow rather than precede the key legislative decision. It would be published 'shortly'. When shortly came and went, we were told that it would appear 'in March', then 'in April', until finally it was published on 28 June (2011), over six months after the legislation it was supposed to prepare the way for, and long after all universities had been forced by that legislation to draw up their financial plans despite not knowing how the new scheme would operate.

Moreover, it became clear during this period that the government had made a serious miscalculation even on its own premises. We now know that when the decision was taken to replace the block grant with a loan system, the Treasury (presumably the real driving force behind the change) calculated that the initial expenditure on loans would more or less match current expenditure on the teaching grant, assuming an average fee not higher than £7,500. The glaring defect in the Treasury's calculations was that it presumed (do officials and advisors understand their own machinery?) that the Office for Fair Access (OFFA), which oversees universities' admissions policies, had the legal power to dictate what fee a university could set, ensuring that fees would be kept down to the desired average level. But OFFA has no such legal power, as its director was obliged to 'remind' the government. A great many universities were setting fees of

£9,000 (as anyone could have predicted they would). Not only was the scheme not going to reduce expenditure, even on the official projections; it slowly dawned on the government that it might actually prove to be a lot more expensive than the present system. Observing ministers and officials in BIS during the first few months of 2011 was like watching a man haplessly trying to reconnect two halves of a hose-pipe while his companion, following instructions, was opening the tap even further. Whether one is broadly in favour of the new fee regime or not, there can be no denying that the process through which policy has taken shape in the last eight months [December 2010–July 2011] has been a risible shambles.

II

This particular Whitehall farce, punctuated by well-trailed leaks about various aspects of the proposals, means that there is now an inevitable sense of anti-climax surrounding the publication of the White Paper. Attention is bound to focus principally on what it reveals about the government's efforts to get out of the hole it has dug for itself, an awkward procedure that involves contradicting its professed market principles at almost every turn. It realizes that it cannot in fact have an open 'market' in the recruitment of students, since any significant rise in overall numbers will entail a corresponding rise in public expenditure given the need to provide funding to pay the fees in the first instance. But if it then keeps the cap on numbers, with, as at present, allocations to each university, it fears that this fails to introduce proper 'market discipline' at the bottom – that is, it wants universities to be in a position where they might fail to be 'competitive' in recruiting students and so go bankrupt. Keeping some version of the current allocation of places would also make it difficult for 'new providers' (including private companies) to enter the field, at least if they were to compete for students eligible for the publicly supported loan system.

We need to pause over this question of student numbers, since it is in this section of the White Paper that the blandest phrases hide the sharpest ideological fangs. Faced with the conundrum of how to create a market within a structure which still reflects a centralized command economy, it has come up with the wheeze of a 'core and margin' model of allocating places. Let's say that there are at present approximately 360,000 full-time undergraduate places at English universities each year for UK-domiciled applicants (all these figures are plagued by difficulties of definition). The government proposes to withhold some 85,000 of these places when making its allocations, with the number each institution is initially allowed to recruit being reduced pro rata. This means that universities will only be guaranteed about three quarters of their present intake. Beyond that 'core', to recruit extra students they will have to compete in one of the two pools that make up the 'margin' of places. In the first of these pools, there will be approximately 65,000 places reserved for applicants with A-level scores of AAB or higher, and there will be no central controls on how many applicants a university may recruit from this pool. So, if an institution's basic A-level offer is AAB or above (which is the case for most of the conventionally rated 'top' universities), it will not need to change its standard admission policies: a quarter of its regular intake can simply be designated as coming from the margin since they possess the requisite qualifications. In fact, it could take more, up to the point at which there were no more applicants available with the necessary A-levels, though there would be, quite apart from increased pressure on staff, facilities, accommodation and so on, a delicate trade-off involved between increased numbers (and hence income) and reduced exclusivity.

The second pool would be made up of 20,000 places that will be competed for by institutions whose average fee does not exceed £7,500. This is explicitly intended to make it possible for 'new providers' to enter the system, organizations (such as Further Education Colleges as well as charities and for-profit companies) which do not at present have an allocation of places, but which would obtain them from this pool by undercutting universities. This also means that students recruited from this pool by for-profit providers will be eligible for government-backed loans, so that public finance will help to boost the profits of the directors and shareholders of these companies. Its implicit purpose, clearly, is to force less highly ranked universities, if they are to fill their places, to reduce their fees below the level at which the Treasury, quite arbitrarily, decided the loan system should be funded. Moreover, since the total number of 'funded' places (that is, students eligible for loans) will stay more or less constant for now, the auctioning off of 20,000 places to the lowest bidder will necessarily be at the expense of those existing universities that are undercut by the new providers. Some universities may even go bankrupt: 'Providers that perform poorly under the new funding arrangements will primarily be those that fail to recruit enough students', but 'the Government does not guarantee to underwrite universities and colleges'. The White Paper is silent on the damage this will do in terms of course closure and the sacking of academics (it presumably thinks the latter can be re-employed at piece-rates by private providers). And this is only the beginning: in each succeeding year, we are told, the 'core' will shrink and the 'margin' will expand.

Markets always reward those who are already advantaged. Since admission to universities is not in fact a genuine market, this plan is designed to produce a rigged market which ensures that the 'top providers' will do well out of it and there will be the usual race to the bottom at the lower end. The new scheme will introduce de facto price controls, a depressing example of the hypocrisy in all the proud affirmations by this government that universities are 'autonomous', that admissions are 'a matter between the student and the university', that the government cannot dictate what fees universities set and so on. Nothing is more indicative of the mess the government has made of this policy than the fact that this system has only been announced *after* universities had set their fee levels for 2012. Universities made those decisions when they believed the system would operate by one set of rules, but they have now been told that the rules have changed, and that some of them will be punished for decisions that they were forced to make by the government's own rushed timetable.

In keeping with its wholly phantasmatic conception of competition, the White Paper declares confidently that this system 'should allow greater competition for places on the more selective courses and create the opportunity for more students to go to their first-choice institution if that university wishes to take them'. But the two parts of this assertion must be in contradiction: if it were really true that this ensured more competition for the most sought-after places, then by definition that would reduce rather than increase opportunities for applicants to get their first-choice places. The actual effect of these changes (here mirroring the likely effect on the social composition of the student body of the introduction of high variable fees) is to make the distribution of resources for institutions match more closely the distribution of A-level scores. Just on fee income alone, students at institutions with an AAB offer or above will be better resourced, by quite a long way, than students at institutions with lower entry requirements. This is a naked example of using the power of the state to entrench hierarchy in the name of 'market principles'. By effectively ruling that a large number of universities must charge considerably less than the level it has itself legally permitted institutions to charge, the government is constructing a system that is bound to further reinforce existing social inequalities. All serious research shows that children at private schools have dramatically better chances of obtaining AAB at A-level than children at state schools. These children of privilege will now be further guaranteed that the universities they get into will be much better resourced as well. Perhaps it's not surprising that at this point the White Paper falls mysteriously silent about its otherwise much-trumpeted goal of increasing 'social mobility'.

These changes mean that, to a considerable extent, HEFCE ceases to be a funding council and becomes primarily a regulatory body and a 'consumer champion'. But there will still be a small residual teaching grant, and here the White Paper, like the Browne Review, reveals a curious unsteadiness about the extent to which the provision of courses by universities is or is not to be determined by 'student choice'. The latter, we are frequently told, is to be the 'driver' of the new system: students will be willing to pay to get what they think is worth having, and universities will have to provide this or perish. Students operating as consumers ensure market discipline works (the 'discipline' is exerted on universities, which are assumed to need it). But then we find that government will still provide a teaching grant direct to universities 'to fund additional costs and public policy priorities that cannot be met by a student-led funding system alone'. Thus, the extra costs, over and above the ceiling for fees, of medicine, laboratory-based courses, and others with high overheads will continue to be met centrally. But why should we assume that such 'expensive' courses would be less attractive to students if they were to be charged the full cost of providing them? The logic of the supposed 'market' is that students will not simply always opt for the cheapest course on offer, but will choose the higher price where they believe the quality, and the return in the form of future income, warrant it. That, after all, is supposed to be 'high-quality' universities' selling point. So why does that logic not apply to higher-cost subjects such as science and engineering? 'Market discipline' surely means that if universities cannot recover their costs in terms of sufficient numbers of fee-paying students, then they should not be offering such subjects.

A similar query may be raised about the proposal to maintain a certain element of the central grant for 'strategically important and vulnerable subjects' that 'require support to avoid undesirable reductions in the scale of provision'. 'Vulnerable' here must mean that not enough students want to study them, but that there are other reasons for maintaining them. Yet the crucial premise of the whole brave new world is that 'providers' will be forced to match their offerings to the wishes of 'consumers'. If not enough students want to do a degree in, say, German, no matter how much a university brings its price down, then the laws of the market dictate that that degree should not be offered. What can 'undesirable reductions in the scale of provision' mean in a market system? Obviously, a different set of criteria are tacitly in play here, and indeed at one point the White Paper concedes that HEFCE should ensure 'a healthy mix of subjects'. Indeed it should, but once *that* is acknowledged it follows that other values are recognized as capable of trumping 'student choice', and that to give effect to these values what we need is something remarkably like the present system of the teaching block grant, which enables 'the scale of provision' to be maintained far more effectively than by trying to pick up the pieces every time there is a shift in fashionable choices among seventeen-year-olds (or, more accurately, among fourteen-year-olds, given the determining effect of curriculum choices made at that age). There are some kinds of so-called 'market failure' which ought to make it embarrassingly clear that what we are dealing with cannot be adequately comprehended as a 'market' in the first place.

Incidentally, the retention of an element of the teaching grant for 'expensive' subjects has given rise to the perception that the policy is a deliberate assault on the arts and humanities, since they will receive no such central subsidy. But it should be said that, while these disciplines may suffer in various ways under the new system, this aspect of the proposals does not in fact single them out for exceptionally harsh treatment, since the recommended fee levels are higher than the current combination of fee and per capita grant for these courses. In purely financial terms, universities may turn out to have more incentive to put on humanities courses, provided they can find enough qualified applicants, than to put on courses in physics and chemistry whose full costs they may not be able to recover, though Russell Group universities will be able to subsidize such courses from research income.

Beyond the warped ingenuity of these Heath Robinson schemes to force 'free' competition to happen in certain closely controlled circumstances, such interest as the White Paper possesses may lie chiefly in its providing a handy compendium of current officialese, a kind of sottisier of econobabble, the conventional wisdom of at-the-end-of-the-day, when-push-comes-to-shove, let's-face-it, bottom-lining, global-competitiveness-speak. One of the most revealing features of its prose is the way in which the tense that might be called the Mission Statement Present is used to disguise implausible non sequiturs as universally acknowledged general truths. For example, one mantra, repeated in similar terms at several points, declares: 'Putting financial power into the hands of learners makes student choice meaningful.' Orwell would surely have admired this cunning parody of Newspeak. Part of the brilliance of the semantic reversals at the heart of such phrases lies in the simple transposition of negative to positive. Here, after all, 'putting financial power into the hands of learners' *means* 'making them pay for something they used to get as of right'. Forcing you to pay for something means enhancing your power, geddit? And then the empty, relationship-counselling cadence of the assertion that this 'makes student choice meaningful'. Translation: 'if you choose something because you care about it and hope it will extend your human capacities it will have no significance for you; but if you are paying for it then you will scratch people's eyes out to get what you're entitled to.' No paying, no meaning. After all, why else would anyone do anything?

Another favoured tense in such official documents is what might be called 'the Dogmatic Future'. For example: allowing 'new providers' to enter the 'market' 'will also lead to higher education institutions concentrating on high-quality teaching'. Not, you understand, in the way they concentrate on it at present, but in the way they 'will' do when Cramme, Chargem and Skimpe has set up shop down the road (Dickens would have recognized the type). Or again: 'Empowering' students by loading high levels of debt onto them 'will stimulate competition between [*sic*] the best academics'. I suppose I must not know any of the 'best' academics referred to here, but I do know and admire many colleagues who at present prepare and deliver their lectures with extraordinary care and imagination. I shall have to explain to them now that, despite their previous efforts, the fact that students are being forced into debt to get an education means that these admirable colleagues will henceforth be expected to trample each other down in the hope of winning a 'best in show' commendation from the drowsy emperors at the back of the hall. As always, despite the disingenuous use of terms such as 'best', the real assumption behind such reasoning is that academics are idle slackers who will only do their job if the whip of competition is applied to their bleeding flanks with some regularity. The clunking machinery of already antiquated New Public Management thinking echoes through this document.

Another notable feature of the current BIS-speak which pervades the White Paper is the way in which the pseudo-measurement of 'consumer satisfaction' replaces argued analysis about desirable goals. The central concept here is 'the student experience', part of the individualist subjectivism by means of which market transactions hollow out human relations. The model may be thought of as the guest at a hotel, filling in the feedback questionnaire on the morning of departure. Was 'the guest experience' a good one? Did you find the fluffy towels fluffy enough? Sometimes, this language is used simply as a meaningless reflex. For example, a perfectly sensible proposal to amalgamate the separate processes of applying for university and applying for loans to pay for university is said to 'provide a seamless customer experience'. In other contexts, the same terminology serves as sales-speak. Magna Carta College in North Oxford, 'an independent Business School offering high-quality affordable degree programmes', promises potential applicants 'the Oxford experience'. Of course, universities marketing 'the student experience' don't need to worry that anyone will take them to be offering a simulacrum of the real thing.

Where all this talk about 'the student experience' starts to betray the purposes of education is in its focus on a narrow form of short-term box-ticking satisfaction. This is spelled out in one of those phrases that can easily delude the busy politician into believing that he is saying something, perhaps even what he intends to be saying. These proposals, we are told, are 'crucial to ensuring that students experience the higher education they want'. But, actually, this will only work as long as we can prevent students from coming into contact with any half-way probing ideas about the nature of human desire. If, however, we drop our guard for one moment, and let them get their hands on ideas that have been influenced by, say, Aristotle or Nietzsche, not to mention Freud, then they will find that 'the student experience' will turn to bitter ashes in their mouths. For they will discover that it is in the nature of desire that it cannot be satisfied: consumer wants are not 'satisfied', they are an endless cycle of temporary pleasure and recurring discontent. Upon graduation ('exiting the student experience' we should rather say), respondents may tick all the boxes to indicate that the goods and services they received corresponded to those promised, and yet still be left with the uneasy feeling that they haven't been, to use a word from olden times, educated. Not that practical things are unimportant or students' views irrelevant or future employment an unworthy consideration: suggesting that critics of the proposals despise these things is just a way of setting up easily knocked-down straw opponents. It is, rather, that the fundamental model of the student as consumer is inimical to the purposes of education. The paradox of real learning is that you don't get what you 'want' – and you certainly can't buy it. I can bustle about and provide a group of students with the temporary satisfaction of their present wants, but in that case they would be right to come back years later and complain that I had not really made any effort to educate them. The really vital aspects of the experience of studying something (a condition very different from 'the student experience') are bafflement and effort. Hacking your way through the jungle of unintelligibility to a few small clearings of partial intelligibility is a demanding and not always enjoyable process. It's not much like wallowing in fluffy towels. And it helps if you trust your guides rather than assuming they will skimp on the job unless kept up to the mark by constant monitoring of their performance indicators.

It also has to be said that, even on the proposals' own cockeyed premises, the system will not actually be driven by 'student choice' but by the decisions of schoolchildren (and their parents). All the paraphernalia of marketing has to be brought to bear on the moment when sixth-formers choose the courses and universities they hope to get into. But even if one tries to elevate these anxious seventeen-year-olds to the full majesty of 'consumers', the analogy doesn't quite hold. For one thing, the 'producers' choose the 'consumers' at least as much as the other way round. And for another, applicants mostly do not have a chance to modify their behaviour as a result of their experience of the satisfactions yielded by rival products. For most school-leavers, applying to university is a one-off event: it is more like getting married than it is like buying soap powder. It cannot primarily be price-sensitive, adaptive, feedback-governed consumer behaviour.

The main proposal in the White Paper to ensure that university applicants act as fully informed consumers (when did you last meet one of those?), and so get the student experience they think they want, is to force all universities to publish a Key Information Set which will include various kinds of information about courses and their requirements (much of which is already available), plus statistics about student satisfaction, employment prospects and so on. The KIS, we are told (in another example of the Dogmatic Future tense), 'will enable higher education institutions to illustrate the quality of the experience that they offer'. But of course, 'quality' is what such crude data cannot illustrate. Learning, for example, the 'salary for that subject across all institutions forty months after graduating' will tell you nothing about the quality of teaching or education, and it will also be hopelessly flawed unless government adopts some more draconian methods to identify named individuals' salaries in the private sector. (One might almost be persuaded there was some merit to this particular proposal if it meant that the exact income of young bond traders and investment bankers would be made public.) As with so much in this document, measures which may in themselves have some merit (who could be against fuller provision of information?) are devalued by being turned into the premises of a tendentious set of claims about 'markets'.

III

Critics of the current policy need to acknowledge that these proposals are designed to tap into the quite considerable levels of anger to be found among middle-class parents about the conditions their children encounter at many universities, principally about the very high student–staff ratio and the consequent low level of contact hours (this is one reason why at certain moments in this document the figure of 'the student' and 'the taxpayer' almost become conflated). But in so far as there is a problem here, it is (as many commentators pointed out about the Browne Review's similar arguments and as I emphasize in Chapter 6, below) due to two factors: first, the deliberate underfunding of the huge expansion of numbers that has taken place in recent decades, especially in the late 1980s and early 1990s; and, second, the distorting emphasis on 'research productivity' caused by the research assessment exercises. Since the White Paper's proposals do not actually address either of these problems, it seems a trifle optimistic to claim (in yet another example of the Dogmatic Future tense) that they 'will put excellent teaching back at the heart of every student's university experience'. 'Back' here refers, as so often in public discussion of universities, to some unspecified moment in the past when everything was so much better, but since the proposals provide no means for the present average student–staff ratio of somewhere around 19:1 to be returned to its early 1960s level of around 8:1, and no suggestion that the exactions of the research assessment process will be reduced or eliminated, the claims that the policy is actuated by a desire to provide students with more contact hours remain bogus.

It has been striking to observe how, although the government has been able to count upon an element of indifference or even hostility to universities among a substantial section of the English electorate, in Scotland a very different political situation obtains. There, the tradition of 'the democratic intellect' and universities' historic accessibility (whether real or assumed) to 'the lad o'pairts' means that tuition fees are an electoral liability. In the elections earlier this year [2011], both the SNP and the Scottish Labour Party (the two serious contenders for office) pledged themselves not to introduce fees on the English model. Since education policy is a devolved matter but revenue-raising is, on the whole, a Whitehall prerogative, the decision by the new Scottish Executive to maintain the line against fees sets up a complex funding problem. The amount Scotland receives from the Treasury is governed by the Barnett formula, which ties it to the level of the budget for public expenditure in England, so unless Alex Salmond can work some other political magic, the funds the Scottish Executive has to devote to its various domestic priorities, including tuition-free universities (for Scottish students), may be correspondingly reduced. The special fees charged by Scottish universities to English students, despite their being EU citizens, may also become a bone of devolutionary contention. It will be interesting, to say the least, if in the immediate future we see two higher education systems which are so closely linked being funded on quite different principles.

Faced with the prospect in England of a hugely disruptive and potentially damaging dismantling of a system that has, by and large, worked well, we have to ask: why are they doing it? It clearly cannot be simply on the grounds of reducing public expenditure. Indeed, David Willetts, the minister of state for universities and science, has proudly maintained that this policy does not represent a cut to universities, but a boost to their income of around 10 per cent by 2015. It is just, he says, that the money is now to be 'channelled' through students. But wait a moment: by 2015 the Treasury will not yet have recouped a penny of the money it will have given out in loans since 2012. Therefore, that 10 per cent rise must be an increase in government expenditure on higher education above the cost of maintaining the present block grant. Now, of course, we all understand that if you can put something under the heading of a 'loan' in the accounts, it becomes an asset not a cost in accountancy terms, but the fact remains that this will still be several billions of public money that has been spent on universities rather than in other ways. After 2015, some students will start to pay some of their loan back, at varying rates, from whenever they start to earn more than £21,000. On the most optimistic figures, it will take thirty years for the Treasury to recoup 70 per cent, at a maximum, of what it provides in loans each year (other economic analysts think the government will never recover more than 50–55 per cent of the amount loaned). And the official figures are premised on the Treasury's arbitrary assumption that the average fee would be £7,500, which even the government must now realize will not be the case. Whatever else is said in favour of this policy, it cannot be maintained that it represents a saving in public expenditure in the short or medium term, even though in the longer term it does signal a significant shift from public to private funding.

The cursory way in which this White Paper, here following the Browne Review, dismisses the case for any kind of graduate tax is revealing of its priorities. It would, of course, be perfectly possible to have a form of graduate contribution that resembled the proposed system in several respects, such as only coming into effect when earnings reach a certain level and ceasing after a certain notional sum has been paid and so on. Such a levy would involve the vaunted 'partnership' of private and public funding and would, in the long run, reduce public expenditure. It would not be a loan for a charge that masquerades as a fee, but a shared contribution, by those in a financial position to make it, to an area of public investment. This would be cheaper to administer, would have none of the deterrent effect of 'debt', and would enable universities to plan on the basis of a teaching grant that was assured over the medium term. Of course, all schemes have their pros and cons, but such a measure has not been rejected because of any of the peripheral problems such as the difficulty of enforcing contributions from those who leave the country and hence the tax system. It has been rejected because under such a scheme, as the White Paper frankly acknowledges: 'Universities would see their dependency on the state increased because they would be reliant on Government for all their teaching funding and this would reduce their responsiveness to students.' This is pure dogma: the rigged 'fee' method of funding is preferred because it promises to introduce more 'consumer behaviour' into the system.

Actually, it also has another, less advertised, advantage as far as the Treasury is concerned. Once the arrangement is up and running, the government can 'monetize the loan book', that is to say, sell the debt to one or more private financial institutions. Any such sale would need, we are told, 'to reduce significantly the government's risk exposure to the loan book and represent value for money to the taxpayer'. But that being so, any private company that takes over the loans will need to find a way to extract *more* money from it than the government is planning to do. Moreover, any such company will also need to make a profit for shareholders as well as pay the huge salaries of its own executives. Does anyone seriously believe that a bank or other private financial institution is going to be able to generate all this extra income from the loan book while maintaining the same terms and conditions for its constituent debtors as the government initially offers?

But these financial calculations do not go to the root of the matter. The inescapable conclusion is that this huge gamble with one of the world's most successful and highly regarded systems of higher education is being taken in order to bring universities to heel. From the mid-1980s, when the then minister for higher education, Robert Jackson, complained that universities were frustrating government efforts to 'reform' them by acting as 'a producers' cartel', successive administrations have sought for ways to make universities conform to their will. But these efforts have run up against the intrinsic tension involved in all higher education policy. Whatever other functions societies have from time to time required their institutions of higher learning to fulfil, universities are primarily institutions devoted to extending and deepening human understanding, and if they are to do this successfully those engaged in such enquiries must be allowed to pursue whatever lines of enquiry seem likely to be most fertile intellectually without being entirely constrained by immediate practical outcomes. From such enquiry, all kinds of benefits may in fact flow to the host society, but they will only do so via a route that is indirect and at one remove. This makes good universities maddeningly resistant to governments' desires for them to contribute more directly to current policy objectives, and the resistance is the more maddening when they are the recipients of large amounts of public money. The policies of UK governments over the past thirty years have constituted a series of attempts to square this circle by means of the spurs and whips of targets and assessments.

The decision in the summer of 2010 (clearly endorsed, and perhaps even initiated, by George Osborne and the Tory inner circle) to remove public funding for university teaching constitutes a radically different attempt to make universities behave in the currently approved manner. Cunningly, students are portrayed as the elite commandos of the new assault: with a ticking loan strapped to their backs, they are to get inside the ivory tower and compel the inmates to do their bidding. 'The reforms we have set out will open up higher education, making universities accountable to the students they serve ... The right regulation should protect students and taxpayers ...' and so on. In reality, universities are already, and necessarily, 'accountable' to society, including students, in all kinds of ways: it is cheap and empty rhetoric to suggest they exist purely to 'serve students', especially when this is really code for 'respond to the expressed wishes of the consumer in the way other businesses have to do'. And who do students and taxpayers (an unlikely pairing, but one which, in the rhetoric of these proposals, it is tellingly difficult to distinguish) need to be protected from? It can only be from those complacent and self-interested universities, hell bent on – well, it's not clear what, exactly, but something undesirable anyway. With 'students at the heart of the system', so the reasoning goes, the 'producers' cartel' will be dissolved.

We get several other glimpses of the future in these pages. One comes in an apparently anodyne section about the use of the title 'university'. It will, we are told, be made easier for 'new providers' to acquire this title. The next paragraph then continues, innocuously enough, by observing that 'where higher education institutions want to change their status, it can be complex'. Well, of course, we're all against complexity, aren't we? And then, as we're chugging through these inoffensive generalities, we are suddenly told: 'We would ensure that, as the assets of a university have been acquired over time, partly as a result of direct public funding, the wider public interest will be protected in any such change of status.' Whoa! Why would this sentence be there unless the 'change of status' envisaged is from public to private, though this is never spelled out? The current corporate landscape is littered with examples of how well 'the wider public interest' has been protected when services and organizations have been enabled to 'change their status' in this way.

Or again, the White Paper commends the programme set up between the large multinational accountancy firm KPMG and three 'partner' universities where, essentially, the company pays all charges on a group of undergraduates following a special programme that leads to a guaranteed job with the firm. We are told that this arrangement was established with these particular universities 'as they were passionate about its potential and had organisational values that fitted well with KPMG's'. Leaving aside the current cant use of 'passionate about' to mean 'interested in' or 'in favour of', what catches the eye here is this alleged consilience of 'values'. I am impressed, if a little surprised, to discover that the priorities of this huge financial corporation are the open-ended pursuit of human understanding, the rigour of close scholarship, and the other 'organizational values' which these universities must, by their nature, be 'passionately' committed to. Perhaps this signals an important turning-point where organizations hitherto focused on making the highest possible profits are now going to be principally committed to the life of the mind, rather than the other way round.

And we get an almost touching glimpse of the White Paper's concern to ensure that the right values prevail in the future when it announces that, because some graduates will 'aspire to run a business', the government wants to see a student 'Enterprise Society embed[ded] in all universities in England'. No one is likely to object if some undergraduates want to spend the odd evening playing a few rounds of Start-up, but why should universities be *forced* to establish such playgroups? Quite apart from the mildly paradoxical character of a proposal to establish, by central diktat, societies for the promotion of 'enterprise', we might ask why there is no comparable insistence on 'embedding' a Contemplation Society in every university, or a Compassion Society or a Cooperation Society or a hundred other interesting and valuable forms of human expression? Could there be just the teensiest sign of anxiety here that universities may, unless constantly brought into line, encourage people to think about something other than how to make a quick buck?

IV

The White Paper twice quotes the celebrated phrase from the Robbins Report which declared that 'courses of higher education should be available for all those who are qualified by ability and attainment to pursue them and who wish to do so'. This appears to be an attempt to associate itself with this once widely admired document and to claim that the radically new policies are in some ways merely a continuation of those inaugurated by its great predecessor. But it may have been unwise for the drafting team at BIS to remind their readers of the cadence of Robbins's prose, since this seems bound to provoke some rumination about how far we have moved from the assumptions expressed by that prose, how that has happened, and whether something valuable may not have been lost along the way. We might, for example, while our ears are still ringing with the off-the-peg phrases about the need for suppliers to compete to produce increased consumer satisfaction, be reminded of the following passage from Robbins:

It is the essence of higher education that it introduces students to a world of intellectual responsibility and intellectual discovery in which they are to play their part ... The element of partnership between teacher and taught in a common pursuit of knowledge and understanding, present to some extent in all education, should become the dominant element as the pupil matures and as the intellectual level of work done rises ... The student needs from the beginning to be made aware of the scope of his subject and to realise that he is not being presented with a mass of information but initiated into a realm of free enquiry ... Most discussion of this subject clouds the issue by setting teaching and research over against each other as antithetical and supposing an opposition that exists only at extreme points, as if teaching were nothing but patient recapitulation and explanation of the known and all research a solitary voyage to discover something that will be intelligible to a mere handful of persons.

Or, before our minds are utterly numbed by the boardroom language of 'efficiency gains' and the need to 'shed surplus staff', we might remind ourselves of the deeper understanding of universities evident in the following:

Universities have an obligation to preserve and advance knowledge and to serve the intellectual needs of the nation. University teachers must keep abreast of new developments in their subjects and need time for reflection and personal study. Many also want to make their own contribution to such developments and this desire must not be frustrated if they are to remain intellectually alive. In addition, the influence and authority of those who have become acknowledged experts in their own fields of study radiate out far beyond the walls of the university in which they teach. Such persons are rightly required to undertake many duties in the cause of learning and in the interest of the country and indeed of the world, for learning is international. These compete for time with duties within the university. Again, it is the duty of universities to foster the study of new subjects and to ensure that subjects that are important but that do not attract great numbers of students are adequately studied. The ratio of teachers to students in the universities thus needs to be more favourable than the ratio in other institutions of higher education that do not have in the same measure the duty to preserve and advance knowledge.

In neither of these passages is the language slack or indulgent: they sternly talk of the 'obligation' on universities and of activities which are their 'duty', as well as how university teachers are 'rightly required' to undertake further tasks and so on. But what such passages display, and what the White Paper so lamentably lacks, is a considered understanding of the character of intellectual enquiry and of the conditions needed to sustain it successfully both across a wide range of subjects and across many generations. Scholars *are* obliged 'to undertake many duties in the cause of learning' and this *is* 'in the interest of the country and indeed of the world, for learning is international'. Universities cannot be glibly said to exist 'to serve students': that neglects precisely 'the element of partnership between teacher and taught in a common pursuit of knowledge and understanding' which Robbins identifies. The language of these passages is well informed and accurate. It is well informed about what the role of a university teacher is actually like, rather than being in hock to the idiom of some second-hand role-analysis imported from management-school textbooks of a generation ago, and it is accurate because it uses the words which best pick out what it is trying to describe – emphasizing that teaching at this level is not simply the 'patient recapitulation and explanation of the known'; university teachers 'need time for reflection and personal study' if they are to 'keep abreast of new developments in their subjects', and so on. Such phrases would stick out in current HiEdspeak precisely because they are modest yet confident, not all outer bluster and inner defensiveness.

Lionel Robbins, it should be remembered, was himself a leading neoclassical economic theorist and no admirer of socialism or left-wing ideas more generally. The case against the

White Paper, and against the whole shift in public discourse that it both reflects and tries to push further, does not involve any repudiation of the legitimate and indispensable role of economic reasoning any more than it involves some supposedly utopian disregard for the financial cost of proper support for public services, education included. Similarly, pointing to the damage likely to be done to universities by the proposed applications of business-school models of 'competing producers' and 'demanding consumers' does not rest on any nostalgic desire to return to the far smaller and more selective higher education system of three or four decades ago. The expansion of the proportion of the age-cohort entering higher education from 6 per cent to 44 per cent is a great democratic gain that this society should not wish to retreat from. Quite to the contrary, we should be seeking to ensure that those now entering universities in still-increasing numbers are not cheated of their legitimate entitlement to an *education* – not palmed off, in the name of 'meeting the needs of employers', with a narrow training that is thought by right-wing policy-formers and Home Counties dinner-party wisdom to be 'good enough for the likes of them', while the children of the privileged classes largely get to attend properly resourced universities that can continue to boast of their standing in global league tables. There is nothing fanciful or irresponsible in believing that this great public good of expanded education can and should be largely publicly funded. This White Paper and the legislation already enacted are not about finding 'fairer' ways to pay for higher education or, in any meaningful sense, about putting 'students at the heart of the system'. Rather, they represent the latest instalment in the campaign to replace the assumptions of Robbins's world with those of McKinsey's.

Sold Out: Privatizing Higher Education

I

It's time for the criticism to stop.[1] Whatever you think about the changes to higher education that have been made in recent years – and in particular the decision in the autumn of 2010 largely to replace public funding of teaching with student fees – this is now the system we've got. Carping about the principle or sniping at the process is simply unhelpful: it antagonizes ministers and officials, thereby jeopardizing future negotiations, and it wins little sympathy from the media and wider public. This country is in desperate need of jobs and of economic growth, and in higher education as in every other sphere we are now competing in a global market. So pipe down, and let's all focus on making this system work as effectively as possible.

If this is your view, you may not wish to read on – or you should at least be warned that this chapter contains material of an economically explicit nature and some strong language (not all of it mine). But everyone else, including those who are being cowed by their local variant of the pragmatist in a suit, may be interested to learn from two exceptionally well-informed new books just how seismic are the changes now under way in British (or at least English) higher education. The provenance of their authors could hardly be more different. Roger Brown has been, successively, a senior civil servant,

---

1 This chapter was first published in the *London Review of Books* in October 2013. The two books under discussion are Roger Brown with Helen Carasso, *Everything for Sale? The Marketisation of UK Higher Education* (Abingdon: Routledge, 2013), and Andrew McGettigan, *The Great University Gamble: Money, Markets and the Future of Higher Education* (London: Pluto, 2013).

the chief executive of the Higher Education Quality Council, and the vice-chancellor of Southampton Solent University; he is currently professor of higher education policy at Liverpool Hope University. Andrew McGettigan did his doctorate at the highly regarded Centre for Modern European Philosophy that Middlesex University summarily closed down in 2010; in recent years he has distinguished himself as one of the best-informed analysts of the legal and financial changes reshaping universities in this country. Brown's book is a sober, data-heavy overview of higher education policy in Britain since 1979, drawing on extensive secondary and comparative scholarship as well as first-hand experience; McGettigan's is a detailed, at times technical, analysis of the funding of English universities since 2010, explaining these arcane matters with exemplary clarity and identifying the longer-term financial implications of the new arrangements. But for all their differences of style and focus, these two books provide a chillingly convergent description of how, once one gets behind the superficial headlines about fee levels and 'access', a huge gamble is being taken with higher education in England and Wales – an unprecedented, ideologically driven experiment, whose consequences even its authors cannot wholly predict or control.

At this point two caveats may be in order. First, it should be clear that previous governments have played their part in promoting the policies described in these two books. The changes since 2010 have been more fundamental than anything before, but in policy-making circles, and especially among officials in the relevant departments, there is some continuity of approach over the past two decades. Secondly, the fate of universities in the UK cannot be considered in isolation. Deep changes in the structures and dominant attitudes of contemporary market democracies are everywhere putting pressure on the values that have sustained the ideals of public higher education. Unfortunately, the UK has put itself in the position of conducting the pilot experiments in how to respond to these changes. Other countries are looking on with a mixture of regret and apprehension: regret because British universities have been widely admired models for so long, apprehension because they fear similar policies may soon be coming their way. In many parts of the world British higher education is, to change the metaphor, seen less as a useful pilot experiment and more as the canary in the mine.

The place to begin may be the US Senate. At the end of July 2012 the Senate Committee on Health, Education, Labor and Pensions presented an 800-page report, the culmination of a two-year investigation into 'for-profit' higher education institutions. The senators found that at such institutions a mere 17.4 per cent of annual revenue was spent on teaching, while nearly 20 per cent was distributed as profits (the proportion spent on marketing and recruitment was even higher). They also found that huge numbers of people from the least advantaged sections of society were stuck with large debts from having enrolled in, and very quickly dropped out of, courses which were never suitable for them. ('Subprime degrees,' observes Andrew McGettigan, 'like subprime mortgages, are sold to communities relatively unfamiliar with the product.') The explosive growth of the for-profit sector in the US dates from the late 1990s and the involvement of investment banks and private equity. For example, in 1998 Ashford University had just 300 students; it was taken over by Bridgepoint Education Inc, and by 2008 it boasted 77,000 students, nearly all online. Bridgepoint was described by the Senate committee's chairman as a 'scam', still collecting profits while having drop-out rates above 84 per cent.

The biggest player in this market is the University of Phoenix, owned by the Apollo Group (of whom more anon). UoP claims to be North America's largest university: at its peak in 2010 it was said to have some 600,000 students and annual revenue in excess of $4 billion (in October 2012, it announced plans to close 115 campuses due to a drastic drop in its profits). The Senate investigation showed that 60 per cent of Apollo students dropped out of their courses within two years, while of those who completed, 21 per cent defaulted on paying back their loans within three years of finishing their course. It also revealed that 88 per cent of Apollo's revenue comes from federal student loans and that it spends twice as much on marketing as it does on teaching. A lawsuit filed in 2003 alleged that UoP wrongfully obtained at least $3 billion of federal student aid funds. In 2009 the Apollo Group agreed to pay $78.5 million to settle the suit, in what American commentators saw as one of the largest pay-for-performance compensation settlements ever reached. In response to a separate investigation in 2004, the Apollo Group paid about $10 million in fines to the US Department of Education, which had been examining UoP admissions practices for being overly focused on boosting enrolment (with recruiters being paid bonuses depending on the numbers they signed up). A parallel investigation by the *Huffington Post* of another 'private provider', Educational Management Corporation, found that after it was taken over by Goldman Sachs, its recruiters were issued with scripts 'which instructed them to find potential applicants' "pain" so as to convince them that college might be a solution to their struggles'.

Of course, this could never happen here, could it? There is, after all, nothing to worry about, is there, in the following points, raised in a written submission to the House of Commons Public Accounts Committee on 6 December 2012, especially about the amount of public money that, through student loans, now goes to private institutions (both for-profit and not-for-profit)? The submission noted, among other things, that the number of students studying with private colleges on unregulated courses has doubled in one year; 23 per cent of the total public money involved was captured by one provider – Greenwich School of Management – owned by the private equity fund Sovereign Capital; Sovereign Capital's co-founder advised the government on public sector reform (and is now [2013] government spokesman on education in the House of Lords).

The institutions in question, including the government, would no doubt prefer to phrase these things somewhat differently. But the figures are a matter of public record. For example, there can be no dispute that in 2007–8, student loans paid as fees to private providers in higher education totalled £15 million. By 2010–11 this had risen to over £33 million, and recently released government figures showed that the total had almost trebled in size to £100 million in 2011–12, the first full year under the coalition's stewardship. In addition, in 2011 the government increased the amount of public money private providers could receive in the form of student loans from £3,000 to £6,000 (with effect from 2012–13), while also dramatically increasing the number of courses designated fit for this form of public support. Private providers in the UK are subject to some regulation, perhaps a stronger regulatory regime than has historically been enforced in the US, but they are still exempt from many of the obligations of public institutions. They have not had to observe controls on the number of students they recruit, nor, it seems, are they legally obliged to publish information about recruitment figures or completion rates.

Private capital has been quick to spot an opportunity here, one indication of which is the growth of specialist consultancy firms such as Meissa, which claims to provide 'research and strategic consultancy services to companies and organisations operating within the UK education industry' and to 'offer an unmatched capacity to put business opportunities within the sector into perspective and to deliver in-depth research across the industry'. As their survey of recent activity put it: 'The most significant transaction across the UK education industry in 2012 was Montagu Private Equity's acquisition of The College of Law for around £200m. The acquisition was the most hotly contested auction of 2012 as the deal included all of The College of Law's accreditations, thus enabling the college to continue to award its degrees and other qualifications.' (In April 2012 a news item in *Private Equity News* had explained: 'Montagu is reported to be looking for a platform company from which to build a leading player in the British higher education sector, and is said to have offered a higher price than rival bidders.') In November 2012 the college was, with remarkable speed, granted full university status and is now known as The University of Law.

In a more straightforward commercial move, the US for-profit giant Apollo (the previously mentioned owners of the University of Phoenix) formed a consortium with the Carlyle financial group to take over BPP College in 2009 in a £303.5 million deal. Part of the attraction was that in 2007 BPP (not a charity but a subsidiary of BPP plc) had been granted degree-awarding powers; it is now known as BBP University College. It has study centres in Abingdon, Birmingham, Bristol, Cambridge, Glasgow, Leeds, Liverpool, London, Maidstone, Manchester, Milton Keynes, Reading, Newcastle, Nottingham and Southampton, as well as European sites in Bulgaria, Czech Republic, Hungary, Malta, Poland, Romania and Slovakia. Similarly, Sovereign Capital acquired the Greenwich School of Management in 2011 for an undisclosed sum. Sovereign Capital describes itself as 'the UK private equity Buy & Build specialist', and in announcing its acquisition it emphasized that the GSoM 'has strong partnerships with the University of Plymouth and the University of Wales and has been an accredited degree provider since 1991'. (Its American BBA degrees are awarded by Northwood University, Michigan, founded in 1992.) In 2012 GSoM launched plans for a second campus in Greenford, west London, to accommodate a further 6,000 students.

Other 'not-for-profit' private institutions are expanding at a similar rate. In July 2012 it was announced that Regent's College (in Regent's Park), some of whose degree-level courses lead to qualifications from Webster University, St Louis, Missouri, had been accorded degree-awarding powers by the Privy Council. In February 2013 Regent's College agreed to acquire the for-profit American InterContinental University London from Career Education Corporation, thereby boosting its offerings. In March 2013 the UK's Department for Business, Innovation and Skills announced that Regent's College had met the criteria to become a university. Since then, Regent's University London, as it is now known, has advertised itself vigorously. For most courses it charges £14,000, far more even than top-charging 'public' universities. It does offer bursaries for some students unable to meet these high fees, but it seems that not enough apply for them. As the head of the university put it: 'The majority of students who come here are from relatively comfortable families, ranging from comfortably middle-class to staggeringly wealthy.' At present, only 18 per cent of its students are from the UK; it is thus regarded as a significant contributor to the 'higher education export industry'. Its plans include 'a projected doubling of student enrolment in the next seven years, the opening of overseas campuses in Hong Kong, Eastern Europe and South America, and the acquisition of a design school and a law school'.

At first sight, the distinctions between 'public' and 'private' institutions, and within the latter between 'for-profit' and 'not-for-profit', may seem clear-cut and inviolable. In reality, both distinctions turn out to be more complicated. Most of Britain's older universities were originally chartered, autonomous corporations, but they are rightly regarded as public institutions in the same way that, say, the BBC is regarded as a public broadcaster, receiving the bulk of their funding from public sources and regulated correspondingly. Private universities do not receive such funding and are, to a considerable extent, exempt from the accompanying regulation. However, the distinction between private and public universities in the UK is becoming blurred given, first, that some erstwhile public universities have since 2012 received very little in the way of direct government subsidy and so are heavily dependent on the income from loan-backed fees; and, second, that approved private institutions can now get the greater part of their revenue from exactly the same source.

The distinction between for-profit and not-for-profit institutions may seem more clear-cut. A for-profit private provider is a business like any other: even though it may make a lot of noise about its 'educational mission' and so on, it is geared to making money for parent companies, directors and shareholders. A not-for-profit institution is different: as an educational charity, it is legally prohibited from directly allocating any part of its surplus to the profit of any other institution or individual. However, as McGettigan shows in a particularly penetrating analysis, the key question where a 'not-for-profit' educational institution is concerned may not be its own legal status but its position within a larger corporate or group structure. A parent company may have several ways of making money from a not-for-profit college without that institution violating its charitable status, including various management fees and the revenue from being the monopoly provider of certain services. Doubtless, most investment companies and private equity groups are actuated solely by a concern for the public good, but the fact that at the moment the waters around higher education institutions are so full of eager predators may suggest, even to the most naive, that they have been aroused by the scent of profit. The government has made it much easier to acquire the title and status of being a university, once so jealously protected; surprisingly, there is no requirement to have a spread of subjects or to offer postgraduate degrees, and it has now been decreed that only 750 students need to be following degree-level courses. It also seems that if an existing college is subject to a private capital buyout it will still be allowed to keep its precious degree-awarding powers, even though the 'charitable' institution may have become part of a larger corporate empire.

Among the various new types of institution, none has attracted as much media interest as A.C. Grayling's New College of the Humanities, though in terms of numbers it is as yet of negligible importance. The announcement of its founding in 2011 was accompanied by some high-toned claims about how it would provide the kind of top-quality liberal arts education that is allegedly disappearing from established universities. But the reality, as McGettigan demonstrates, is that NCH is merely an upmarket crammer, a kind of sleek private tutoring organization for the age of the global elite. It is not a university and does not award degrees. It 'prepares' students for existing University of London International Programme examinations – as a variety of private tutoring institutions across the world have long done. It promises small-group tuition, and several academic superstars who hold full-time appointments at universities in Britain and the US figure in its advertising as 'visiting professors'. For this, it charges fees of £18,000 a year, twice the maximum that even the most famous British universities are currently allowed to charge. Thus far, its students do not qualify for publicly backed loans nor has it obtained 'trusted sponsor' status from the visa authorities (and so cannot bring in students from beyond the EU), which may cramp its business plan somewhat. One has to wonder why UK applicants with the qualifications necessary to get into a good UK university (where they will be in greater demand than ever now that the government has rigged the market for students with the top A-levels) would choose instead to go to this curious institution. It may develop a certain *social cachet* – central London premises, 'Oxbridge-style tutorials', the company of other children of the wealthy – though it's not obvious why serious academics with posts elsewhere would wish to assist in such a purpose, especially since it can only succeed by draining talent away from the hard-pressed publicly supported universities from which they themselves benefited so much.

But the real bite of McGettigan's analysis lies in its unravelling of NCH's corporate structure. In essence (the story is complicated), the not-for-profit college is now a subsidiary of a parent company called Tertiary Education Services Limited, which can distribute its own profits (when there are any) to directors and shareholders. Despite Grayling's protestations to the contrary, this is the reverse of the position in which existing universities set up spin-off companies which then make profits, because in those cases the surplus goes up the chain *to* the charitable body, the university, at the top, whereas with NCH the money moves *from* the charitable institution up the chain to the profit-distributing company. At present the prospect of actual profits seems some way off; in McGettigan's view, 'the College is unviable but for the deep pockets of its private equity backers', principally a Swiss family who run a venture-capital company based in Lucerne. McGettigan's analysis of NCH is a telling illustration of his more general point about the need to analyse the corporate *group* structure, rather than simply accepting that, if the actual teaching institution is described as a not-for-profit charity, there can be no question of profits for private investors further down the line.

A crucial step for any 'new provider' is to get its courses 'designated' so that its students are eligible for government-backed loans, another process that has seen a marked acceleration in the past few years. There are now such courses at over 150 private institutions – a number greater than the total of UK universities – and as an example of the acceleration McGettigan reports that 'approval was recently given to 98 Edexcel courses at London College UCK within four days of their application being received'. I admit that I had not heard of this last institution, which is based in Notting Hill, and offers several degree-level courses as well as many lower qualifications. Its website announces that 'The London College UCK is an Approved Partner of the University of Derby', though it is not clear whether Derby actually validates any of the degree courses (and at present London College UCK does not figure among the list of Approved Partner institutions on Derby's website). I am not suggesting there is anything improper about these arrangements, merely that there has grown up, mainly in the last two or three years, an extensive network of private provision in this country, the exact character and standing of which is not always immediately apparent. Its appeal to private investment firms, however, is all too apparent. The international law firm Eversheds recently identified the commercial attraction of higher education for prospective investors in brisk terms, including 'research commercialization projects, revenues from overseas campuses and from selling access to the institution's degree-awarding powers'. Perhaps it is not surprising that a market consultancy group has described the higher education sector as 'treasure island'.

II

But why, it may be asked, go on so much about private providers when they are still such a relatively minor presence in higher education in the UK (though not as minor as many people seem to think)? Surely the changes in funding since 2010 have not really altered the character and functioning of mainstream universities? Surely our children and grandchildren will still have the same chances of a good education at a good public university?

If you think that the change in 2010 was merely 'a rise in fees', and if you think things have settled down and will now carry on much as usual, then you simply haven't been paying attention. This government's whole strategy for higher education is (in the tired cliché it so loves to use) to 'create a level playing-field' that will enable private providers to compete on equal terms with public universities. The crucial step in this strategy was taken in the autumn of 2010 with the unprecedented (and till then unannounced) decision to abolish the block grant made to universities to support the costs of teaching – abolish it in its entirety for Band C and Band D subjects (roughly, arts, humanities and social sciences) and in substantial part for Band A and B subjects (roughly, medicine and the natural sciences). From the point of view of private providers, that change removed a subsidy to established universities which had hitherto rendered private undergraduate fees uncompetitive in the home market. With that removed, and with all types of institution that offer these subjects being largely dependent on student fees, the way is open to rig the market to drive down the price. In McGettigan's view, 'the short-term restrictions on the majority of institutions are a deliberate step in a process designed to destabilise them prior to the entrance and expansion of the alternative providers, who in contrast will be nurtured into the new terrain'. On this matter, at least, David Willetts, the minister responsible for higher education, has been clear about his aims: 'The biggest lesson I have learned is that the most powerful driver of reform is to let new providers into the system.'

Note that use of 'reform': the implication is always that there is something wrong with the present arrangements that these changes will put right. And observe the logic of such 'reform'. If you reclassify people as 'consumers', you have already reduced them to economic agents in a market. The cunning of government propaganda, in higher education as elsewhere, is to pose as the champion of 'the consumer' in order to force through the financialization and marketization of yet more areas of life. And who do the student-consumers need assistance against? Who is preventing them from getting what they want and therefore should have? Universities, it seems. In the Browne Review and in all subsequent government rhetoric, the tacit assumption is that giving financial force to consumer demand through the fee system will *force universities to change*. No case has been made that they were failing generally in their purposes before or that these changes will enable them better to fulfil those purposes: the rhetorical pressure has been entirely focused on implying that it is universities that obstruct student wishes, obstruct the legitimate demands of employers, obstruct efficient management of the sector and generally just, well, obstruct. But being forced to swallow a good dose of private equity, it is gleefully claimed, will soon unblock the system. Unfortunately, the metaphor all too accurately points towards what may thereby be produced.

Just as the replacement of public funding by fees is the vehicle for remaking universities in the image of consumer-oriented retailers, so it is also the Trojan horse which allows private capital to find ways to make profits out of higher education. But perhaps existing public universities could meet them halfway? A straw in the wind here is the University of Central Lancashire's application to change its legal status so as to open itself to private investment. UCLan also announced plans to adopt a 'group structure' from August 2013, whereby its international branch campuses in Cyprus, Thailand and Sri Lanka would be managed separately, with its vice-chancellor running only the UK university and reporting to a group chief executive (though it subsequently appeared to have shelved these plans). As the *Times Higher Education* reported, switches to company status and changes in structure were both advocated in a 2009 report to Universities UK by Eversheds, UCLan's legal advisers for their application, as ways for higher education institutions to attract private investment (its author, Glynne Stanfield, a partner in Eversheds, has reportedly described himself as a 'legal, non-party political' adviser to David Willetts). The Eversheds report said that under such a structure 'distinct higher and further education and even school brands' could be 'intermeshed with commercial companies within the group which could have funding and interest from outside stakeholders'. Professor Malcolm McVicar, the current vice-chancellor, who was to become interim head of the group, said that the group structure idea came from the university's board, which considered it to be 'a model ... used in many medium-sized companies which have ambitious plans for the future'. Ah yes, 'medium-sized companies which have ambitious plans for the future' – perhaps an apt description of one of the 'mission-groups' of UK universities?

The pressure to pursue commercial opportunities is not, in itself, new. For some time now, the major money-spinner has been overseas (i.e. non-home or EU) student fees. In the last decade alone, the number of full-time overseas students at UK universities has increased from 175,000 to nearly 300,000. As a result of this enormous expansion, one in six of the students at UK universities now comes from outside the EU, the largest number (67,000) from China. Higher education is currently classified as the UK's seventh-largest 'export industry'. But after 2009 the UK Border Agency (before its recent abolition) began to take a different view of matters, seeing universities and colleges as a weak point in its efforts to cut immigration. In August 2012 UKBA revoked London Metropolitan University's status as a 'trusted sponsor' for visa purposes, potentially threatening the right to stay of several thousand students and a loss to the university of some £30 million a year. It appears that in April this year [2013] an agreement was reached, and LMU is again being allowed to recruit overseas students, but obviously there are conflicting messages coming from two government departments on this issue, BIS urging more recruitment as part of its 'export drive', the Home Office tightening the rules as part of its 'clampdown' on immigration.

If the immigration authorities are an obstacle to bringing in yet more overseas students to study at a university in Britain, why not simply take the university to where the overseas students are? 'Campuses' of British universities in other countries have mushroomed in recent years, some in partnership with local institutions, some free-standing. They are not always in the largest or most obvious countries. Take, for instance, the University of Central Lancashire Cyprus, whose marketing slogan is 'Get a UK Degree at a UK university – in Cyprus' (degrees, that is, in business, law and some aspects of engineering). UCLan Cyprus markets itself to UK as well as overseas students. It charges fees of £9,000, though home students who choose to go there do not (at present) have access to the UK student loan scheme. Cyprus seems to be a favoured location for these new campuses (presumably the possibility of some kind of 'joint venture' with Club 18–30 cannot be ruled out). In June 2012 the University of East London Cyprus was 'promising to offer high quality British degree programmes in one of Europe's most popular study destinations' at a 'stunning new campus', but then in April 2013 it was announced that after recruiting just seventeen students UEL Cyprus would be closed. A spokesman for the university, the *Times Higher Education* reported, 'would not disclose how much money the university will lose'.

Then there are bonds. Universities can raise a lot of money in this way, if investors think they are secure enough. For example, in 2012 De Montfort University raised a bond for £110 million, a figure that represents over 70 per cent of its annual income. McGettigan does the sums – and they are frightening. With a coupon of 5.375 per cent on its bond, De Montfort needs to find £5.9 million a year just to pay the fixed annual return to bondholders. In recent years the university has in fact been running a deficit, so either costs will have to be cut savagely or income significantly raised. In 2042 it will need to repay the capital, a huge sum, if it is not to default. This potentially puts future decisions in the hands of the bondholders, especially if the university's position changes significantly in the meantime in ways considered prejudicial to its financial viability (if it were, for example, to lose 'most trusted' sponsor status for visas). The risks look large and, as McGettigan points out, whatever happens, DMU 'has certainly abrogated some of its institutional autonomy to a dynamic that we do not yet fully understand'. The more bonds are issued, the more the markets have an interest in maintaining and then raising fee income, which is ultimately the 'security' against which the bond is largely issued. On all these matters, McGettigan's general observation is indisputable: 'Additional private income runs in parallel with the interpenetration of values and practices of business and commerce into universities.'

Many of the financial problems faced by UK higher education date back to the really shocking underfunding of university expansion in the 1980s and early 1990s. The Dearing Report found that 'public funding per student for higher education had declined from a value of 100 in 1976 and 79 in 1989 to 60 in 1994'. That is, it nearly halved in just eighteen years. Later improvements in funding never fully repaired this damage: between 1979 and 2011 student numbers increased by 320 per cent while public expenditure on higher education rose by only 165 per cent. Roger Brown, scarcely given to rabble-rousing, concludes: 'In effect, market-based policies have partly compensated for – and even been a (deliberate?) distraction from – a failure to consistently invest an appropriate proportion of national wealth in higher education.'

III

So what about the core business of HiEdBiz PLC? The centrepiece of the coalition's 'reforms' is, as we have seen, the abolition of the greater part of direct public funding of university teaching and its replacement by fees. How is that policy looking, almost three years after it was announced and after one year of operation?

Even in its own terms, the coalition's policy is struggling with a contradiction between its two chief priorities: it wants to introduce an 'efficient market' in higher education and it wants to control government expenditure in this area. If market forces are supposed to do their work of driving down prices (while, of course, 'driving up quality'), then there has to be real competition at the bottom: institutions that are undercut by cheaper providers will need to lower their prices or go bust. (Or, as the 2011 White Paper ominously put it in a passage partly quoted in Chapter 4, above: 'The government does not guarantee to underwrite universities and colleges. They are independent, and it is not Government's role to protect an unviable institution.') But for that to happen not only must the cheaper providers have access to student loans on pretty much the same terms as their more expensive rivals, but the demand for such places must not significantly outstrip the supply, since otherwise 'market discipline' will not operate. However, to introduce its revolutionary changes and to get them accepted by waverers (such as the Lib Dems), the government agreed to provide the capital necessary for a massive system of student loans, one which, for the present at least, involves an element of public subsidy. But this means that the Treasury, at least as powerful a driver of policy in this government as in any of its predecessors, has a keen interest in the cost of this system. Once the terms are set, the main determinant of cost is student numbers. The Treasury therefore insists that numbers be capped. (They have in fact been reduced, first by the removal of a temporary increase of 10,000 places introduced by the previous government, then by a further reduction of 5,000 places.) But this fact alone renders the project of a genuine 'market' incoherent, since it is known in advance by all parties that demand for university places is thus bound to considerably exceed supply. The entry of yet more low-cost private providers at the bottom end of the system offering additional places could remedy this, but for them to succeed they would need to be guaranteed access to student loans for all the extra students they recruit, which would send the costs of the system in the short and medium term through the roof. So a way has to be found simultaneously to lower prices *and* restrict numbers.

The device the government came up with in 2011 was the 'core and margin' system for allocating university places (discussed more fully in Chapter 4 above). As a chorus of commentators immediately pointed out, this arrangement is almost bound to have socially regressive effects. Brown quotes Sir Peter Scott, one of the most respected of these commentators (and a former vice-chancellor):

> To rely on A-level grades alone is, in effect, further to privilege the already privileged, to give disproportionate rewards to those whose way in life has been smooth. The correlation between school performance and social advantage is too plain to deny. For years universities have attempted, feebly perhaps, to level the playing-field by making differential offers. Now, on the fiat of David Willetts, they are no longer free to do so.

As Brown observes, more quietly but no less damningly: 'The stratification of higher education contributes to and reinforces the stratification of the school system, and vice versa.' The injustice is exacerbated in that the universities in a position to recruit more of the children of the already privileged are thereby better financed than the institutions that end up taking even more of the children of the less privileged. The introduction of this mechanism, presumably at the behest of the Treasury, makes a mockery of the government's frequent lectures to universities about their failure to widen access.

The core and margin wheeze was introduced hastily by the government when it belatedly realized that the Office for Fair Access (OFFA) did not have the power to order universities to set lower fees. This meant that many universities that had already announced their fees and negotiated (where necessary) their access agreements were suddenly being told that the ground had shifted retrospectively. The new measure had some of its desired effect immediately, since it forced twenty-four universities to announce, after they had published their admission materials, a reduction of their fees in order to be eligible to bid for places in the margin that had been taken away from their previous allocation. Even the pin-striped language of the HEFCE report on 2012–13 recruitment could not entirely hide another aspect of the shambles: 'The core and margin policy led to the redistribution of 20,000 student places in 2012. 9,643 of these places were allocated to 35 higher education institutions, while 155 further education colleges took 10,354. At present, it appears that 35 per cent of these margin places (around 7,000) remain unfilled.' This means that these places were withdrawn from the core allocation of universities which had presumably filled them quite satisfactorily in previous years, and awarded to other institutions that were, for whatever reason, then unable to fill them, so that there was in the end a further reduction of 7,000 in the number of places for applicants.

Another potential snag shows how these policies can come to bite their authors. HEFCE currently controls total numbers of university places (and hence likely total demand for loans) by setting quotas for each university. But if, as we are constantly being told by ministers, universities are autonomous institutions, how is this unelected quango in a position to enforce the quotas? In the past, the mechanism, of course, was that HEFCE provided a block grant and could impose penalties, in the form of hefty reduction of that grant, for institutions that exceeded their targets. But in the brave new world of fees some institutions may receive practically no funding from HEFCE (if, say, they don't teach medicine or the expensive laboratory subjects and did not do well in the research assessment exercises): their teaching costs are supposed to be financed by student fees. In that case, an institution would have no reason to abide by any notional numbers cap prescribed by HEFCE, as long as their applicants could access the loan system. Once again, in its own small print HEFCE is forced to acknowledge this uncomfortable truth: 'Our current ultimate sanction is withdrawal of funding, which may not in the future be an effective mechanism.' That's bureaucratese for 'Yikes! What do we do now?' In all probability, the Treasury will have insisted that accepting a cap on numbers is the quid pro quo for an institution's students being eligible for loans, and a recent announcement by David Willetts has now confirmed that such a cap will be applied from 2014–15 in most cases. The result, therefore, is that private providers that were previously entirely independent will now be subject to central planning, thus illustrating the sweet ironies of enforced marketization.

As McGettigan rightly notes, the core-margin system is not only a clumsy way for the government to try to restrict numbers and to redistribute places from less selective to more selective universities. It also has the political advantage of enabling the government to claim that *it* is not to blame – though in fact it is – when there is a significant fluctuation in the number of applicants getting places at English universities. Instead, universities can be blamed for somehow mismanaging their admissions. This is consistent with so many other aspects of the coalition's higher education policy: new hoops are rigged up by the government for universities to jump through, and then universities are blamed for choosing to jump through said hoops – which, as 'autonomous' institutions they are 'absolutely free' not to do. It is the same fallacy as in age-old conservative and individualist thinking: actual circumstances are disregarded in abstract affirmations of possibility – the homeless person is equally 'free' to sleep under Westminster Bridge or at the Savoy.

The reality is that universities, though possessing certain forms of legal autonomy, have in effect been public institutions for at least two or three generations now. Many were founded entirely with public money, and all have long been largely financed by public money. There are bound to be tensions in such an arrangement, but it worked well enough all the while governments abided by the 'arm's length' policy of leaving universities free to determine their own academic policies and intellectual activities. The state does not, for example, tell universities, unlike schools, what and how to teach. But in recent years governments of both parties have become restive, keen to harness universities to whatever is deemed the priority of the moment.

As Brown puts it: 'In Britain ... the main threat to academic control of research has come from a series of state initiatives since the early 1990s to promote what successive governments of all parties have deemed to be in the national economic interest.' These 'initiatives' are now being extended to the fine detail of the undergraduate admission process: never before, I believe, has a government department (working through HEFCE) specified the exact grade of outstanding A-levels which a university must require before an applicant can be accepted. But universities, we shall be told, are free to ignore this requirement – and pay the penalty; in other words, they may choose to sleep under Westminster Bridge.

Despite these short-term fudges, the central logic of the coalition's policy is clear enough, and it is emphasized in the data it now requires universities to provide for applicants, the Key Information Set. The value of a university education is the income it enables you to earn minus the cost of acquiring that education. The message to applicants is therefore equally clear: compare the salaries of graduates from two or more institutions, deduct the different fees charged by those institutions, and your university choice makes itself. A great deal of attention, both within universities themselves and especially in politics and the media, is focused on questions to do with the precise level of fee. Universities are being told to 'compete on price', and they are therefore supposed to make decisions about what the 'market will bear': the merits of £8,250 as opposed to £8,750 are keenly debated. Consumers are then supposed to make choices on the basis of value for money.

This, as an array of well-qualified analysts have pointed out, is impossible because the 'good' on offer is not one about which consumers could make such fine discriminations of quality. The Browne Review announced, with the same breath-taking confidence with which it announced so many things, that price is the 'single best indicator of quality'. The fact that price in this case is actually a feeble proxy for true judgements of quality is one of the confusions that bedevils the new scheme at every step. For one thing, a university education is what some analysts have called a 'post-experience good': a full understanding of its benefits cannot be had in advance. In so far as it can be assimilated to economists' standard categories, it has to be regarded more as a 'positional good' than a 'consumer good'. A place at a particular university is *not* (at least at present) available to all with the desire and the finances to purchase it, and the 'value' of any given university place will partly depend upon the existing status hierarchy among institutions, something that changes with glacial slowness, even in a time of rapid change in the sector in other ways. This is, incidentally, another reason why it is in the interests of the most selective universities not to expand their numbers significantly. David Willetts berates them for this, and the open season on AAB+ applicants was intended to encourage expansion 'at the top', but sensible institutions resist this pressure, and it is rational for them to do so even in market terms. (It is clearly right for them to do so in terms of protecting the quality of education they can offer.) The much-lauded – not least by coalition spokespersons – Ivy League universities understand this very well: undergraduate numbers at Harvard, Yale and Princeton are kept down to around five or six thousand, fewer than half the twelve or thirteen thousand at universities such as Oxford, Cambridge and other leading British universities.

Thus, under the new fees regime, applicants are supposed to take decisions based on information that can only ever be proxies for quality – for example, statistics about individual universities' spending per head or league-table places (themselves proxies for the impossible task of ordinal ranking by quality). In reality, of course, applicants are making decisions on other grounds, as they have long done: general reputation, the 'fit' with the kind of course they think they would like to take, the social amenities offered, the part of the country and so on. But if this is what they did before fees were ramped up in 2012, what part *should* price now play in this decision for the 'rational consumer' (i.e. the seventeen-year-old sixth-former)? The surprising truth is that, even within the terms of intelligent consumerism, it would be

foolish for typical applicants to let price be any significant determinant of their choice (quite apart from the deeper reasons
why this is an undesirable way to try to run a higher education
system).

To make this clear, let us assume that an applicant is hesitating
between making University A or University B her first choice (the
majority of UK applicants are female). The courses and amenities at the two universities are very similar, but University A,
the somewhat older foundation, has traditionally had a slightly
higher reputation than University B, though it may not be entirely
clear why this should be so, based on the information about the
two institutions contained in their respective Key Information
Sets. However, while University A has set the fee for its course at
£9,000, University B, attempting to situate itself in the market in
the approved way, has set its fee at £8,000. So, given that they
seem to be pretty much identical in every other way, this whop-
ping difference in sticker price must be decisive, mustn't it? And
indeed, there seems to be anecdotal evidence that some members
of the first generations of applicants under the new fee regime
are responsive to precisely this consideration.

But should they be? What are the financial consequences of
each decision? Here is where it is crucial to understand that the
student loan system is not at all like credit card debt or even
a mortgage. It is more like a tax, paid at a fixed rate, until the
notional capital of the loan is paid off. Let's assume that the
financial circumstances of our applicant and her family are such
that she will borrow the maximum for maintenance costs, and
thus the only variable would be the different fee. So, if she goes
to University A, let's say she takes out loans totalling £42,000
and if she goes to B, loans totalling £39,000. Now, let us assume
that whichever of the two universities our applicant goes to,
she subsequently gets a job with the same salary. (In reality it is
more likely that having attended the university with the slightly
higher reputation she will get a slightly higher starting salary,
but let us disregard that for the sake of argument. We can also
leave aside the unrealism of the assumption that the graduate

will get *any* job after graduating, though the fact that so many won't is another serious problem with the scheme.) Then, once the graduate's salary exceeds £21,000, 9 per cent of the amount by which it exceeds that threshold will be taken through the payroll tax system. This will not vary depending on how big the loans were that they took out. It is a flat-rate tax. (Interest will have been charged on all loans during student years and then at a sliding scale in relation to subsequent income.)

Now let's assume, in order to make the sums easy, that the graduate earns £30,000 per year averaged over the first ten years after graduation, £40,000 per year averaged over the next ten, and £50,000 per year over the next ten (all at today's prices). Let us also assume, though this may be the most unrealistic assumption of all, that the terms on which she took out the loan are honoured and not changed with retrospective effect. This means that the 'repayment' accelerates as she gets older: 9 per cent of £9,000 (the amount by which her £30,000 salary exceeds £21,000) reduces the 'debt' by a lot less per year than 9 per cent of £29,000 will do (remember also that the notional capital will actually increase a little in the early stages because of the interest charges). The fact, then, is that our graduate would pay *exactly the same amount each year* for, let's say, twenty-five years after graduation whichever level of loan she had taken out. The only difference will be that when she is in, say, her late forties and earning a substantial salary, she will carry on paying the 9 per cent tax for a little longer (perhaps up to two years – there are too many variables to be more exact) if she went to University A rather than University B, in order to pay off the notional capital-plus-interest on an initial loan of £42,000 rather than £39,000. Any applicant serious about getting a good university education would be foolish to let that distant and relatively minor extra period of additional tax determine their choice of university at the age of seventeen.

None of this is to say that the principle of variable fees is a good one or without damaging side-effects. It is not. Nor should we forget that a large proportion of applicants are not 'typical', or that the scheme is likely to have damaging effects on the class composition of the student body at the most highly regarded universities. But it is to say that there is not a genuine market here; that many, perhaps most, applicants would be right to recognize that price should not be a major determinant of their choice; and that universities should not be seduced by market rhetoric into thinking it will necessarily be to their long-term advantage to charge slightly lower fees.

For the applicant, the plethora of scholarships, bursaries, fee waivers and the rest can be bewildering, further adding to the difficulty of making a rational market choice. It is obviously right that universities should do whatever they can to reduce the expense of getting an education for those who can least afford it, but fee waivers are actually a foolish misuse of money, apart from a possible, but unproven, advantage they may have in recruiting students from straitened financial backgrounds who do not really understand the loan system. When the logic of the loan-repayment system is better understood by applicants, they will see that it is far more in their collective interest to have financial aid now rather than a promise of a reduction in their possible tax rate at some distant point in the future. It is certainly much better for the university to have the income from the fee and for some of that money to be used to provide additional maintenance scholarships for those in need, thereby materially improving students' finance in the present. The chief beneficiary of fee waivers is the Treasury, since universities are thereby relieving it of the need to make available the finance to pay the fees. This is doubly foolish, since universities cannot know whether the students to whom fee waivers are granted will be among those who will end up not repaying all or any of their loans, in which case the university may have used its scarce resources merely to help reduce the government's future costs on the loan system. The government is trying to force universities to offer fee waivers rather than scholarships by allowing waivers to count in calculations about the average fee that institution is charging. Thus, even though every undergraduate enrolling at Loamshire University who is paying fees is in practice being charged, say, £8,000, the 'average' fee can be calculated as, say, £7,499 if the fee waivers are taken into account, which may be crucial in terms of avoiding the constraints or penalties the government may impose on institutions charging over £7,500. Is this really an intelligent way for universities to have to operate?

Of course, one way, the economists will tell us, that the sticker price may quite rationally enter into the applicant's calculations is that University A, catastrophic mismanagement aside, is bound to have a higher income per student than University B, and so what it spends on education and amenities is likely to be correspondingly greater (at least until Britain's universities are run by for-profit companies, in which case the higher fees may just go to enrich the bonuses of top executives and the cash pile of the private equity partners). Beyond this, and especially towards the top of the reputational range, the higher 'price' may, as with various luxury goods, become a *positive* incentive to opt for what is, as we have seen, partly a positional good. Meanwhile, applicants have every reason to make their choices on the same basis as their predecessors did; the 'price' differential is a phantom factor which says more about the confidence of particular universities than it does either about the 'value for money' of particular courses or (to any great extent) the future financial burdens of the graduate.

This being so, the government will presumably do whatever it takes to try to make the choice a 'properly' rational market choice, for institution and individual alike. In all probability, the terms of both the loan scheme and the allocation of places will at some point be changed. It would certainly be naive in the extreme to believe that the terms on which student loans are currently offered will not before long be altered for the worse. The government's official guide for students to the terms and conditions of the loans explicitly says: 'You must agree to repay your loan in line with the regulations that apply at the time the repayments are due and as they are amended. The regulations may be replaced by later regulations.' In other words, you cannot know what your repayment terms will be; they will be whatever the government of the day decides. This clause may be of considerable interest to any private financial firm considering buying a chunk of the loan book. And note that this does not simply mean a change of terms for new loans: the terms of existing loans can be varied once they have been taken out. Such changes would not require fresh legislation: the government is now empowered to vary the terms, as long as the interest rates charged do not exceed 'commercial rates'.

But do we really think that this or any future government would even contemplate such changes? Well, earlier this summer, the government was forced to reveal its exploratory plans to change the terms of pre-2012 loans retrospectively in order to make the loan-book more attractive to private financial institutions. And if you are still in any doubt, listen to the source quoted in the press at the end of June this year [2013] about the discussions between the Treasury and BIS leading up to the Spending Review:

> There was a paper circulating from the Treasury that wanted all [further education] provision put on to a loan basis. Even people with little more than GCSEs would be put on to student loans. It would have been massive cuts in the FE budget. They were wanting, in some places, to get rid of student grants and convert them all into loans. Reopening the question of the student loans scheme – dropping the threshold to £18,000 was one of the proposals.

As with every aspect of these revolutionary changes, the present version is only the tip of the iceberg. Apparent safeguards are incorporated in the first form of these measures as a way of winning support from well-meaning but credulous groups (e.g. some Lib Dem MPs). But once the system is in operation, these 'safeguards' are summarily removed since they function as obstacles to the pursuit of profit by private sector corporations and finance houses, which the government wants to become more and more involved in the enterprise and to which it would like ultimately to hand over the running of the system. Presumably it is wholly consonant with the crazed market vision driving these changes to expect that anyone taking out a student loan under the new scheme will in future also take out an insurance policy against the day when the repayment terms are retrospectively altered for the worse. They would, as the economists say, be rational to do so. (In fact, since there may anyway soon grow up a flourishing little secondary market in lecturers taking out some form of malpractice insurance along the lines familiar to doctors and others in the US, the indirect boost to the stock market prospects of the big insurance companies should shortly figure as part of the economic 'impact' of higher education.)

The reality of the economics of the loan scheme in its present form must cast doubt on any claim that this enormous change has been brought about in order to reduce public expenditure. We all understand the accounting convention by which, since loans count as an asset, this system can be presented as reducing the deficit in public finances in the present, even though in practice the outlay is going to be enormous, and will increase at alarming speed. There has been little discussion of the medium and long-term effect of this on public debt; McGettigan has some particularly good pages on this. The Office of Budget Responsibility itself calculates the *additional* outlay between 2012–13 (the first year of the loans) and 2017–18 as £25 billion. And it will go on increasing until repayments begin to match outlay. When will that be? Not until the mid-2030s, according once again to official calculations. Some graduates will never reach the income threshold that triggers repayments; others will never pay off the entire sum. A prediction of how much will have to be written off in this way constitutes what government accountants call the Resource Accounting and Budgeting (or RAB) charge, that element which has to be counted as expenditure because it will not be recovered. Independent analysts thought the government was optimistic in suggesting this could be kept to 32 per cent of the total loaned; Willetts has recently admitted it could be

35 per cent or even higher; others have suggested it could be 40 per cent. Unpaid loans are written off after thirty years. At that point, the government's liability/asset will start to be reduced both by repayments and by write-offs. BIS itself calculates that by 2046, thirty years after the earliest cohort paying these fees will have begun to make its first repayments, the outstanding debt will be around £191 billion.

This is, by any standards, a colossal level of outlay, but since it also represents, in accounting terms, a considerable asset, it is another reason for thinking that this or future governments will be tempted to 'sweat the asset', by, for example, raising repayment rates. But if you are lying awake at night worrying that the government might be bankrupting the country in this way (a rarefied worry, perhaps, especially in view of what else they are doing), then rest assured: there is a lot that this or future governments can do to reduce the problem. Everyday administrative fiats, such as freezing the repayment threshold at £21,000 or reducing it (instead of, as promised, raising it in line with inflation) will bring in quite a bit more money. But how long can it be before a *Daily Mail*-responsive government decides that 'loan-spongers' should be flushed out? Why should they not repay anything if their earnings do not exceed £21,000? Why should the outstanding balance be written off after thirty years? It will not be hard to change those terms either.

In fact, let's take it further. After a while, there will be statistics about the repayment rates for graduates not just from different universities but from different courses. If one course shows a very low repayment rate, why not harness 'anti-scrounger' feeling and cease to treat it as eligible for publicly backed loans? The joke is that a fee system is justified, in government rhetoric, as making universities more independent of government. The reality is that it may give an alternative lever for forcing 'market' judgements on universities in deciding what courses to offer. This, as McGettigan spells out, will 'achieve what direct government control could not ... and it will appear that universities are doing it to themselves. The pull of access to the loan scheme may be so strong that institutional autonomy becomes a chimera.' As with university-issued bonds, the long-term effect is to make aspects of higher education provision in this country reflect the priorities of for-profit financial institutions. These will thus be further steps towards achieving the government's unstated aim: to convert universities into market-driven corporations that are governed by the financial imperatives of global capitalism. McGettigan calls it 'the creative destruction of mass higher education', undertaken in the name of an unspecified future: 'Education is being re-engineered by stealth through a directed process of market construction, each move designed to protect the elite and expose the majority.'

The international evidence of improvement of standards as a result of increased marketization is, to say the least, mixed. As Brown notes, this form of competition

> may also damage quality by commodifying knowledge, creating or reinforcing student 'instrumentality', and lowering standards through grade inflation, and acceptance of plagiarism and other forms of cheating. It may also lead to a diversion of resources away from learning and teaching to activities like marketing, enrolment, student aid and administration (and in the US, athletics).

But the UK experiment is being conducted in a hurry, with no time to consider such evidence; as Brown notes, the *average* of the fees introduced in 2012 is already 'higher than that of nearly every "public" university in nearly every comparable system'.

Many national systems of higher education consist, designedly, of different types of institution with markedly different functions. In the UK, there is very little explicit differentiation of function: almost all established universities pursue teaching and research, educate undergraduates and postgraduates, offer a range of subjects, cater to other than local students and so on. What we have instead is a definite, if informal, reputational hierarchy – or what Sir David Watson, another respected commentator on higher education (and another former vice-chancellor) calls 'a controlled reputational range' – and the 'mission-groups' into which most universities have now sorted themselves are at least as much to do with status as with function. As Brown points out, this was clearly signalled by the announcement in March 2012 that four members of the 1994 Group of 'smaller research-intensive universities' (Durham, Exeter, Queen Mary and York) would be joining the Russell Group. They had not changed their function at all: they were, in effect, cashing in on their success in recent research assessment exercises and, above all, on the strength of their undergraduate applications, as places where large numbers of well-qualified applicants thought it was desirable to go. The existing members of the Russell Group are, on the whole, larger institutions with big professional and medical schools and a higher turnover, but the new fees regime, and especially the attempt to rig undergraduate admissions via the AAB+ clause, means that the pattern of undergraduate applications may come to matter somewhat more in determining what counts as a 'top' university because it now has such financial consequences. The new entrants were reported as paying an entrance premium of £500,000: a spokesman for Exeter said that 'membership of the Russell Group is a brand asset ... so it is well worth the cost of joining'. The favoured institutions are thus triply advantaged: they get nearly all the research funding, they get more money per student from fees, and they get the reputational advantage. As Brown puts it, 'we need to consider whether the benefits of such preferential treatment outweigh the costs to the system and the country as a whole'. The 'controlled reputational range' has been one of the huge strengths of the UK system, not least in terms of its standing abroad, but the free-for-all at the bottom end of this range will now severely damage that standing. As Brown continues, in best 'stiff memo' terms: 'It is strongly arguable that what we need is not more "world-class" universities but a "world class" higher education system.' Exactly so.

IV

You might think that one of the cardinal principles of higher education policy-making should be that any new measure must be assessed not just in terms of its professed and immediate purpose, but in terms of its impact on the practice, culture and ethos of the system as a whole. Current Whitehall in-house assessments may not be particularly good at this because they are now cast in a too narrowly economistic form. The classic illustration here is research assessment. 'The Research Selectivity Exercise' introduced in 1986 had an appealingly simple rationale, it seemed: how should the money available to support research in universities be distributed, given that the funds are limited and the money may not be used to best effect if awarded to all universities (or departments within universities) regardless of the scale and quality of their research activity? This was an issue for the experimental sciences above all, where there can be obvious economies of scale in terms of expensive equipment and where large concentrations of researchers can be intellectually beneficial in ways not so true for other disciplines. So, a system was established by which the research quality of all university departments was periodically assessed by national panels, and the research funding then distributed according to the resulting rankings. But what an all-devouring monster was thus created. As a result of successive research assessment exercises in 1989, 1992, 1996, 2001, 2008 and (now renamed the Research Excellence Framework) in 2014, preoccupation with research ranking has come to dominate academic life, from appointments, promotions, choice of research topics and so on to universities' strategies, marketing and publicity. It has also become, of course, one of the principal mechanisms for stratifying the system. On this, Brown is uncharacteristically outspoken:

> Because of the interrelated nature of teaching, research, and scholarship, impact assessments need to cover the effects on all university activities, and not just on the activity at which the policy is directed. The consistent failure to do this in relation to

the RAE – on the frankly sophistical grounds that selectivity was only about improving research performance and other impacts were irrelevant – is a serious blot on the Funding Council's stewardship of the sector since 1992.

This is another matter on which the ministerial cry of 'it's nothing to do with me, Guv' rings so hollow. Ministers like to say that the whole process is in the hands of academics, but it transparently is not. It is a bureaucratic process, run by HEFCE, which tries to give effect to the wishes of its political masters. And sometimes those wishes are expressed with revealing frankness. For example, the 2008 RAE was a large-scale exercise, as a result of which funding for research would be allocated (in fixed, diminishing proportions) to departments that came in the top three quality bands. Except that it wasn't: once the (expensive and labour-intensive) exercise had been completed, the government decided that it would prefer a higher proportion of the funding to go to the top-rated institutions, and it altered the ratios accordingly. Indeed, in 2012–13 funding for those departments which had succeeded in being placed in the third band was withdrawn completely. Why? 'The removal of this stream of funding was in response to direction from the Secretary of State in the annual grant letter.'

A procedure run by academics for academics? Brown authoritatively piles up the counter-evidence. For example: 'The changes to the RAE which resulted in the creation of the REF were the result of business lobbying of the Chancellor, Gordon Brown, in the run-up to the 2006 budget statement, about the apparent privileging of "pure" over "applied" research.' It is heartwarming, isn't it, to know that busy business leaders were willing to donate their precious time to helping universities decide what kind of research they ought to be doing? By contrast, one feels a little abashed that the press isn't fuller of stories about senior academics comparably using their great influence with chancellors of the exchequer to urge that fiscal regulation force companies to stop privileging profit over social function. The truth is that 'impact', the requirement introduced as a result of this intervention, is another metric designed to redirect academic research in politically approved directions. One of the strengths of Brown's book is its familiarity with a very wide range of international evidence, and he cites a study based on OECD data which found that 'when staff are given more autonomy, they do more research and are more productive. Trying to control research at the input stage by resource allocation conditions, as with the RAE and similar exercises, is actually counter-productive.'

Underlying so many aspects of the policies discussed in these two books is the fallacy of uniformly measurable performance. Human life involves many incommensurable forms of value. A parent's love of a child is not the same kind of thing as a painter's attempt to capture shape and colour or a scholar's interpretation of complex sources or a soldier's act of bravery and so on. The logic of punitive quantification is to reduce all these activities to a common managerial metric. Every other human agent has to justify their activities in the terms used by the businessman (or, to be more exact, an abstracted model of commercial calculation that managers are taught in business schools to use, whether or not actual successful businessmen may have operated according to other more diverse, and sometimes more intuitive, criteria). There are some activities for which these alien metrics only partially distort or fail to represent their true character; and there are others where 'false metrics' are ubiquitous. The activities of thinking and understanding are inherently resistant to being adequately characterized by quantitative metrics, which can only ever measure something measurable, and so in this case proxies have to be found for qualitative judgements.

This is part of the explanation for the pervasive sense of malaise, stress and disenchantment within British universities. Some will confidently declare that such reactions merely reflect the necessary jolt to the feelings and self-esteem of a hitherto protected elite as they are brought into 'the real world'. Like postmen complaining about changes to their work practices or head teachers retiring early in droves, grumbling academics are, it will be said, merely a symptom of the modernization of their industry, always a process that produces squeals. But there is obviously something much deeper at work here. It is the alienation from oneself that is experienced by those who are constantly forced to describe their activities in misleading terms. The managers, by contrast, do not feel this and for good reason, for the terms which suit their activities are the terms which have triumphed: scholars now spend a considerable, and increasing, part of their working day accounting for their activities in the managers' terms. The true use-value of scholarly labour can seem to have been somehow squeezed out; only the exchange-value of the commodities produced, as measured by the metrics, remains.

Various justifications have been offered for current policies, not always with conscious cynicism: 'the need to reduce public expenditure'; 'the need to secure a sustainable financial future for our universities'; 'the need to make student choice effective'; 'the need to make students bear some of the expense of their education'. However valid as goals in their own right any of these may be, as justifications for what is being done to higher education at the moment they are simply not persuasive. In reality, the overriding aim is to change the character of universities and make them more closely conform to market ideology. The innocuous phrase 'private providers' represents the shark in sheep's clothing: profit-seeking capital is to be allowed to run higher education in the way that it increasingly runs (ruins?) so many aspects of our common life. Universities must thus be made over into businesses, selling a product to customers: if they reduce costs and increase sales, they make a profit; if they don't, they go bust. Profit is the only indefeasible goal, competition the only effective mechanism.

From their very different starting points, the authors of these two books largely concur in their assessment of what is happening. Brown begins by declaring: 'The reform programme announced by the coalition government in November 2010 and incorporated in the subsequent (June 2011) White Paper is the most radical in the history of UK higher education, and amongst the most radical anywhere.' And he ends, more in sorrow than in anger, one suspects, by observing that

> higher education in England (and, to a more limited extent, in the other countries of the UK too) is now the subject of a 'real time' experiment which is being implemented without any 'control' or fallback position. This is in spite of the copious evidence from America, Australia, and now Britain, summarized in this book and elsewhere, showing the very clear limitations of markets as a means of providing an effective, efficient, and fair higher education system.

McGettigan strikes a similar note: 'An experiment is being conducted on English universities, one that is not controlled and that in the absence of any compelling evidence for change threatens an internationally admired and efficient system.' We are left to hope against hope, he concludes, that we shan't simply be left with 'a handful of selective universities (privatized to all intents and purposes) and a selection of cheap degree shops offering cut-price value for money'. And in case anyone in those 'selective' universities thinks that outcome might not be too bad, we should add the wise words of Sir David Watson, writing in 2007: 'It is important to recognise that even the most powerful institutions can't really go it alone. At some stage, and for some important purposes, every institution is going to rely on the strength and reputation of the system as a whole.'

The students who took to the London streets on 10 December 2010 may not all have been well informed about the imminent changes to university funding and they may not always have made the best choices about tactics, but their intuitions were largely sound. Under the cover of a vote to extend the level of a financial cap stipulated in an existing regulation, in conjunction with a series of other administrative decisions, the coalition succeeded in launching a fundamental and unprecedented revolution in higher education in England, a revolution whose long-term consequences are not easy to identify. The government was scarred by the scale of the protests in 2010, and it seems to have determined to avoid bringing forward new primary legislation whose progress through parliament would provide a focus for renewed opposition and protest. Instead, it has been changing things in a piecemeal way through budget decisions and the use of statutory instruments. After almost three years, there has still been no proper parliamentary debate about the new system of higher education that is being implemented.

Future historians, pondering changes in British society from the 1980s onwards, will struggle to account for the following curious fact. Although British business enterprises have an extremely mixed record – frequently posting gigantic losses, mostly failing to match overseas competitors, scarcely benefiting the weaker groups in society – and although various 'arm's length' public institutions such as museums and galleries, the BBC and the universities have by and large a very good record (universally acknowledged creativity, streets ahead of most of their international peers, positive forces for human development and social cohesion), nonetheless the policies and the rhetoric of the past three decades have overwhelmingly emphasized the need for the second category of institutions to be forced to change so that they more closely resemble the first. Some of those future historians may even wonder why at the time there was so little concerted protest at this deeply implausible programme. But they will at least be able to record for posterity the fact that, alongside its many other achievements, the coalition government took the decisive steps in helping to turn some first-rate universities into third-rate companies. If you still think the time for criticism is over, then perhaps you'd better think again.

CHAPTER 6

Higher Purchase:
The Student as Consumer

I

In his 1981 book, *After Virtue: A Study in Moral Theory*, Alasdair MacIntyre raised a disquieting possibility.[1] What we take to be 'the' language of morality now amounts, he proposed, to little more than a collection of verbal remains, the husks from which the kernels of coherent moral beliefs have long since been removed. 'What we possess ... are the fragments of a conceptual scheme, parts which now lack those contexts from which their significance derived. We possess indeed simulacra of morality, we continue to use many of the key expressions. But we have – very largely, if not entirely – lost our comprehension, both theoretical and practical, of morality.' The most we can do is to transpose the traditional issues of morality into the vocabulary of a barren utilitarianism.

I would be inclined to resist the more apocalyptic strain in this account, not least because it encourages conservative or nostalgic fantasies about 'returning' to a lost state of coherence or harmony in our beliefs (MacIntyre appeared be looking to some kind of revived Aristotelianism or Thomism). But I do wonder whether we may not be approaching a point where our usage of terms such as 'universities' and 'higher education' may, similarly, be best understood as the deployment of an inherited vocabulary without the underlying assumptions that for a long time made sense of it. This thought does not entail treating a particular phase of the historical development of such institutions as normative. There is no one 'right' understanding of the term

---

1   A slightly shorter version of this chapter was first published in the *London Review of Books* in January 2016.

'university' that would have commanded assent in eleventh-century Bologna, twenty-first-century Beijing and all points in between. But there is a recognizable family resemblance among the assumptions that sustained thinking about universities between, roughly, the development of the first modern versions of that institution in early nineteenth-century Europe and the great enlargement of what was still essentially the same form in the three decades or so after 1945. Much of our contemporary discourse about universities still draws on, or unwittingly presumes, that informing pattern of assumptions – the idea that the university is a partly-protected space in which the search for deeper and wider understanding takes precedence over all more immediate goals; the belief that, in addition to preparing the young for future employment, the aim of developing analytical and creative human capacities is a worthwhile social purpose; the conviction that the existence of centres of disinterested enquiry and the transmission of a cultural and intellectual inheritance are self-evident public goods; and so on.

While that conception of a university and its purposes is still very much alive – and may, I suspect, continue to underlie the intuitive convictions held by a great many 'ordinary' citizens about what universities are for – we may be nearing the point, at least in Britain, where it is starting to give way to the equivalent of MacIntyre's barren utilitarianism. If 'prosperity' is the only overriding value which politicians in market democracies can assume commands general support, then universities have to be repurposed as 'engines of growth'. The value of research has then to be understood in terms of its contribution to economic innovation, and the value of teaching in terms of preparing people for particular forms of employment. There are all kinds of tensions and inconsistencies within this newer conception, just as there are in the larger framework that posits a constant 'global struggle': neoliberalism assumes and promotes 'free competition' in international markets, while the rhetoric of national advantage often echoes mercantilist assumptions. But, through the debris of the older conception, what we still call universities are coming to be reshaped as centres of applied expertise and vocational training that are subordinate to a society's 'economic strategy'.

Universities are in some ways minor victims of the great mudslide that increasingly sees the vocabulary of exchange-value sweep aside the vocabulary of use-value in almost every area of life. It is becoming difficult to find a language in which to characterize the human worth of various activities, and almost impossible to make such assessments tell in public debate. Instead, contribution to 'growth' monopolizes the field. The public case for any proposal has to be couched in terms of the billions it will eventually add to the GNP. Whether the topic under discussion concerns the extension of human understanding or the enjoyment of the aesthetic, the preservation of the countryside or the provision of sports facilities, speculative and often bogus statistics have to be assembled to make the case in purely quantitative economic terms. (One pressing task for critique here is to help people to see that such statistics are not objective, reliable and fungible, but are often crude and tendentious generalizations cast in the form of one kind of language, i.e. numbers, though both their basis and the use made of them are wholly dependent on another form of language, i.e. words.)

To those who find the newer conception persuasive, even self-evident, existing universities can seem to have been disappointingly slow to recognize their proper role. Their archaic structures of self-government, their gentry-professional ethos and their blinkered devotion to useless knowledge are, in this view, leftovers from an earlier history. Since the 1980s much has been done to 'reform' (i.e. destroy) such features and to render these once inward-looking and obstructive producer-cartels 'fit for purpose'. But more remains to be done. In particular, some more effective and sustained method than repeated government diktats needs to be developed to ensure that universities function in accordance with the demands of a modern market economy. The key to this transformation, it turns out, is to be found in that unlikely embodiment of right-wing market thinking at its purest, the student.

The general logic of such thinking depends upon treating people exclusively as economic agents. The central social relation is that between buyer and seller. Hitherto, the primacy of these roles has been disguised by various inherited mechanisms that shielded individuals from direct participation in markets. These mechanisms – ranging from, at the collective level, direct state ownership to arm's length public bodies, and, at the individual level, from defined-benefit pension arrangements to student grants – are progressively being eliminated. Consumer 'choice' is now sovereign, and each agent is responsible for his or her own economic salvation. The role of government in this conception of modern society is thus largely confined to making sure that markets work. The institutional expression of public interest is largely reduced to the office of a 'regulator': hence the rise of all those agencies which in Britain are called 'OfSomething-or-Other' (OfCom, OfWat and so on). Prevailing dogma states that if markets work 'properly', consumer interest is maximized: real competition will 'drive up quality' and 'drive down prices'. Since, of course, in actual markets this is not what tends to happen – competition more often leads to near-monopoly power for the largest producers who can then fix the markets to their own benefit – the government, in the form of the regulator, is constantly having to step in to make competition work properly, and it does so as the champion of the consumer.

It is the application of this model to universities that produces the curious spectacle of a right-wing government lauding and championing students. Traditionally, of course, students had been seen by such governments, at least from the 1960s onwards, as long-haired layabouts, clearly part of the problem, not the answer. But now, from being depicted as some kind of anarchist militia bent upon disrupting society while sponging off it, students have come to be regarded as the front-line troops of market forces, storming the walls of those obstructive bastions of pre-commercial values, the universities. If students can be made to pay for what universities provide, then they acquire the rights of consumers and the government becomes, not their demonized oppressor or political antagonist, but their champion. If students will set aside airy-fairy old-fashioned notions about getting an education, and will instead focus upon finding the least expensive course that will get them the highest-paying job, then the government wants them to know that it will go into bat for them.

But who will it go into bat *against*? The logic of consumerism dictates that it is the producers, or more encompassingly 'the providers', who will, if unchecked, threaten the consumer interest. So, on the side of the angels, are the students, the taxpayers and the government. Arrayed against this formidable alliance must be, by elimination, the universities and, more particularly, the academics, who, unless kept up to the mark by constant assessments and targets, will revert to type as feather-bedded, professional-class spongers. A curious inversion has taken place whereby the academics now occupy the demonized role formerly assigned to the students, who are consistently spoken of in commendatory terms as striving to make appropriate economic choices guided by their wholesome desire to get 'value for money'.

Of course, in itself, 'value for money' is an entirely empty notion: it says nothing about what you should get or how much you should pay. It is also empty because no one, presumably, is in favour of not getting value for money. Nonetheless, the phrase occurs four times in the one-page foreword by Jo Johnson, the minister of state for universities and science in the current Conservative government, to the new Green Paper, *Fulfilling Our Potential: Teaching Excellence, Social Mobility and Student Choice*, and it is then repeated over and over again in the body of the document (the NUS has counted twenty-seven appearances, topped only by thirty-five for 'what employers want'). Its incantatory use signals official endorsement of consumerist logic: if you pay for something you acquire rights, and the government will help enforce those rights against those who

threaten to obstruct or deny them. Appearing to align the interests of students with those of taxpayers and the government in
this way is a neat trick. There had already been several moves
in this direction over the last decade or more, but the Browne
Review of 2010 made the logic chillingly clear, and the new fee
system that came into effect in 2012 was an attempt to opera-
tionalize it. Still, as Johnson rather ominously announces, 'the
job is not yet complete'. The proposals set forth in this document
are explicitly intended to complete the job.

It should be said at the outset that one of the central goals
the Green Paper's proposals are ostensibly designed to achieve is
unquestionably a good and important one. Universities should
provide good teaching. There has long been anecdotal evidence
that they do not always do this. It would be desirable if means
could be found, where they do not already exist, to check, as
far as is possible, when universities are and are not providing
good teaching and in the latter cases to see whether there may
be ways to nudge or encourage them towards improvement.
Restated in these more modest terms, the aims of this part of the
document seem unimpeachable. Certainly, it will be very difficult
for its critics to avoid being labelled as wilful refuseniks who
are resisting what is presented as the entirely proper exercise of
public scrutiny. But, as so often with changes justified in terms
of 'accountability', some of the measures proposed will not in
fact achieve the stated goals, and they will have unintended
consequences that may be more damaging than the ills they are
intended to remedy.

The specific proposals in the Green Paper are a curious
mixture of the sensible, the well-meant but misguided, the pig-
headed and the potentially sinister, but, when seen as part of the
broader developments sketched above, they all fall into place
as ways of 'completing the job'. The central proposal is to set
up a Teaching Excellence Framework (TEF) which will parallel
the existing Research Excellence Framework (REF). In theory,
the REF periodically assesses the quality of the research done
in all university departments and accords them scores. On the

basis of these scores, league tables are constructed, both at discipline level and at overall institutional level, and central funding for research is distributed accordingly. The TEF will, also in theory, do something similar for teaching. Ways will be found to measure the quality of teaching, and similar kinds of league tables will be based on the results. But teaching is now financed almost entirely by means of student fees, so the financial consequences will have to be implemented somewhat differently from the REF. The proposal, roughly, is that higher scores in the TEF will enable an institution to set higher fees.

This part of the proposal is complicated and not entirely clear at this stage. Four levels of teaching quality attainment will be specified, with fee levels corresponding to each one. Getting a higher ranking would enable an institution to 'raise fees in line with inflation'. The government will set the maximum that can be charged at each TEF level. 'The Government would not pre-set a formula for this fee uplift, but would set the uplift each year, maintaining the current model of basic and higher amounts, and not exceeding real terms increases.' It is not altogether clear whether this means that even the maximum increases that could be achieved for a top-level rating would not exceed the rate of inflation, or that the government would set a series of fee bands that would thereafter increase in line with inflation. If it is the former, the whole laborious process would lead to only minuscule increases at current rates of inflation, especially for the lower levels. The Green Paper states that if a university gets the first level TEF rating (as it acknowledges pretty much all existing universities are bound to do), they can 'increase their fees in line with inflation from the 2017–18 academic year'. With inflation currently well below 1 per cent, that would, in the first year, be the difference between a fee of £6,000 and, at most, £6,060, or £9,000 and £9,090. But in that case the three higher levels would have to involve more substantial increases, well above inflation. 'After the first year, and over time, we would expect fees to increasingly differentiate according to the TEF level awarded.' This seems to suggest the government will set a series of new fee caps for the three higher levels, with a maximum well above £9,000, and then increase those in line with inflation – or until it decides to increase them for other reasons of its own. No figures are mentioned, but it is hard to shake off the suspicion that part of the function of the new proposals, together with all their accompanying rhetoric about improving teaching quality, is to cover or legitimate substantial hikes in the top fee levels.

It is worth pointing out, especially to those still clinging to the idea that the Lib Dems helped get a fairer settlement on fees, that George Osborne gave students a sly stab in the back in the November Spending Review when he slipped in, unannounced, that the terms of loans taken out since 2012 are to be varied retrospectively. The earnings level at which repayments start will not in fact be increased in line with average earnings, as was solemnly promised at the time, thus at a stroke adding several thousand pounds to many students' eventual repayments. As one of the government's own advisers on student finance pointed out, a company that retrospectively changed the terms for existing borrowers in this way might attract sanctions, perhaps even prosecution. But this government, we must not forget, is there to 'champion' the interests of students. An undercover cell of social critics wanting to contrive a stunning exhibition of the Tories' bad faith in these matters could hardly have devised a more striking *coup de théâtre* than the publication of the Green Paper's ringing statement of the government's role as the students' champion at almost the same moment as it slips out news that the terms of their existing loans have just been retrospectively changed for the worse.

So, how will teaching quality be assessed, and assessed with the precision that will allow for ordinal ranking of institutions, with fee levels calibrated to match? The Green Paper acknowledges that there will have to be further discussion with universities about how to do this, but in the first instance it proposes three metrics: 1) data on 'retention' (i.e. drop-out rates); 2) National Student Survey (NSS) scores; 3) data on graduate employment. These all come in neatly quantitative form and so are, of course, objective and reliable. Beyond these indicators, there will be 'institutional evidence', that is, universities will describe in great detail the means and processes through which they 'assure' teaching quality, under designated headings such as 'The Learning Environment', 'Student Outcomes and Learning Gain' and so on.

Even if these initial metrics are eventually supplemented or superseded, the Green Paper's flirtation with them is revealing of the confusions at its heart. Consider, for example, the implicit premise that higher rates of employment among a university's graduates are evidence of better-quality teaching. Is there any evidence that this is the case? If one leaves aside the effects of home background and social connections, which are very considerable, the main determinants of a graduate's employment prospects are 1) the perceived standing of the university they attended, 2) their field of study, and 3) (but a distant third) the class of their degree result. The relative standing of universities only changes with glacial slowness and continues to involve elements of pure social snobbery. For employers, the most salient differentiating feature of universities is how difficult they are thought to be to get into: a university's admission scores are taken to provide prima facie evidence of the general ability level of its graduates. If reports on 'the student experience' consistently point in one direction, that may, eventually, have some effect, and how 'satisfied' students were with their teaching makes up one part of that experience. Even then it is hard to know whether such reports involve much direct relation to the *quality* of teaching, as opposed to issues such as workload, ease of getting high marks and so on.

The deeper problem is that this document doesn't know what it means by 'teaching quality'. It treats it as the equivalent or sum of a number of things that can be measured. So, if a course provides a clear description in advance of its aims and procedures; if the number of contact hours and requirements for written work are as advertised and such work is marked and returned promptly; if few students drop out; if students from that course have in the past had a good record of subsequent employment;

and if many students say they were 'satisfied' or 'very satisfied' with the course – then all that is taken as proof that high-quality teaching has taken place. Or, more exactly, that is what, within the proposed framework, quality of teaching will now *mean*. But it will be immediately obvious that these conditions might all apply without necessarily providing any reliable indication of the *quality* of teaching at all, though they may provide evidence of certain kinds of efficient functioning in a university or department. For the most part, the required information will merely demonstrate that certain procedures have been properly followed. Actually, all they really show is that a particular institution is good at presenting what we used to call a 'paper-trail' suggesting that those procedures have been properly followed.

In fact, the problem is a deeper one still, since it is not easy for anyone to say, in other than the most blandly formulaic terms, what good teaching consists in, and very difficult indeed for anyone, even sometimes for those involved in the interaction, to say in any given case whether good teaching is happening (it may be easier to identify and describe certain kinds of bad teaching). I am not suggesting that there is some unfathomable mystery here, nor that a Green Paper should be expected to resolve some of the most profound issues in the philosophy of education. But it should not try to kid either the public or itself that the measures prescribed in this document will necessarily improve the *quality* of teaching in universities. They may improve some aspects of some procedures and some record-keeping, and those may be real if limited gains. They may also create yet another bureaucratic burden (on already bureaucratically overburdened institutions) that actually makes it less likely that good teaching will get done.

If you really wanted evidence about the quality of teaching, one of the least imperfect mechanisms would be some equivalent of inspection by the now-abolished Her Majesty's Inspectors of Schools. That is to say, a visit by an experienced and impartial observer who actually sits in on a teaching session, even though that can be intrusive and distracting, may provide some worthwhile evidence. Above all, what such a mechanism makes clear is that any genuine evidence can only ever be a matter of judgement not measurement. The TEF will not involve visits or any direct observation of teaching. It will rely on metrics and on institutions' self-descriptions.

However, the Green Paper then goes on concessively: 'We recognise that these metrics are largely proxies rather than direct measures of quality and learning gain and there are issues around how robust they are.' Indeed. In fact, the term 'proxies' in this sentence might be glossed as 'largely irrelevant as indicators'. Some of the metrics may be based on information that is useful in itself, including the number of contact hours and data about 'training and employment of staff', where it says 'measures might include proportion of staff on permanent contracts', which is an interesting indication that even the government recognizes that the drift towards a largely casualized teaching body does not produce good teaching, however much it may be in line with market dogma about 'labour flexibility'. (In the US, sometimes taken as a guide to our future in these matters, approximately 70 per cent of those doing the teaching in colleges and universities are now not tenured or in tenure-track appointments, and there is widespread recognition that this is damaging the system.) Still, overall, it is clear that the bulk of the material submitted to the panels will consist of 'institutional evidence', that is, systematic boasting by universities as in the comparable sections of the present REF.

It takes no great insight to foresee that, as a result, a form of TEF-guff will develop to parallel the existing REF-guff. A handy rule-of-thumb test to apply to any new requirement for a form of institutional boasting is the following simple law: the usefulness of any document is in direct proportion to the ease with which a parody may be distinguished from the real thing. Warning bells should ring loudly when it proves difficult to tell whether a given piece of prose is genuine or a spoof. In describing a department's 'strategy for impact' within the existing REF, for example, one can bolt together all the currently approved clichés to produce an impeccable statement which may only differ from actual submissions in the unsullied purity of its managerial diction and its completely, as opposed to partially, fictitious character. Clearly, the statement of the 'institutional evidence' of teaching quality will be similarly likely to fail the test. Even just cribbing phrases from a couple of pages of the Green Paper produces a plausible opening: 'Rigorous procedures are in place for enhancing the learning environment and ensuring knowledge-gain and positive student outcomes. A focus on the acquisition of transferable skills ensures all courses deliver added value and employment-ready graduates, while providing a level playing-field for those from disadvantaged backgrounds...' There will be frequent appearances by our old friends, Robust and Transparent, the Rosencrantz and Guildenstern of HiEdBiz prose, attendant lords that will do to swell a progress. And the already top-heavy administrative echelons of universities will expand to include, if they do not already possess, Directors of Learning Quality Strategy, Teaching Excellence Coordinators and so on ('You will be passionately committed to using robust metrics to ensure transparent evaluation of student-centred knowledge-gain...').

'A panel of independent experts' will then assess all this information. 'The proposed panels will be made up of a balance of academic experts in learning and teaching, student representatives, and employer/professional representatives.' This immediately suggests two questions: 1) in what sense are these people 'experts', and 2) who is not there? Presumably the 'experts in learning and teaching' will be drawn from the world of 'quality assurance' and perhaps from university education departments, the latter of which would at least signal the presence of one kind of expertise. Presumably 'student representatives' means a number of current students; their expertise is less obvious. And presumably the representatives of employers are, at best, 'experts' in what employers want, rather than anything to do with teaching quality. As to the most striking absence, it is surely the kinds of people who actually *do* the teaching – subject-specific, front-line academics. This may change as the consultation progresses, but in this form it does raise the suspicion that the panels will not really be judging teaching quality: being seen to meet certain external expectations looks a likelier goal.

Along the way, some interesting light is shed upon the role that could be played by data on the employment history of a university's graduates. 'Section 78 of the Small Business, Enterprise and Employment Act 2015 now enables higher education data to be linked with HMRC income and employment data, and DWP benefits data to inform understanding of the labour market outcomes of graduates.' The suggestion here is that the government will use the tax and benefits systems to compile data on the employment patterns of graduates from each university, and perhaps each course, so that in time this can 'inform' the assessment of teaching quality. Not enough graduates in jobs, or in the right kinds of job, may result in financial punishment: courses that perform poorly by this measure, leading to a low rate of repayment of loans, could be denied eligibility for future loans and so on. In addition it raises the possibility, noted by Andrew McGettigan a couple of years ago, that tranches of the student loan book could be sold off at differential rates depending on the 'credit worthiness' of an institution's cohort of graduates, something that could also affect a university's ability to raise money in the capital markets.

At a more concrete level, a few perfectly sensible suggestions appear along the way. For example, it is obviously desirable that universities publish clear information for potential applicants about their courses, including details about contact hours, expected written work and so on. Most places seem to do this already, but perhaps provision could be improved. The Green Paper also touches, though in a somewhat cursory way, on two other related matters. First, there is the question of whether the current degree classification of Firsts, Upper Seconds and so on is sufficiently discriminating to be informative; and, second, there is the issue of so-called 'grade inflation'. I suspect many academics would testify from their own experience that there is now something amiss with the current system in these respects. In

2013–14 I chaired my department's exam board. I was yet again impressed by the remarkable thoroughness and care exercised through a long process of paper-setting, double-blind marking, use of external examiners, extra scrutiny of borderline cases, rereading of scripts, lengthy meetings and so on. But then there was the bathos of the outcome: 93 per cent of the candidates got a first or upper second. Those candidates certainly deserved their good results, but, faced with such a figure, it is hard not to feel that at least some standardized form of supplementary information about a student's performance should be developed to give students themselves, parents, employers, grant-giving bodies and others a better indication of the real level of achievement. It looks as though the TEF will be used to encourage moves in this direction, probably by adopting some form of grade point average similar to that used in the United States and elsewhere, though that system has some well-known drawbacks of its own.

Elsewhere, the Green Paper touches on problems that are real enough but beyond its power to remedy. National surveys of student opinion repeatedly confirm that the two improvements students would most like to see are more contact hours and smaller-sized teaching groups. In so far as the TEF is intended to put more emphasis on teaching rather than research, it may be that it will encourage improvement in these directions. But the two root causes of the present unsatisfactory state of affairs (discussed in Chapter 4, above) are beyond the reach of any TEF. The first is the drastic underfunding of universities from the mid-1980s to the early 2000s which has only been partially remedied in recent years. In the 1960s, the average staff–student ratio was claimed to be around 1:8; now (in so far as meaningful averages can be obtained in a much more diverse sector: the figures are much disputed) it is said to be around 1:19. The second cause is the culture created by the REF itself and its predecessor assessment exercises. Institutions and individuals have been pressured and incentivized to give research priority over teaching. The Green Paper is right to identify the resulting patterns of behaviour as a problem, but, in suggesting that the TEF will help to 'rebalance' things, it is acting like the kind of doctor who first prescribes one kind of unnecessary medication (the REF), which produces various undesirable side-effects, and then triumphantly adds a second medication (the TEF) that will, it is claimed, reduce them. It is possible, though implausible, that a university tyrannized by the REF *and* the TEF will be better than one tyrannized by the REF alone, but a simpler and much more economical remedy suggests itself.

So what will the TEF actually produce? At least the following:

1. More administrators to administer the TEF.
2. A greater role for business in shaping the curriculum and the forms of teaching.
3. A mountain of prose in which institutions describe, in the prescribed terms, how wonderful their provision and procedures are (cf. REF).

It also seems pretty certain to produce:

4. More efforts by universities to make sure their NSS scores look good.
5. More pressure on academics to do whatever it takes to improve their institution's overall TEF rating (cf. REF).
6. More league tables, more gaming the system, and more disingenuous boasting by universities about being in the 'top ten' for this or that.

And what is it *un*likely to produce?

1. Better-quality teaching.

Although the proposals for a TEF are what have attracted most attention, the Green Paper has substantial things to say about at least three further topics. The first concerns what it calls the 'architecture' of the higher education sector. Here again, what it proposes may appear, at one level, to be pursuing a perfectly sensible aim, though the most likely outcome has a sinister aspect. In recent years, the quangos involved in running higher education have proliferated (now, why might that be?), and the main one, the Higher Education Funding Council, England (HEFCE), has in effect lost its central function since it no longer distributes a block grant for teaching. So the proposal is to abolish it, along with the Office for Fair Access (OFFA) and the Office of the Independent Adjudicator (OIA), and replace them all with one new super-quango – the Office for Students, which the Green Paper queasily avoids calling by the obvious 'OfStud', preferring instead the unpronounceable OfS. 'This would be the first time that a higher education regulator has been explicitly designed to promote the student interest, and approach higher education regulation through a student lens.' The Green Paper does not speculate whether perhaps the NUS, and even possibly individual student unions, might now want to dissolve themselves, secure in the knowledge that the student interest is in such good hands, but the government wants everyone to know whose side it's on. In fact, OfStud's remit will include the protection of other weak and vulnerable groups: it will 'empower, protect and represent the interests of students, employers and taxpayers'. By this point in the exposition, it should be clear how protecting the interests of employers is simply another way of 'putting students at the heart of the system'.

Although most public funding of teaching was withdrawn in 2012, there remains a residual teaching grant to be allocated to support high-cost STEM subjects and other 'priorities', so if HEFCE is abolished a new mechanism for doing this will have to be found. One method that seems to appeal to the government (now, why might that be?) is 'for BIS ministers to set the strategic priorities for teaching grant ... This will enable ministers to strengthen incentives for higher education provision that supports the needs of the economy.' More significantly still, a new mechanism would have to be found to distribute the research funding that results from the REF, currently done by HEFCE. At present, the so-called 'dual-support system' means that this basic funding for research goes directly to universities, in line with their REF performance, while funding for particular projects is distributed, on a competitive basis, through the research councils, which are quite separate organizations. The Green Paper ostensibly reaffirms the traditional commitment to maintaining these two separate strands of funding, but it raises the possibility that both might be administered by a single 'overarching body'. A review of the role of the UK research councils, conducted by Sir Paul Nurse, President of the Royal Society, has been taking place alongside the discussions that have issued in the Green Paper, and one of that review's main recommendations appears to be that the research councils should be under the general aegis of a new 'ministerial committee chaired by a senior minister, so we have the political will for science and can use it for the good of the UK'. (It has been plausibly reported by the *Times Higher* that 'the most likely candidate to chair this committee would be George Osborne'.) It is not hard to see how putting all the eggs of research into a single funding basket will make it easier to direct that funding to what ministers decree to be 'strategic needs'. As the political grip gets tighter, it would not be mere nostalgia to recall the 'arm's length' arrangements of the old University Grants Committee as a more intelligent means of giving universities the freedom necessary to benefit humanity in the long run.

The second topic concerns what the document generically terms 'new providers'. The government wants to make it much easier for outside bodies to set up a university and acquire degree-awarding powers, and it wants to ensure the existence of the fabled 'level playing-field' for both existing and new universities in terms of regulation, access to student loans and so on. It has already gone some way towards supporting such 'alternative providers': in 2010–11 about 6,500 students were getting their higher education from such institutions, whereas now 60,000 do so. The reasons given for expanding this sector further and faster are the usual market-speak: increased competition will 'drive up quality' and 'drive down prices'. The Green paper is emphatic that it is 'a clear priority for the Government to widen the range of high quality education providers'.

Until recently, it was not easy for an existing educational institution to become a university and even more difficult for a commercial enterprise to set one up from scratch. There were strict controls on the use of the title; degree-awarding powers were only granted with the approval of the Privy Council; fledgling institutions often had to endure a longish period during which their courses were validated by an established university; and so on. One might have thought that these safeguards had contributed to the generally high reputation of British universities across the board for the greater part of the twentieth century, but now we are told 'innovation and diversity in higher education provision are crucial to maintain our international reputation'. Moreover, it is axiomatic that increased competition means increased innovation (and provides better value for money). So the Green Paper proposes to do away with many of the existing checks. There will be no need for Privy Council approval; no requirement about minimum student numbers (and therefore no longer any status of 'university college'); all institutions that pass rather minimal requirements will be free to call themselves universities. They would not even have to be teaching institutions: 'Degree awarding powers could also potentially be made available to non-teaching bodies meeting appropriate standards.' And they would not need to pass the present tests on their track record and financial sustainability, which could all be speeded up. The Green Paper notes in passing that henceforth the accounts that meet the financial sustainability test may be 'the accounts of a parent company, if the provider is a wholly-owned subsidiary' – just so we know what sort of animal these 'alternative providers' are likely to be.

So, Cramme, Chargem and Skimpe will now be able to set up EasyUni without too much difficulty; its students will be eligible for the publicly backed loans, the profits from which will pass to the parent company, CCS Holdings Ltd. EasyUni will innovate like crazy, completely up-ending hidebound ideas about education, and its offer of Quick 'n' Cheap degrees will help drive the long-established University of Loamshire out of business, thereby, it will be claimed, raising the reputation of British higher education abroad. For it is central to government thinking that there should be losers as well as winners. 'In a changing and more competitive sector, providers that innovate and present a more compelling value proposition to students will be able to increase their share total – in some cases this may be at the expense of other institutions.' The Green Paper outlines arrangements for what it coyly terms 'provider exit', whether as a result of 'financial failure', or because they are closed down by OfStud, or 'as a result of voluntary exit by the provider' (presumably this doesn't mean the VC buying a one-way ticket to Dignitas). So, the plan is to have lots more organizations calling themselves universities, more cut-throat competition, and more closures. We shan't be able to say we weren't warned.

The third topic touched on is 'social mobility and widening participation'. This contains the usual mix of well-meaning confusion and blank evasion. The Green Paper sorrowfully reports that a smaller proportion of the age cohort from 'disadvantaged' backgrounds goes to university than from more 'advantaged' groups, and of those who do, a still smaller proportion goes to 'highly selective universities'. Gosh, who knew? But the document's gloss on 'disadvantage' is inadvertently revealing. As far as simple university entrance goes, gender is not the problem, except in so far as the fact that female students now comprise the majority may be taken to indicate underachievement by certain groups of male applicants. Nor, in a straightforward way, is ethnicity, though those described as of 'black Caribbean heritage' are significantly under-represented. No, it's 'white males from disadvantaged backgrounds' who are losing out most dramatically: only around 10 per cent of them go into higher education, whereas the figures for males of 'Indian heritage' and 'Chinese heritage' are 50 per cent and 60 per cent respectively.

Of course, the great unmentionable word here, as in government pronouncements more generally, is class. These boys are, by and large, the children of the unskilled white working class, and their cumulative social and economic disadvantages are indeed deeply unjust. At first, your heart might leap at the thought that the government is going to do something about this unacceptable state of affairs. At last, a government that is determined to tackle inequality at source. After all, the only lasting way to make university recruitment (and much else) more equitable would be to reduce these structural disparities in background. But that, you won't be altogether dumbstruck to learn, is not the government's preferred route. While implicitly recognizing that the inequalities between the 'advantaged' and the 'disadvantaged' are the defining feature of the problem, they propose to leave those as they are, and instead to force universities to give more places to people from such disadvantaged backgrounds, by, for example, setting targets and financially penalizing universities that do not meet them. After all, the present social imbalance in intake must be the fault of the universities, which need to do more to correct it. The fundamental circumstances of advantage and disadvantage are, apparently, fixed, perhaps even sacrosanct. What we must ensure, it seems, is that coming from a disadvantaged background is no, er, disadvantage.

The Green Paper concludes with a remarkable couple of pages on the REF, pages which have little organic connection to the proposals in the main body of the document but which should not be missed by anyone who savours life's little ironies. What is most striking about these two pages is their note of surprise, even shock, that the REF should turn out to be a) extremely expensive to run, and b) so burdensome that it 'attracts such negative views from some in the sector'. What is so disingenuous here is that the costs and the bureaucracy are indeed shocking, but they were the inevitable, indeed widely predicted, results of the measures successive governments imposed on universities. One small indication of the monster that has been created is provided by the following pair of figures. The 2008 research assessment exercise, which was already widely criticized for its expense and bureaucracy, cost approximately £66 million to run. The 2014 Research Excellence Framework, in which the most notable innovation was the requirement to demonstrate certain kinds of social and economic 'impact', cost approximately £246 million. In other words, a procedure imposed by the government was already expensive, and now, as a result of additional requirements imposed by government (including, it should be said, laudable equality and diversity safeguards), it has become nearly four times as expensive.

It is at this point that the disingenuousness reaches almost comic proportions. The Green Paper declares, nicely mixing outrage and amazement, that 'we must ... address the "industries" that some institutions create around the REF and the people who promote and encourage these behaviours. There are cases of universities running multiple "mock REFs", bringing in external consultants and taking academics away from teaching and research.' The similar response of Captain Renault in *Casablanca* comes irresistibly to mind: 'I'm shocked, shocked to find that gambling is going on in here!' The indisputable fact is that these 'behaviours' have not been 'promoted and encouraged' by some mischievous elements in universities: they are the direct result of the system imposed by the government. Yet the Green Paper shows no sign whatever of drawing the obvious moral. Indeed, it casually speculates that perhaps *between* the regular REFs more use could be made of metrics to 'refresh' its results in the intervening years – or, in other words, to add yet further processes of data-gathering and assessment. And whatever changes any review of the REF might produce, tackling its most obvious and expensive failing seems to have been already ruled out: the Green Paper stubbornly maintains that any future exercise must continue to 'provide a clear sense of strategic priorities (for example around the introduction of impact)'. At this point, Captain Renault is revealed, not altogether implausibly, to be a descendant of the Bourbons, learning nothing and forgetting nothing.

But don't worry: the Green Paper is only a 'consultation' document. So that must mean, mustn't it, that if cogent objections are put forward to the premises, reasoning and conclusions it contains, then none of these proposals will come to pass. Well, mustn't it?

PART III

OCCASIONS

CHAPTER 7

The 'English Problem' and the Scottish Solution

I

Let me begin with three brief preliminary remarks.[1] First, I am certainly not presuming that I am in any position to tell anyone what should be done about the funding of universities in Scotland. I have, of course, read the Green Paper (*Building a Smarter Future: Towards a Sustainable Scottish Solution*, 2010) and followed the debate in Scotland with some interest, but I'm sure there are various dimensions of the situation here that I, as an outsider, am under-informed about or simply not aware of. Second, although I am going to offer a few reflections on the changes under way in the funding of universities in England, we have to be clear that they are not, or at least not yet, a clear and definite set of arrangements. Since November 2010, aspects of higher education policy in England have been changing on almost a weekly basis as the coalition rather desperately seeks to devise a workable system on the back of the radical upheaval that was rushed through parliament. It is quite possible that things I believe at the moment to be the case with English policy will be out of date by the time I sit down. And third, I am not speaking here as any kind of expert in higher education policy. That is, of course, a flourishing scholarly field in its own right, and I have only dipped an unpractised toe in the extensive and sometimes rather technical literature that has grown up in the last couple of decades in particular. I'm tempted to say that mine is the view from the trenches, but I recognize that a chair at Cambridge may seem to be a pretty well-upholstered and protected trench some

---

1 This chapter was first given as a lecture in Edinburgh in February 2011.

way behind the front line, so I'll just say that it is the perspective of a working scholar in the humanities with a special interest in the history of universities.

Despite that reference to history, I'm not in fact going to spend time today on retracing the development of the system in England, though I have to say that public debate on this subject is, I think, bedevilled by unanalysed assumptions about 'what universities used to be like' which then so easily slide over into assertions of 'what universities should be like'. Rather, I want to begin by drawing attention to some of the central features of the changes taking place in England, before going on to raise some questions about the current debate in Scotland. The policy in England may be 'post-Browne', but in various ways it cannot be said to be 'ergo propter Browne'. The coalition has unpicked the recommendations of the Browne Review which, whatever its failings (and they were many and serious), did possess a certain skewed logic. I think there is no point, therefore, in going over Browne again; we have to work from the policy that is struggling, piecemeal, to get itself made as we speak. The policy is very widely referred to in the media as 'a rise in fees', but that is misleading. It is not a 'rise' in fees: it is, of course, a radical transformation of the system in which public funding for teaching will be replaced by contributions paid retrospectively by graduates. The more or less complete withdrawal of the block grant for teaching is the centrepiece of the strategy – and the one, I may say, about which there was no warning and no democratic discussion. It is the likely effects of this on universities that I shall concentrate on, since these have been rather neglected in the understandable focus on the question of the effects of the new repayment system on recruitment and social mobility.

The premise governing my reflections is that we simply cannot at this point know for certain what the consequences of these changes will be. Those more expert than I am in the history of universities say that no country has, in modern times, taken such a leap in the dark with its higher education system. So, for that reason, it may be helpful to borrow an infamous distinction and talk about the 'known unknowns' and the 'unknown unknowns'.

Among the most obvious of the known unknowns is the behaviour of applicants and students in response to the new funding arrangements, and this is where the question of assumptions comes in. Obviously, we all realize that actual policies are not arrived at through a process of strict logical inference from a set of abstract premises, but in both the Browne Review and in subsequent government statements much is made of the claim that if students are in effect treated as consumers, then they will be more demanding about the education they receive and the result of this will be, in a favoured phrase, to 'drive up quality'. But is this claim convincing? One assumption here is that if people are in effect spending or investing their own money in something, they will care more about the outcome and feel more empowered to complain when that outcome is not to their liking. But in so far as this is true, it surely only applies to certain aspects of life. We don't, by and large, think people care more about their spouses if they met them as a result of paying a fee to a dating agency, and although all argument by analogy is open to immediate and obvious objection, putting it like this should at least make us pause to reflect on what the psychological mechanism is supposed to be where education is concerned. It is obviously not true that people *only* care about what they pay for, and in fact I doubt that my students could care more about their education than they do now.

The slightly more plausible version of this claim is that students who are in effect assuming a considerable burden of future tax liability will thereby feel empowered to be more critical or more demanding, and that this will force universities to improve the quality of the education they offer. But again, the reasoning here seems to me very doubtful. The student is in some respects already a complaining animal – complaining about issues such as accommodation or the price of beer in the student bar. But complaints that result in the quality of *education* being improved are altogether more problematic. To begin with, students are not usually in the best position to know in advance what it is that a particular educational experience should be like or should do for them. They may complain about things they do not like, such as heavy workloads or difficult ideas or properly strict marking, but it is far from clear that any university would be improving the quality of its education if it simply provided what, in relation to such matters, these consumers say they think they want. I am not, of course, denying that students can sometimes be well placed to point out where something about the process of their education seems to be inadequate, but I am saying, first, that they do this already and there is no reason to think they will do it more wisely or more effectively under the new arrangements, and, second, that there is no necessary link between so-called 'student satisfaction', as measured by meeting expressed wants or diminishing expressed complaints, and educational *quality*. Because the quality of education is not easily represented in tables or brochures, it is likely that other features of 'the student experience' will become the focus of increased pseudo-competition among universities, leading to what one observer has nicely called 'an amenities arms race'.

But the truth is surely that universities will still, as they do now, have to make decisions about which of these consumers' demands it is appropriate to satisfy and which it is not. If, say, students were to start to demand which members of staff they would be prepared to be taught by, or which requirements for a course they wished to see dropped, or, at the limit, to insist that their paying large fees entitled them to top degree results, universities would quite properly say that meeting these demands would not 'drive up quality'. I am not suggesting it is likely that students will henceforth make such demands in large numbers, not least because I don't believe in the consumer model in the first place, but we should recognize that the essential link in the claim that charging students much higher fees will 'drive up quality' is, in this respect, simply not persuasive.

In support of the changes it is also said that they will help to give a proper emphasis to teaching, something that has suffered or been undervalued in recent decades. But in so far as the historical premise is true, what are the causes? They are, surely, first, the long period of deliberate underfunding in the 1980s and 1990s that saw student numbers expand hugely without a corresponding increase in resources, and, second, the effects of the culture produced by the research assessment exercises. It is, once again, not obvious that the new funding arrangements will alter these conditions significantly. As we know, the proposed basic fee represents a substantial cut even on present funding levels, while the REF perpetuates the bad effects of the over-rewarding of a certain kind of research productivity. It is hard to see why replacing the income that universities get for teaching at present with slightly less income in the form of fees (unless they charge the £9,000 maximum) will lead them to invest more in teaching or to reward it more highly. There will, presumably, be increased attention paid to the presentation and marketing of teaching, but it is hard to see these changes, by themselves, affecting the governing imperatives of career advancement as they are presently reinforced in English universities.

But let us press further, into the 'unknown unknowns', and assume for the moment that applicants will be influenced by the new arrangements into making different course choices from those they make at present. The premise of the new arrangements is that the system should be driven by student choice, but would ministers and others actually be willing to stand by this principle if applicants overwhelmingly choose, say, media studies? Or, indeed, what will happen if applicants more or less entirely desert subjects such as physics and chemistry? In other words, I do not think our society will, or should, be willing to endorse *whatever* pattern appears to follow from sixth-formers' choices, and in that case the signals sent out about which subjects may need to be encouraged or supported is a crucial aspect of policy.

The present system of the block grant signals, albeit in a clumsy way, that there is a public interest in maintaining a spread of disciplines in higher education, and that the amount universities receive for teaching the different subjects varies simply because the actual cost of teaching these subjects varies. The logic of the new system, we are repeatedly told, is that student choice will henceforth decide what subjects particular universities teach. But if that is so, then there is no justification for the continued public subsidy of the extra costs of subjects in Bands A and B, essentially the medical and scientific subjects. If student choice really were sovereign and if students were rational consumers, then, it should follow, they would calculate whether the cost of any given course represents value for money. They would choose, say, science courses even though they may be more expensive because the likely returns are also correspondingly higher. And if not, not. But the proposed system does not in fact adhere to this logic. Reference to these disciplines in the Browne Review and elsewhere as 'priority subjects' gives the game away. There is an incoherence here which is potentially very damaging.

There has been much anxiety over the fate of the humanities under the new dispensation, some of it perhaps based on misunderstanding. Ministers may, with some justice, say that the changes do not represent an attack on the arts and humanities: they may say, rightly, that funding for research is being maintained for *all* disciplines, and, more ambiguously, that the teaching of *all* subjects is now to be funded by fee income, with simply the extra laboratory costs of medical and other STEM subjects still being supported centrally. But what, staying at the level of perceptions, has been *seen* to be the case is that the arts and humanities are to be entirely subject to the vagaries of student choice while some central support will continue to be given to STEM subjects. This is bound to look like a declaration that STEM subjects are a greater national priority – but then that may, of course, be what some of those responsible for the policy believe. Personally, I do not find any version of 'two cultures' talk either accurate or helpful; society has no less of a need for the humanities and social sciences than it does for the natural sciences, just as all branches of scholarship and science have a common interest in the health of the university system.

In practice, of course, applicants' choices may be at least as much determined by changes in school curricula and associated forms of assessment as by anticipation of future earnings or some other allegedly rational calculation. For example, we have yet to see what effect the new GCSE league tables based on the so-called 'English Bac' will have, though it seems possible that it may eventually feed through some increase in the number of applicants for courses in history and languages.

Although the future of universities in ten or twenty years' time may come under the heading of 'unknown unknowns', what surely *is* known is that the next few years will be marked by considerable instability and changes of course, which may themselves do damage that will take a long time to repair. Just as funding that goes as a block grant directly to each university (so-called QR or 'quality-related' funding) is, in my view, far more essential to the flourishing of research in the humanities than is research council funding awarded on a competitive basis for specified projects, so stable internal budgets are more vital to creating and maintaining good teaching departments in the humanities than are alternating periods of boom and bust, even if the boom outweighs the bust. A particular worry I have is that those institutions, and they are the majority, that are heavily reliant on income from teaching may be driven to respond to short-term fluctuations in the apparent popularity of various subjects by eliminating courses and posts at short notice. We may well see some contraction in the range of subjects offered in such institutions, and an increase in temporary and short-term teaching contracts.

In addition, the fate of small subjects themselves, already at risk in some areas of the humanities, may become still more vulnerable if universities come to feel that any element of cross-subsidy is unsustainable. Individual universities will make what may be, within the terms of their own budgets, rational decisions to close such departments, but it is not clear whether there will be any national oversight of the pattern that may result. A certain amount of centrally organized support and consolidation may be necessary if certain subjects are not to disappear inadvertently.

And finally, practically no attention seems to have been given to the possible effect of these changes on recruitment to postgraduate courses, particularly PhDs. It is clearly possible that some high-achieving students who might otherwise have undertaken PhDs will now feel unwilling to add to the burden of debt they have already incurred and will choose another career path. Again, it is possible that some of those responsible for this policy may welcome that effect, but it raises serious questions about the recruitment of the next generation of scholars and teachers, especially in subjects perceived to be marginal or unpopular.

Let me end this part of my remarks with one very general reflection. Having witnessed the scenes in London and elsewhere last November [2010], no one will be likely to underestimate the enormous importance of the *symbolic* aspect of these policy changes, whatever view one takes of their *actual* benefits or drawbacks. This very substantial shift from a form of public funding to a form of individual funding is bound to be read as signalling a loss of belief in the public, as opposed to the individual, value of higher education, even if ministers and others repeatedly affirm that this is not the case. The larger problem here concerns the whole language of justification that currently dominates public discussion of universities. It is scarcely an exaggeration to say that the greater part of public discourse about higher education at present reduces to the following dispiriting proposition: universities need to justify getting more money and the way to do this is by showing that they help to make more money. This presents itself as realism, but it sells the case short – in particular, the case for having an educated population rather than merely an employable workforce.

Since there is a risk that my arguments in this vein will be misinterpreted, let me say emphatically here that I – and, I believe, pretty much everyone else who works in or cares about universities – do not for a moment underestimate the expense of these institutions or presume that they have some God-given right to be lavishly funded. Of course the case for their value and importance needs to be made. But it needs to be made in appropriate terms, and these terms are not chiefly, and certainly not exclusively, economic. They are intellectual, educational, scientific and cultural. In addition, it has to be emphasized that higher education is a public good, not simply a set of private benefits for those who happen to participate in it, and therefore that it is a mistake to allow the case for universities to be represented as a merely sectional or self-interested cause on the part of current students and academics. For government, for universities – and, I would add, for individual scholars such as myself – the task of effectively making this case in its *proper* terms is now more pressing than ever.

II

So, what bearing do these reflections have on the current debate in Scotland? I should say that the Scottish government's Green Paper, whatever its limitations, is at least potentially a more constructive document than that fashionable mix of bottom-line managerialism and free market fundamentalism which so marred the Browne Review. I shan't try to cover all aspects of the Green Paper, but let me just make a brief comment on each of four areas.

The first concerns the role of the block grant for teaching and its impact on universities. At various points in the Green Paper we encounter the assertion that 'critics have said' that the block grant 'encourages conservatism' or (in another formulation) that 'it could be criticized for inhibiting innovation'. It does not surprise me that these claims are unattributed since I believe that there is no evidence for their truth. It is surely more likely, first, that the removal of the block grant would make institutions more anxious and twitchy, over-hasty in eliminating any activity which they fear may cost them income in the very short term, and therefore that it would encourage a kind of institutional conservatism; and, second, that, by comparison to a system in which universities can have some confidence in the funding council's continued support, 'empowering student choice', as the cant phrase has it, is much less likely to lead to worthwhile educational innovation. In Britain as a whole, hostile political and business interests have in recent decades propagated an assumption that universities are old-fashioned, introverted, self-stymying organizations incapable of 'dynamic' and 'forward-looking' change and so on. This claim is now treated as part of the received wisdom of public debate, and is, I'm sorry to see, repeated in the Green Paper; but it is in fact false, and we should not allow policy-makers to rely on such lazy stereotypes. Both politicians and the public in Scotland need to be persuaded that the block grant is an important part of the conditions favouring worthwhile innovation rather than an obstacle to it.

Secondly, there are various points in the Green Paper where it hankers after a way of measuring and rewarding what it calls 'teaching excellence'. Anyone familiar with recent official literature on higher education policy will know that 'excellence' is the term reached for by the bureaucratic mind when it has no idea how to identify real achievement in the activity in question. It scarcely needs a Plato to point out that if we are to judge in a given case whether an activity is being done well, then we must have some understanding of the point or purpose of the activity in the first place. On this score, the Green Paper doesn't come very well out of a little mildly Socratic questioning, and it rather desperately hopes that a measure of 'excellence in teaching' might be found in statistics about how that otherwise elusive quality leads to 'graduate employment opportunities'. Sensing, as stooges in the Socratic dialogues often do, that perhaps this is not the right answer, the Green Paper tries another tack and announces that 'student choice or the Student Satisfaction Survey might also be used as a proxy for determining excellence'. But of course it can't, because in so far as that flawed mechanism registers anything, it registers something other than the quality of teaching. As Professor Roger Brown (no relation) has pointed out, in England the actual proxy for 'determining excellence' is now to be price, and anyway a proxy is always a substitute for the real thing. One step in the right direction might be to recognize that good teaching can be judged but not measured; another would be to recognize that the business consultant's model of setting benchmarks by which to measure 'continuous improvement' is internally inconsistent as well as destructive of good teaching.

Thirdly, the Green Paper is rightly more ambitious than the Browne Review in including the funding of research in its scope, but here again there are some very doubtful premises built in to the questions it asks. At this delicate political moment it has to be said emphatically that not only is QR funding more valuable to universities in their long-term research activities than research council funding, it is also more protected from immediate political interference. ('QR', to repeat, stands for 'quality related' – that is, funding distributed in a lump sum to each university, largely as a result of its performance in research assessment exercises, as opposed to 'project funding' awarded on a competitive basis by the research councils in response to individual proposals by teams of researchers.) The research councils come directly under the control of BIS, and anyone who has studied the recent development of, for example, the Arts and Humanities Research Council (AHRC) will tell you that it has been falling over itself in trying to set up programmes and research themes which it thinks will appear to its paymasters to be signs that it is supporting 'government priorities'. Although the funding council, HEFCE, comes under the general aegis of BIS as well, and is dependent on it for funds, it is, in constitutional terms, a Non-Departmental Government Body, which means it has certain statutory protections against direct ministerial meddling. A few special-programme funding streams apart, HEFCE does not tell a university which areas of research it must spend its QR funding on, whereas in effect research councils increasingly do exactly that by earmarking project funding for favoured themes.

If in Scotland some form of block grant for teaching is maintained, as I believe it should be, then after 2013 the Scottish Funding Council will have a more substantial funding role than will HEFCE. But that makes it all the more important to challenge the rather glib phrases in the Green Paper about directing research funding to 'national priorities'. If Scotland wants high-quality research done in its universities then it must allow the scholars and scientists in those universities to decide what the intellectually interesting and important areas of research are in each field or sub-field. Trying to specify those areas as part of some populist political programme is only likely to direct funds away from the most intellectually fertile projects.

Under the same heading, I also observe that the Green Paper entertains the potentially disastrous suggestion that in Scotland greater weight could be given to the 'impact' element in distributing funds in the wake of the REF. Anticipation of the impact requirement is already having a distorting influence on scholarly research, and there are strong pressures in England to have its weighting reduced not increased. But the superstition appears to be growing that what is classed as 'impact' under this flawed procedure is some kind of indicator of the worth of academic research to the wider community. That is simply untrue, and I hope that Scotland will in this case limit rather than magnify the damage already done by this confused policy.

Fourth and finally, the Green Paper shows several worrying signs of what I call 'Champions League syndrome'. It fears, or purports to fear, that the top Scottish universities will lose their place in the meaningless world rankings unless they are funded on a basis comparable to the leading English universities. This is like the logical regress used to justify the spiralling salaries of chief executives, and there is no reason to be bullied by such claims made on behalf of Edinburgh or Glasgow or St Andrews any more than there is to cave in to similar claims made in England about Oxford or Cambridge or Imperial College. World rankings are of little value: they are chiefly a guide to the level of expenditure on big science, not to the quality of the education universities provide, and certainly not to how well they serve the culture of their host country. Moreover, when universities are being true to their intellectual purposes they are far more supportive of each other than they are competitive, since they all have a stake in a flourishing culture of teaching and research. Institutions such as Edinburgh and St Andrews are and can remain wonderful universities without having to try to match the investment in big science of Caltech or Singapore, and as the California system showed across several decades, doing what they do well is enabled rather than obstructed by being part of a network of institutions (which in Scotland includes the likes of Heriot-Watt or Robert Gordon or Napier and others) that are, within the terms of their own somewhat different missions, also supported at the highest possible level. The case for higher education in England has been fatally weakened by internal divisions among vice-chancellors as the most powerful institutions pursue an entirely selfish course. It would be nice to think that the more compact nature of the sector in Scotland will prevent rival interest groups frustrating the larger purpose in this way, but I suspect that thought just shows what an innocent outsider I really am.

Let me conclude with one final observation. When I was preparing these remarks, I weighed up the risks involved were I to cite George Davie's classic work from 1961, *The Democratic Intellect*. One risk is that this is by now a hackneyed and overworked allusion; another is that of seeming to forget that the story Davie had to tell was, as far as nineteenth-century Scottish universities were concerned, a story of decline. But it is not entirely wishful thinking to observe that some version of the tradition to which Davie's celebrated title has come to refer does still have a resonance in current debate in this country, and in that respect Scotland has at least one crucial advantage over England.

South of the border, the intellectual and educational case for the distinctive value of universities is poorly articulated, and as a result it is not a political force with which the government has to reckon. Instead, we get third-hand clichés about promoting economic competitiveness and training an adaptable workforce. Of course, you get a lot of that in Scotland as well, and it is obviously easy to fall into a cheap romanticization of the 'lad o'pairts' tradition and all that. Nonetheless, the advantage lies not just in having such a tradition to appeal to, but in the fact that it is a tradition with built-in democratic purchase and appeal. It is very cheering – and, for an Englishman these days, all too rare – to come across a sentence in an official document that declares as roundly as the Green Paper does when discussing where the main burden of funding higher education should lie: 'The Scottish government believes that the prime responsibility should lie with the state.' I wish my Scottish colleagues every success in translating that admirable sentiment into a workable system that shows up the narrow-minded philistinism of the 'English solution' for what it is.

CHAPTER 8

Public Higher Education:
An Undefensive Defence

I

Until recently, the sense in which higher education in Britain could be described as 'public' seemed so self-evident as to need little analysis.[1] But, as with several other aspects of social and cultural provision, we are moving towards a situation where a variety of hard-to-classify hybrid species may grow up. This will change the ecology within which putatively 'public' institutions operate, and will thus complicate what might be at stake in 'defending' them. We need, therefore, to consider the senses in which universities in Britain might be thought of as 'public' institutions and to identify the chief kinds of public interest involved in the provision of higher education. For this purpose, it may be helpful to lay out some basic distinctions where so-called public or private provision of higher education around the world is concerned. We can distinguish four main categories:

1) A directly state-run department, as in France, where universities are under the immediate control of the relevant minister and academics are *fonctionnaires*, part of *le service publique*. A broadly similar situation obtains in several of the developing economies where universities are set up to further a specific element of state policy, such as the mechanization of agriculture or the exploitation of information technology.

2) A largely publicly funded institution where the finance and general policy but not the educational activities are subject to a

---

[1] The first section of this chapter was given as part of a presentation to the All-Party Parliamentary Universities Group at the Houses of Parliament in February 2012; the second section was delivered as part of a paper to a conference on 'Shaping Higher Education Fifty Years After Robbins', held in October 2013.

certain element of direct local democratic control, as is the case, for example, with the large American state universities.

3) An autonomous but regulated charity dedicated to providing education and research, independent of government but in receipt of considerable indirect public funding in the form of grants for research and special programmes, such as the American Ivy League universities and similar institutions.

4) A for-profit business, unrestrained by public policy or charity regulation, and only subject to the same legal constraints as any other commercial enterprise.

Now, it will be immediately clear that universities in Britain had their origins in more than one of these forms, and that they have long been hybrid types, not directly corresponding to any one of these four models. Historically, British universities mostly evolved as self-governing corporations, protected in some ways by their charters, but increasingly reliant in the course of the twentieth century on public funds and hence subject to close oversight and regulation, though some of them also have their own endowments as well. They are not directly state-run, as in France, but nor are they wholly independent charities. If anything, they have been closer to certain other cultural institutions that, though in receipt of substantial public funds, operate on the arm's length principle as semi-autonomous bodies, such as, say, the British Museum or the BBC. The BBC is emphatically not run by the government, but nor does it depend on commercial transactions with individual customers. Thus, the somewhat complex sense in which we may want to say that Oxford, unlike Harvard, is not a private university may seem quite like the sense in which we say that the BBC is not a private broadcaster.

The point of spelling out this little taxonomy is just to emphasize that the form in which we may say we have 'public higher education' in Britain at present is not straightforward: it is not a matter simply of where the bulk of its funding comes from, and therefore it is not immediately obvious how fundamental a change to that status the new policy on undergraduate fees will make. I'll come back to the question of the public funds that go to universities for research, but just staying with under-graduate teaching for the moment, the government says that it is continuing to invest large sums in supporting such teaching, but that this funding is now to be routed through loans rather than grants. However, in terms of the distinctions I have just drawn, this is rather like saying that there should be no more public subsidy to the British Museum or, through the licence fee, the BBC, and that instead the government will loan to any citizen who wants to use those services a sum equivalent to the charges that those institutions would then be forced to make to their users. In public perception, such a change would surely make a big difference to whether we thought of, say, the British Museum as any kind of public body, especially if the vouchers could also be spent in alternative venues that were run entirely for profit.

One of the consequences of this perceived public status, cer-tainly over the past fifty years, has been a greater sense of public entitlement and belief that admission to a university should depend only on intellectual aptitude. Debates in the past decade or more about 'access' suggest that some people perceive that, in practice, class background gives some applicants an unfair advantage, as it surely does, but clearly this criticism presumes and reinforces the standing of the general principle. There is no general social acceptance in this country at present of the idea that one should simply be able to buy a place at a university. Indeed, it is a curious and little remarked fact that in Britain today entrance to a university is one of the few widely desired social goods that cannot be straightforwardly bought. And it would, I believe, still be generally thought quite unacceptable for a place at a selective university to be awarded on the grounds that the applicant was the child of either an alumnus or a donor, though we must remember, amid so much selective citing of US models, that both of these are explicitly acknowledged categories of intake at the most prestigious American private universities and colleges. So, 'public', in this case, signals some idea of oper-ating according to collectively agreed criteria that apply to the whole relevant population, not just to a wealthy sub-section thereof who can afford to buy what they want.

I think it is very difficult to tell, at this point [2012], just how far the new fee arrangements will modify or undermine the popular perception of this idea. The 2011 White Paper's claim to 'put students at the heart of the system' is unpersuasive in various ways, in part because they are already there. It would be more accurate to say that it tries to 'put the price mechanism at the heart of the system', where a university place then partly depends on what a customer is willing to pay for it: education becomes a transaction between a seller and a buyer, and this may be what indicates a key move from 'public' to 'private', despite the continued public underwriting of the loans system. The introduction of 'for-profit' private providers into the system extends the logic of purchasing a university place even further, and it will be interesting to see how far erstwhile public institutions may feel impelled to move in this direction in the future, including differential fees for different subjects and discounts for early completion.

Another way to look at the operation of this distinction might be to think of a public rather than a private model of graduate contribution. Let's suppose for a moment that graduates were asked to make retrospective payments to a national higher education fund rather than pay fees up front to a particular university. This could involve the same amount of money as they will contribute under the new system and it could involve calibrating payments to earnings in a similar way, up to a fixed level, but it would represent a different principle (as well as being cheaper and simpler to run). Graduates would retrospectively contribute to the maintenance of the national higher education system, not prospectively pay for a product from an individual service provider.

I'm not for the moment concerned with the practical advantages or disadvantages of this, and I recognize that many universities might reject it because they would fear that they would have less control over future income, and anyway the so-called 'top universities' may believe they have more to gain from the government's model that, like all market models, rewards the already advantaged. From the point of view of the present government, the key difference would be that my imagined scheme would not subject universities to the same kind of notional 'market discipline' as does dependence by each individual institution on fees paid directly to them by individual students. But perhaps this highlights another aspect of the crucial dividing line between public and private as far as British universities are concerned. In my imagined model, there would be more room for collective long-term planning about how to direct the expenditure of the system as a whole to protect the public interest in maintaining certain types of provision. In my view, if I may say this to a gathering that includes many vice-chancellors, there has been too little concern in the recent debates with the values represented by a national *system* of higher education as a whole, and too much concern about the competitive advantage which particular mission-groups or individual universities think they may gain.

The question of 'public higher education' is usually taken to be a question about undergraduate teaching and how to pay for it, but the question of research is no less important here. Once again, this is not simply a matter of who pays for it, directly or indirectly, but of the relation between public and private goods. For example, in terms of the science involved, there may be many overlaps between the research undertaken in a university department and that undertaken in a company's R&D lab, but they differ fundamentally in their aims and governing criteria. Intuitively, it is not hard to see what would be lost if the only research carried out in various fields were that carried out by commercial companies: this is another way of saying that there is a public interest in disinterested science, and here, again, it is not simply a matter of who pays. One can see how an independent university with charitable status may, in some cases, find its research activities being indirectly determined by certain sorts of donors, thus jeopardizing the disinterestedness of its science, but one can also see how, in other cases, such a university may be better placed to protect the freedom of research than a state-funded institution forced to support the agenda of a dirigiste government.

In fact, developments in Britain in the past couple of decades have caused widespread alarm on this score, especially as more and more public funding for research has been channelled through the research councils which are more directly responsive to the will of government than are the universities themselves. In theory, the research councils operate according to 'the Haldane principle' (named after the early twentieth-century minister, Lord Haldane) which lays it down that government, though providing the funds, should have no direct say in what research is undertaken, since that decision is better left to the research community itself. However, recent practice has signalled a marked modification, at the very least, of how this principle is interpreted. Consider, for example, the way in which labelling certain areas of research as 'national priorities', earmarked to receive preferential funding, risks harnessing research too closely to the transient political agenda of the day. Or consider the way that the emphasis on shortening the innovation chain between fundamental research and commercial application tends to make the needs of the latter determine the agenda of the former. Or, again, consider how the 'impact' requirement not only steers research in certain directions, but strongly encourages universities to pursue commercial exploitation for themselves and, in particular, to set up a protective ring of intellectual property rights. As the physicist Philip Moriarty put it recently: 'far from improving accountability and transparency, this [policy] will embed a culture of intellectual property protection and commercial exploitation entirely at odds with the ethos of academia, and, ultimately, compromising public trust in science.' Or as an editorial in the *Lancet* put it a few years ago, this agenda faces academics with a choice: 'to develop their entrepreneurial skills or to maintain a commitment to public-interest science – and we do not accept that the two options are mutually compatible'. In other words, the 'public' value of research lies a) in its agenda not being wholly determined by the short-term needs of any one powerful group; and b) in its processes and results being in principle available for scrutiny by any other qualified researcher in the field. The right kind of public funding is more likely to secure this than even the best kind of private funding, but actually the principle of the autonomy of research may be even more important than the source of the funding as far as securing the public interest is concerned.

There is an interesting parallel between the two parts of this topic. Just as meeting the perceived needs of corporate or similar customers will not safeguard the public interest in creative long-term research, so meeting the expressed needs of school-leaving customers may not safeguard the public interest in balanced long-term education. Reverting to my earlier comparisons for a moment, we could consider whether, if the British Museum were wholly dependent on the income from entrance charges, we would reason that the expressed preferences of the paying customers should determine the long-term collection policy of the museum. It is a standard assumption in various forms of political and economic theory that public provision attempts to sustain those long-term values which can become casualties of the necessarily short-term perspectives of profit-driven private provision. However, I would have to say that there are aspects of recent policies, from both this government and its predecessor, that may in fact be undermining this function. There is always a risk that well-meant attempts to demonstrate the 'relevance' of universities to society's needs can end up being counter-productive. Society actually obtains the greatest benefits from universities by encouraging them to concentrate on doing the things they are particularly good at, and not by trying to turn them into some form of company laboratory or apprenticeship scheme. This is the nub of the public interest here, and it may be threatened not just by changes in the funding of undergraduate teaching but also by an over-zealous insistence on universities satisfying prevailing ideas of national priorities or the needs of business. This in turn suggests to me that we in universities should not be so defensive: more is to be gained, by everyone, if universities explain *in their own terms* the character of what they do and why it is significant and worthwhile, rather than repeating and colluding with a discourse which always risks becoming reductive and short-termist. There is more at stake in the question of 'defending public higher education' than simply the issue of undergraduate fees.

II

This is one of the many topics on which it can be helpful to return to the 1963 report on higher education chaired by Lord Robbins. One of the most striking things about the Robbins Report, viewed from our present perspective, is its lack of defensiveness. By this, I don't mean that it is not careful in its reasoning or alive to the difficulties its proposals might face – it is both of those things. I mean that it is written throughout from an assumption that universities don't need to apologize for themselves, that they have a value and a role in society that can be argued for and that society by and large recognizes. Clearly, the tone and address of the report owed something to the barely challenged dominance of the values historically associated with a governing elite, even something to the persistence of patterns of cultural deference. But in its general as well as its specific statements, the report was not apologetic or embarrassed about assuming that in 'developing man's capacity to understand, to contemplate and to create', universities served what it repeatedly called 'the needs of society'. It was not afraid to say that they did so *because*, not in spite of the fact that, education 'ministers intimately to ultimate ends', and *because* 'what is taught should be taught in such a way as to promote the general powers of the mind'. Nor was it apologetic about emphasizing that, of course, preparation for future employment was a proper concern of universities and of their students. These were taken to be complementary, not antagonistic, goals.

This lack of defensiveness comes out particularly strikingly, I think, in a section of the report that has been rather neglected compared to those dealing with student numbers and finance. For Robbins and his colleagues it was one of the most crucial parts of the report: 'We have now to approach the most important and the most difficult of all the problems we have had to consider – what machinery of government is appropriate for a national system of higher education in this country?' Here, the report emphasized essentially two features. First, the vital importance of the 'arm's length' principle – that is, that universities should not be directly controlled by government but should be administered through an independent institution, made up largely of senior university figures, to act as a buffer, as the University Grants Committee was seen to do at the time. And, second (as mentioned in Chapter 4, above), that responsibility for this domain should be assigned to an appropriate government ministry. Here, the report recommended not the continuation of the existing, rather incongruous, relation to the Treasury, nor the inclusion of universities in the responsibilities of an enlarged ministry of education (and of course the conceit of assigning them to a department of business was a category-mistake whose time had not yet come). Instead, it recommended the formation of a new ministry, a ministry of arts and science, that would include what it called 'other autonomous state-supported activities that are at present administered on principles resembling those of the grants committee', such as museums, galleries, the Arts Council and the research councils. Here is part of what the report said in favour of this arrangement:

> Since much of the work would be done through grants committees, the whole would tend to be informed by the special degree of detachment and respect for the autonomy of the institutions and individuals ultimately concerned that is so necessary if the connexion of the State with creative activities is to be a quickening rather than a deadening influence ... [This] would recognise the importance to the spiritual health of the community of a proper organisation of state support for learning and the arts.

Well, as we know, this was one of the report's recommendations that was not acted upon, and it appears from Susan Howson's biography of Robbins that this was an outcome he himself particularly regretted. In picking out this aspect of the report, I am not trying to vindicate Robbins's position or wishing that we could, impossibly, return to the conditions of that time. I cite it because, in its tone as much as its content, the report raised the fundamental questions of what universities are for, by what indirect routes they meet the 'needs' of society, and what is the right way to ensure some form of democratic accountability for them.

One of the most striking features of policies towards higher education over the past three decades has been their increasing departure from the principles that Robbins set out in this area. I shan't dwell on the question of the appropriate ministry, except to say that both the game of pass-the-parcel that has been played with the higher education portfolio, and the lodging of it, by both the previous and present governments, in the Department of Business, indicate how far we have moved from what Robbins recommended. Objections can, of course, be raised to any of the various divisions of ministerial responsibility, but a ministry that brought together culture, science and higher education would surely have a better chance of representing universities adequately than the recent and current arrangements.

The move away from the 'arm's length' principle has been no less significant. The University Grants Committee was abolished in the late 1980s precisely *because* it acted as a buffer between government and the universities; the funding councils that replaced it were explicitly intended to be means of implementing government policy. And when we learn, for example, that the 'impact' requirement was introduced into the assessment of research as a direct result of business leaders lobbying Gordon Brown, we can see how far we have moved from what Robbins called 'the special degree of detachment and respect for the autonomy of the institutions ... ultimately concerned that is so necessary if the connexion of the State with creative activities is to be a quickening rather than a deadening influence'.

But there has also, of course, been a larger change in the character of public discussion about these and other matters, especially in the criteria or values that are appealed to. All the while a populist version of 'economic growth' is so dominant, we are, in my view, almost bound to misunderstand the fertility of the tension between intellectual autonomy and democratic accountability.

A further aspect of the same problem is that contemporary public debate about universities (though not, of course, universities alone) is bedevilled by the pressure to substitute measurements of quantity for judgements of quality. I'm sure we can all think of numerous examples of this, but the uncomfortable truth is that the prevalence of the use of Key Performance Indicators and all the other quantitative gobbledegook of New Public Management-speak represents not just the imposition of the agenda of the managerial and business class, but a loss of nerve within universities as well. Again, a restrained but justified confidence and a corresponding lack of defensiveness may be both more appropriate and, eventually, more effective.

The risk is that 'democratic accountability' becomes a shorthand for the never-ending loop of anxiety-driven attempts at legitimation in terms of criteria and categories that *other* people are assumed to be committed to. Academics seek to characterize their activities in terms that they hope will be approved of by their managers; university managers seek to present a picture of their institution's activities in terms that they hope will be approved of by officials in Whitehall and in educational quangos; officials seek to make the case in terms they hope will win the endorsement of their ministers; ministers characterize their policies in terms they hope will win the approval of the electorate. The fact that in their actual lives most people act in accordance with various values other than that of maximizing economic gain, and the fact that they would in many cases like to see universities as natural homes of some of these other values, then gets squeezed out of public debate altogether.

One outcome of this anxiety-driven deferral is that familiar and easily stated practical benefits that are by-products of universities' central activities are latched onto to serve as substitutes for the unfamiliar and elusive values that are the true purpose of the activities in question. It is the kind of logic that leads us to say that the value of playing Beethoven's piano sonatas is attested by the way it helps to make us better typists – a logic from which 'impact' in its currently required form is not wholly exempt. For similar reasons, we are led to connive in the fiction that an auditable paper-trail is evidence of the presence of the relevant form of quality. Out of the well-intentioned urge to exhibit to society the worth of the universities that society supports come these measures which only succeed in short-circuiting the most fruitful forms of relation between universities and society. In turn, this encourages both defensiveness and bad faith among academics who then attempt to conform to these measures, though they know that the true nature of their activities is thereby misdescribed, and out of this comes the familiar idiom of pious euphemism, the empty register of institutional boasting, and the self-defeating game of 'chase the indicator'.

The Robbins Report was of its time, and its time is not our time. But I have singled out its mixture of confidence and public-spiritedness because something like that blend is surely likely to result in a more enlightened perspective than the current mixture of defensiveness and narrow economism. Robbins, as we've seen, was not afraid to speak of 'the importance to the spiritual health of the community of a proper organization of state support for learning and the arts'. In this connection, it is not enough for a government to say it is recognizing this truth by providing state funds to support research. Much depends on the kind of strings that are attached. What Robbins called that 'special degree of detachment and respect for the autonomy of the institutions concerned that is so necessary if the connexion of the State with creative activities is to be a quickening rather than a deadening influence' is not there when a research council feels that it can only justify its existence if it directs a large proportion of its funds to themes bearing on economic growth in the hope that these will be approved of by ministers and their officials. Its proper goal would be better met by using those funds to sustain the kind of sabbatical-supported bottom-up research which nourishes intellectual creativity so much more effectively than attempting to second-guess what an electorally twitchy government might regard as a socially useful topic.

The decades since Robbins have seen a massive educational enfranchisement take place in this country, notably of women and to some extent of those of both genders from less privileged backgrounds. But we risk denying the true benefits of higher education to those newly recruited students, including large numbers of mature and part-time students, if we try to concentrate the activities of universities on what the government considers promotes economic growth. Of course, those new cohorts of students also want their education to be, among other things, a preparation for employment, but policy-makers risk a kind of condescension when they say in effect that although they themselves benefited from the culturally rich education they received, current and future generations, at least outside a few elite institutions, will have to be content with something more narrowly practical. We exercise true democratic accountability not by trying to subordinate universities to the currently favoured form of economic policy, but by ensuring that universities are enabled to concentrate on their principal task of extending and deepening human understanding, because it is from the successful pursuit of that task that, in the long term, society as a whole derives the greatest benefit.

CHAPTER 9

Speaking Out:
Strategies and Their Publics

I

Those who perceive the damage currently being done to British universities by various misconceived policies and other less noticed changes feel a strong desire to speak out, to protest against these follies, to make a better case for how universities should be understood and dealt with.[1] But it is not always easy to see how this might best be done. In my view, one of the essential first steps has to be the identification of the relevant audiences, since this must surely help to determine the choice of occasions and modes of address. In speaking to a meeting of the Council for the Defence of British Universities (CDBU), I can obviously presuppose a largely sympathetic audience, though even here I would like, at the risk of seeming ungracious, to register one reservation. I have always been made uneasy by one word in the title of this organization and that word is 'defence'.

Of course, I understand why it was adopted, and of course the fact that universities have felt under certain kinds of attack in recent years makes it seem desirable to try to come to their defence. But I think one of the greatest difficulties in terms of public perception that the CDBU faces – and some of the responses to the launch event last year [2012] perhaps confirmed this – is the risk of seeming to be complacent, or backward-looking, or even nostalgic. In making the case against various ill-judged higher education policies, it is very important not to seem to suggest that all used to be well with British universities, or that all would now be well if we could just get back to the

---

1 This chapter was first given as a lecture to the Council for the Defence of British Universities in October 2013.

day before yesterday. It is also, in my view, vital to be seen to be speaking up for British universities as a whole, and not just for the more traditional or more selective or more well-favoured among them. Since public debate is, for better or worse, so much a matter of perception, it will obviously be bad news if the CDBU is seen as being too much the voice of disgruntled academics from the older universities who hanker after a world in which dons were treated with some deference. 'Defence' can easily conjure up in the public mind the idea of the self-protectiveness of vested interests; and that, in turn, can easily be twisted into the accusation that it is defending sectional interests against the legitimate demands of democratically elected governments (I'll return to the oversimplifications embedded in these all-too-familiar phrases, but here I am just addressing the question of perception).

As I shall explain, I think it is crucial to be able to exploit the gap or tension that exists on the question of universities between what we might broadly call policy-making and media circles on the one hand and various wider publics on the other, but you risk losing that battle before you start if you allow critics to paint you as resisting changes which are seen as being part of a wider democratization of our society. When that happens, you have been positioned in opposition not just to policy-making and media circles but to those wider publics, too – and that is obviously fatal. There have already been sneers about the over-representation of 'the great and the good', so called, in the CDBU, and while that may just be the inevitable sniping of media commentary, I think it is important to challenge that perception, and I shall suggest ways of doing so by trying to make common cause with wider publics.

One last preliminary observation: here I only have room to discuss one central aspect of the task of making the case for Britain's universities. This certainly does not mean that I dismiss or undervalue all the other routes which this and other organizations are trying to pursue. This is a campaign that has to be conducted on as many fronts as possible and using as many persuasive tactics as we can, including the working out of detailed alternative policy proposals in some cases. But a central fact of our situation is that what we may for brevity's sake call 'the policy-making class' is currently in thrall to two related, though separate, convictions: first, that the only consideration that has indisputable electoral legitimacy is that of contributing to economic growth; second, that the most effective means to do this will always involve some attempt to simulate the conditions of an economic market. My remarks will concentrate on ways of challenging these dogmas and of making a more adequate case about the nature and purposes of universities to a wide range of publics.

I've been speaking casually about 'publics' in the plural, as I do in my title, but perhaps I had better say a little about why I find that somewhat ungainly form so helpful. In his book *Publics and Counterpublics*, the American scholar Michael Warner offers a very useful analysis of the category. Everyday invocations of 'the public' in the singular, and still more imputations of agency to that beast, as in claims about 'what the public wants' or 'what the public believes', are often tendentious or even ideological attempts to dress up one sectional view as having a larger legitimacy. As Warner shows, publics are not collections of predefined empirical individuals, but notional indications of a particular world of discourse. Publics are constituted by participation, even if only passively, in that particular world of discourse, and are therefore always open-ended and anonymous. Seen in this way, it becomes easier to recognize how actual individuals may belong to various different publics depending on the nature and level of discourse in question. It is crucial not to fall into the trap that some forms of identity politics can encourage, namely that of defining someone wholly in terms of one salient characteristic or affiliation. But by the same token, it is important not to let others get away with tendentious reifications of a supposed public defined in terms of one highly selective gloss on a particular shared feature. The obvious example here, which I've written about elsewhere, is invocations of 'the taxpayer' which are used to suggest that the entire country is united in its single-minded rejection of any activity or expenditure other than that which can be represented as contributing directly to a reduction in their own rate of income tax.

I am making what may seem to be slightly heavy weather of this general and rather basic point because I think that recent debates about higher education have been bedevilled by a simplistic and misleading way of talking about this matter. It is very common to hear the world divided into three parts: there are those who work in universities; there is the government and associated policy-shaping groups; and there is 'the public', often, as I've said, redefined as 'the taxpayers'. If that tripartite structure is allowed to pass unanalysed, the game is lost: sooner or later, 'the universities' will find themselves manoeuvred into a minority position faced by an alliance of 'the government' and 'the public'.

But if we think of publics in the plural, then the configuration becomes far more complex and far more dependent upon the particular type and level of case being made. In truth, 'the universities' do not for most purposes constitute a single public either: in recent years there has been a very obvious divide between the majority of rank-and-file academics and the various organizations of vice-chancellors. The managerial revolution that has transformed the administration of British universities in the past twenty years or more means that it is rarely the case that we can assume a coincidence of opinion or interest between academics and administrators, now renamed managers. Nonetheless, the plurality that I particularly want to focus on here is that plurality of publics outside universities to whom any case about those institutions' true nature and purpose might be addressed.

Now, as I've already hinted, one of the slack features of much debate is the way it represents people as being defined by just one attribute or affiliation, rather than recognizing that what is to count as an individual's defining characteristic is both context-dependent and argument-dependent. When we think in empirical terms about possible addressees or interlocutors we often define people in terms of roles – legislators, parents, foundation administrators, journalists, schoolchildren, donors, government officials, students, taxpayers and so on. Any actual individual may belong to more than one of these and similar categories, of course, and there may be purposes for which it is also relevant to define them in terms of other types of category. We can, needless to say, think of them in terms of some of the major markers of class, gender and ethnicity; we can think of them in terms of affiliation, cultural, religious, sporting or whatever; we can think of them in regional or national terms (far too little is heard in this debate about, for example, the different traditions and social attitudes sustaining universities in Scotland); and we can think about them in terms of the type and level of medium through which they are to be reached: tabloid-reading publics can be distinguished from broadsheet-reading publics and so on. And within those categories still finer distinctions can be made that are relevant to argumentative address or literary tactics: it is not true, for example, that the *Guardian*-reading public is identical with the *London Review of Books*-reading public, despite overlaps. But it also means thinking about other media than print – what commentators lazily call 'the Facebook community' involves a whole series of different markers from what may be called the '*Today*-programme public', which is different again from the 'literary-festival public' and so on.

There is no such thing as 'the public' and hence no such thing as 'the public's view of higher education'. But that being so, it is crucial to identify and seek out or address those publics who, in one way or other, do not share the reductive market dogma that currently dominates among the policy-making classes. And here I am not only talking of the kinds of variation recorded in, say, the annual *British Social Attitudes* survey, which might show such and such a percentage of people with a specific set of characteristics being in favour of greater welfare spending or greater redistribution of wealth or something of that kind. I am also talking about all those publics who, by the actual conduct of their lives, demonstrate that they implicitly recognize the standing of values other than narrow economic prosperity. People who care about the quality of schools, and who care about them as doing something other than manufacturing employment fodder for the economy, can be drawn into a case about the quality of universities. People who want to see museums and galleries maintained even if they rarely or never visit them themselves can be drawn into an argument about public goods that transcend private benefit. People who care about the beauty of the natural environment or the preservation of biodiversity can be drawn into arguments about what it means to think of something as 'a good in itself'. I don't mean glibly to assert that arguments about universities are on a par with these other issues or that such tactics will always be successful. I mean, simply, that recognizing the plurality of values by which people do in fact lead their lives gives at least a handhold for the kinds of arguments by which, ultimately, more adequate accounts of higher education need to be supported.

It goes without saying that different media and various literary forms are needed to successfully reach this plurality of publics. There is no single document – or lecture – that can be expected to do duty for all occasions, and no one person is going to have the gifts or the experience to successfully deploy all these different forms. If the CDBU contains people who are effective in the four-minute roughhouse of *Newsnight* or the *Today* programme, then you should cherish them, for those skills are, I think, rare among academics. By temperament and education, most of us tend to be better suited to the extended prose presentation of an argument, and perhaps we should play to that strength wherever we can. Although there isn't room to talk about it here, I also think there is a lot to say about the different pitfalls of tone in relation to these different publics – the difficulties in some situations of not seeming patronizing or the risks in others of adopting what has been called 'false democratic bonhomie'. A fine line separates the prudent modulation of one's style of address for a particular audience from the adoption of a false manner or tone; in practice it may be less damaging for academics to be thought a little remote in style rather than to be convicted of a jarring phoniness.

It is also helpful, I think, to remember that our goal should not be confined to the highly ambitious one of changing people's fundamental convictions – our goals can rightly be more plural as well as less daunting than that. One purpose that can be too easily undervalued is that of sustaining or fortifying those who are sympathetic but dispirited, helping them to get through bad times. Another is that of encouraging people to articulate what they half believe already. And here, too, we shouldn't be afraid of recognizing that those who work and study in universities are also among our publics. Helping the young temporary lecturer at a post-1992 university feel that there is a worth and dignity to what he or she is trying to do that is not captured by the 'performance indicators' against which they are being measured each day is not a negligible purpose, and nor is helping a first-year student not to feel so defenceless in discussions with relatives and peers over his or her choice of a so-called 'useless' degree subject.

Let us also not forget that many of our publics are international, and that these are not without their effects on policy and discussion in Britain. The managerialization of universities has not, for the most part, gone as far in continental Europe as it has in Britain, and any gathering of European university rectors reveals their deep concern about what they see going on here, concern not just because it was a system which, though different from their own in various ways, they nonetheless largely admired, but also because they see that Britain is the guinea pig in an experiment in extending free market dogmas into higher education, an experiment that cost-cutting market-oriented parties in their own countries may wish to emulate. European systems differ among themselves, of course, but broadly the European university tradition can provide some more natural but generally overlooked allies than either the luxuriant free-for-all of American higher education or the top-down scientific and business-studies forcing-houses of South and East Asia.

In this context, another important argument for several of our publics is the question of the selective comparison with the supposed characteristics of American higher education. Speaking to this audience, I can be brief about this because Howard Hotson has treated it so tellingly in his widely cited articles on the topic, but it is a case that we need to repeat and repeat. American higher education is not only hugely diverse, it is also, however construed, not the success story that ministers and advisers often like to represent it as being. It is, for one thing, hugely expensive and highly wasteful, and in many cases it certainly does not provide good teaching – the casualization of academic employment has now reached the point where two-thirds of those doing the teaching in American higher education as a whole are not only not tenured but are not even tenure-track appointments. Moreover, much of it is driven by a consumerist focus on student satisfaction and amenities that is destructive of genuinely educational ideals, and in many places it is tied to commercialized and (in all but name) professionalized sport in a way that nowhere else in the world is and that nowhere else would want to emulate. But at the same time, it goes without saying that there are many strengths to higher education in the United States, not least the opportunities it provides for second and third chances, something the British system has historically been bad at, and most obviously the huge concentration of resources and talent in its major research universities. All of these things are rooted in different cultural traditions and social circumstances, and we should continue to repeat the point that they cannot simply be replicated in a society with very different traditions and circumstances.

The recent mania in Britain for abolishing departments – I gather that in some places the very term is now officially proscribed – and replacing them with various ersatz 'schools' or 'colleges' is driven by a particular kind of managerialist dogma (discussed in Chapter 2, above). The result is to break down the ties that actually bind colleagues to a discipline and a shared professional experience, and replace them with that constant competition between strangers which is part of the essence of a market. Such larger units are run by managers in accordance with managerial rather than academic values. Of course there is much of this in the United States and elsewhere – these fashions are contagious – but in the major American research universities departments are strikingly strong and durable, and we do have a case to make about the role that that durability has played in developing and sustaining the high quality of much of their research and scholarship.

II

I have tried to express elsewhere some thoughts about the nature and purposes of universities that I think we should be aiming to communicate to the various publics I've mentioned, and I don't want to repeat all that. But perhaps one thing about, as it were, the content of our messages, as opposed to their form or occasion or audience, is worth noting here, especially since it is something that academics seem to me particularly well placed to articulate. And this is, very roughly speaking, that there are many occasions when we need to focus on the long-term effects on the system as a whole, rather than engaging on what is in effect our opponents' terrain of the immediate need that a particular measure is supposed to meet. Generally speaking, public debate about universities in Britain in the past few years has not been good at attending to the character of the higher education system as a whole, partly because it has been plagued by the sectional interests of various mission-groups and the like, and equally it has not been good at identifying the long-term damage done by measures justified in the most narrowly pragmatic and immediate terms.

It may seem obvious to say that for any proposal or measure under discussion, we should consider the overall effect, including effects on values and ethos, not just the immediate practical gain. But this is a perspective that is constantly neglected and which academics are well placed to emphasise. For example, the principal question about the new fee regime is not whether it will deter this or that category of potential applicants, but whether attempting to install a 'provider/customer relationship' at the heart of higher education will produce the kinds of universities we want to have. If we find ourselves discussing the merits or otherwise of some form of graduate contribution, we do not need to be trapped into debating the practicalities of, say, measures that would need to be adopted to obtain contributions from those who had left the country or similar details. What we need to focus on is the character of the relationship between students and university, and also the nature of the institutions that result if graduate contributions are in some way made to contribute to the costs of maintaining a higher education *system*, rather than each individual student being turned into a customer of a particular university. The key question is not 'isn't it right that those who directly benefit from higher education should make a direct contribution to its costs?', but rather 'what kind of higher education system will result from one mode of financing it rather than another?'

Similarly, the question about the research assessment regime is not whether this provides a pragmatic way to distribute limited funds, but whether it has deleterious effects on the intellectual and scholarly culture of universities overall. The question about devoting more money to research council 'themes' and similar large-scale initiatives is not whether any one of these is an important topic, but whether this diverts time and resources from the bottom-up, sabbatical-supported intellectual culture on which creativity depends. Over and over again what is at stake is what the US Defense Department likes to call 'collateral damage', and it is those within universities and those who understand an intellectual culture from the inside who are best placed to point this out.

Currently in Britain, universities are discussed almost exclusively in terms of undergraduate education, often of undergraduate training, and our focus on the larger picture can help to show how good-quality undergraduate teaching cannot be sustained in a void. You cannot merely find a person who knows a lot of information about something and put them on the lecture podium or in the seminar room and expect that what will result will be good teaching. I am not now talking about an element of training in the mechanics of teaching practice and so on, but rather how, for the contagion of minds that is involved in good teaching to work, the teacher needs to be the product of a whole cultural and intellectual tradition, needs to understand the nature and status of the knowledge they are seeking to communicate, needs to be informed by a certain kind of professional ethos and sense of membership of the scholarly guild and so on. Universities are one of the main ways that those characteristics are nurtured and transmitted from generation to generation, but they do that collectively, indeed as part of a larger international scholarly fraternity, not as self-contained rival companies seeking to profit from competitors' weaknesses. Postgraduate education, always neglected in these debates, is irreducibly collaborative in this way. As I've already mentioned, it is not right to say that everything about teaching in British universities in the past was hunky-dory: it obviously wasn't. But it is right to say that the high reputation for teaching which British universities had until recently was a reflection of something more complex and pervasive, if also somewhat nebulous, than the 'efficient delivery of course content' or 'the rising curve of measurable outcomes'. Again, the holistic perspective is needed: universities have to be functioning healthily across the range of activities that constitute them if they are to successfully fulfil the task of undergraduate education at all.

While I'm urging that these messages need to be tailored to different audiences and communicated through a variety of genres and media, let me take a genre that is close to home for me. It is sometimes said by grave official representatives of our universities that detailed criticism of government policy and official documents is not 'constructive', indeed that it is (to use one of the most damning phrases in the lexicon of such official gravity) 'positively unhelpful'. No good purpose is served, they say, by dissecting the prose of government White Papers and HEFCE position documents and so on: it only succeeds in antagonizing ministers and officials. But this is one of those areas where having a clear idea of our target audiences and our goals is crucial. I have no doubt that an extended critique of the language of an official document does not endear one to the authors of such documents, but that, of course, is not the primary audience in such cases. One of the reasons why we should engage in such critique is precisely because the impoverished language used in those documents expresses and conveys an impoverished conception of the activity they are seeking to regulate, and there are discriminating publics who are perfectly capable of appreciating that fact if the criticisms are effected adroitly enough.

But, more important still, mechanical and inadequate language becomes, through repetition, so familiar that it takes some kind of critical effort – that effort of estrangement that is involved in all genuine critique – to prevent us from letting it become naturalized. Terms and concepts colonize our minds, and even we within universities, who were shocked at first by those terms' inadequacy or reductiveness, eventually become habituated to conducting our affairs by means of them and thus contribute to making the reality of what we do approximate more closely to this language's misleading representation of it. It is worth saying again that other academics are also among our publics. Obviously we don't want to be accused of simply talking to each other, but we do nonetheless need to talk to each other from time to time, and we do need to keep more accurate and more expressive language and better concepts alive in our everyday interactions and conduct of business. In this, maintaining an alert ear for the way a diluted version of the sub-dialect of the business school misdescribes what we do and what is valuable about our activities is one indispensable tactic.

As an up-to-date example of how not to do it, let me take a report, recently issued by a university that shall remain nameless, which analysed changes in the pattern of employment of its humanities graduates between the 1960s and 1990s. Underlying the report was a perfectly useful and unexceptionable piece of descriptive empirical social survey work, but that was not how it was presented. What this report *claimed* to show was that the university's humanities graduates were making a 'contribution' – this word occurring with disturbing frequency – and what they, or many of them, were making a 'contribution' *to* were 'sectors driving economic growth'. In fact, across the relevant decades these graduates had shown themselves to be 'highly responsive to national economic needs'. The truth behind this claim was, roughly, that as the financial sector grew over these decades, the proportion of this university's graduates getting a job in finance increased correspondingly. And this was important because some people, it turns out, make a larger 'contribution' than others if they work in sectors that produce more of GDP. If you make a quick killing in currency trading you are obviously making more of a 'contribution' than if you teach a child to read. So the university gave itself a hearty slap on the back, since the figures showed that a rising number of its humanities graduates 'contributed' in just this way.

The question of whether it's a good thing that more graduates work in commercial finance and fewer in education or public service is obviously a large and complicated one that we should not expect such a report to address. But note that the results of the underlying survey could equally have been presented in a mournful rather than upbeat mode. The report might have said: 'Despite our best efforts to get them to prize other values, an increasing proportion of our humanities graduates have followed the trend of deciding that their priority is to make a lot of money quickly.' The case made in those terms might be neither more nor less arguable than the case the report actually made, but where this becomes germane to my theme is if we ask who such a report is addressed to, what assumptions it is attempting to challenge or rebut, and how effectively it represents the work of the university in question.

Clearly, no one involved in teaching humanities subjects in that university actually believes that this report shows their task to be more worthwhile than would otherwise have been the case, and so this presentation of it risks a kind of bad faith as well as condescension. In fact, viewed from *within* the university, it is in effect saying: 'Yes, we know that this is not the real justification for studying these subjects, but there are some people out there who can only understand the question in these terms. Not us, of course, and not the students who choose to study these subjects. Our actual practice when teaching them about Milton or Manet or moral philosophy has nothing to do with becoming a derivatives trader, but there are powerful groups out there who will only be persuaded that it's worth letting students study such subjects if we can show that, despite the apparent irrelevance of their studies, the graduates go on to make a jolly big "contribution" to the economy.'

But is it really the case that there was anyone in a position of responsibility in government or the City who didn't already know that a significant number of the humanities graduates from one of our leading universities now went to work in finance? And was there really anyone among them who thought the case for supporting these studies was strengthened by this revelation? The vice-chancellor of this university 'contributes' a Foreword that commends the report for making 'a bold first step in articulating the importance of the tradition [of the Humanities] in economic terms, and a compelling justification for the Humanities' continued relevance and importance'. It is hard to know who exactly is supposed to believe that the statistics contained in this report make a 'compelling case for the importance of the Humanities'. I suspect even its authors do not believe that, but they do believe that by *pretending* this is their view they will be looked on favourably by those with public and private largesse to distribute. I have to say that I take this report as a saddening illustration of how not to do it precisely because it represents simultaneously a loss of nerve and an exercise in condescension. Moreover, those who live by the sword of 'contribution to economic growth' will die by that sword, because in the medium and long term only those activities that can be demonstrated to make this contribution will be deemed significant and worthy of support. What is fundamentally wrong with this argument, as with 'impact', which is its bastard child, is that something that is an indirect by-product of the true nature of intellectual activity is treated as its principal direct purpose.

III

As I've made clear on other occasions, I am not an optimist about policy change in the short term. But, as I hope I've also made clear, I by no means despair of successfully making our case to certain publics, and I do want to end by saying that I think we have a duty to try. I use that rather formidable and high-toned word 'duty', which in general I'm not terribly fond of using, because in the case of universities we, as I have said elsewhere, are merely custodians for the present generation of a complex intellectual inheritance which we did not create and which is not ours to allow to be destroyed. The duty that we cannot altogether evade, therefore, is a duty to future generations.

At the risk of seeming both mawkish and self-serving, let me close with a small vignette which I have found helps me, at least, remember this obligation and makes it vivid. At a literary festival where I had been talking about my book *What Are Universities For?*, a man (who was not an academic and had not, it turned out, been to university himself) presented me with not one but two copies of my book for signing. When I asked if he wanted me to make them both out to him, he gave me a reply which has stayed with me. I should say that I don't think there is anything in this vignette that is distinctive to me or my book – it might have happened to any of us – but that is precisely why I mention it because I do think it serves to remind us why we should not give up on the task of making the case for universities, however discouraging the circumstances may sometimes seem. The man replied to my question about signing the books to him by saying: 'No, could you make one out for each of my two children, please. You see, this gives them hope.' That's why we should try.

Postscript

We get a small glimpse into the quality of much education journalism in the report of this lecture that was carried a few days later by the *Times Higher Education* (24 October 2014). Under a large picture showing two medieval knights jousting came the heading 'Collini Lambasts Oxford's Defence of the Humanities'. The report began: 'A leading critic of government higher education policy has launched a stinging attack on the University of Oxford...', and went on in the same vein. That is to say, the main argument of my lecture and 95 per cent of its content were ignored: what had been designed as a meditation on the tactics of persuasion in public debate was represented as an attack by an academic from one institution on its historic 'rival' (hence the jousting knights, presumably), even though that was, transparently, not the point of the passage in question and even though the latter institution was never named in the lecture. The *Times Higher* is, of course, a specialist publication, exclusively devoted to higher education, and it is therefore able to present issues with greater detail and sophistication than can always be done in the mainstream media.

CHAPTER 10

The Future of the Humanities

I

The humanities form a relatively small part of the modern research university, but they bulk very large in all discussions about the 'idea' or the 'future' of universities. This may not simply be because those who dilate on these matters are drawn disproportionately from humanities disciplines. It may in part be because the discourse about the humanities has become a locus – and in some respects a placeholder – for wider anxieties about the changing relations between culture and democracy, between society and economy. These anxieties have real objects as well as, like all anxieties, their exaggerated or phantasmatic features, but in these brief remarks I do not wish to encourage this only partly conscious use of the category of 'the humanities' as a way of addressing these wider issues, not least because it tends to make so much of the discourse about the humanities simultaneously too defensive and too pious. Instead, I just want briefly to register some cautions and then to offer one or two informed guesses about what our crystal ball may suggest in regard to the future of these disciplines.

Almost any event or discussion with 'the humanities' in its title risks seeming both predictable and depressing. Predictable because we suspect that, after running through various travails and accusations, the humanities will by the end emerge in their full redemptive glory as the indispensable means of living a satisfactory human life (and as the grand and pious adjectives pile up it becomes hard to suppress a yawn). And depressing because, despite the inevitable arrival of the 'deepest human values' cavalry to save the day at the end, the story along the way is always one of being beleaguered and besieged, involving a tone that varies somewhere between the self-justifying and the complaining.

Since I don't wish to encourage this tone, I shall take a rather quizzical look at both the activity of 'justifying' and the category of 'the humanities' in an attempt to scrub away some of the congealed abstractions. I'll then quickly suggest one or two ways of engaging in this public discourse that are less defensive and more specific. Obviously, the greater part of my own direct experience relates to the situation in Britain, and I am certainly not presuming that this applies in any simple way to the very different public cultures and the much more diverse higher education systems in the rest of the world. But there are some trends and elements here which, if not strictly speaking global, are already common to Britain and the United States and may soon be coming to many countries of continental Europe.

Let me begin with a very obvious point about justification. The activity of justifying something is highly context-dependent. It depends, first, on the kind of criticism or scepticism that is being responded to or at least anticipated; and, second, it always depends upon being able to establish some commonality of values somewhere, some bridgehead in even the most hostile critic's assumptions, if the attempt at justification is to gain any purchase at all. For these reasons, it doesn't seem to me very helpful to try to develop some all-purpose justification couched in highly abstract terms: it may be better to think of particular forms of resistance we want to overcome on the part of particular publics (often in comparison to particular other preferred activities or purposes), and this means that the form and argumentative strategy of our exercises in characterization and persuasion need to be tailored accordingly. The relevant publics, as we know, include various categories – legislators, parents, foundation administrators, journalists, schoolchildren, colleagues, donors, government officials, students, taxpayers and so on – and of course any actual individual may belong to more than one of these categories.

Quite a lot of the well-meaning statements that are issued about the humanities tend to reduce to a series of abstract nouns, in which 'imagination', 'empathy' and the other usual suspects invariably figure. Justification at this level of abstraction can have its uses, especially if it has been preceded by some much more detailed and nuanced characterizations, but one obvious weakness of this strategy is that it is fatally easy for any interlocutors to enthusiastically endorse these large-sounding claims while not actually being persuaded about, or conceding anything to, the more local or institutional or financial case that the claims are meant to support. Another, perhaps slightly less obvious weakness, is that such high-flown claims don't seem to entail the array of often knotty, detailed and usually empirical enquiries that make up the actual practices of our various disciplines. The most elevated claims for the humanities end up sounding as though their goals could be met if everyone would just read *The Odyssey* and *King Lear* with an open heart.

This is one of the places where the logic of justification can lead us astray. There is a tendency for defenders of universities in general and the humanities in particular to want to present them as contributing to every approved social good. This seems to me a mistake both as a matter of fact and as a matter of tactics. We may certainly hope that in helping to extend cultural understanding we are broadening, not narrowing, human sympathies, but there may be no *necessary* connection in either direction. Almost all arguments that seem to suggest that scholarship, science or culture turn their practitioners into 'better people' are awkwardly vulnerable to obvious counter-examples – just think of the inhabitants of any departmental corridor. The fact that someone can make a dazzling breakthrough in the understanding of human behaviour while at the same time behaving abominably in other aspects of life and holding deplorable political views may make us uncomfortable, but it is a combination that universities have to live with because such extension of understanding is their primary activity, not the manufacturing of right-mindedness. The disciplined free play of the mind over a given topic that is at the heart of scholarly and scientific enquiry is principally an intellectual achievement, not a moral one, at least not directly.

Turning to the category of 'the humanities' itself, my first caution is to suggest that we must be careful that by focusing on this category we don't inadvertently reinstate some version of the supposed 'two cultures' divide. Great swathes of work in all disciplines are broadly analytical and factual in similar ways, where standards of accuracy, rigour and evidence are closely related. What all the disciplines share is at least as important as what differentiates them, and they all have much to gain by articulating their common interest in the university as an enterprise devoted principally to the extension and deepening of human understanding.

Secondly, there are many purposes for which we do better to speak of individual disciplines rather than use the category of 'the humanities'. The latter is chiefly an organizational or classifying term, and that is, of course, one reason why it may be a mistake to be too essentialist about it. We should certainly not speak as though it were a timeless category. Not only is it a term that did not come into general currency in its modern sense until the mid–twentieth century, but it did so largely by way of reaction to the imperial claims of the scientific positivism of that period as supposedly embodied in the natural and the social sciences. Perhaps it has never quite shaken off the aura of conservatism and defensiveness that was inherited from these origins, and it seems to me important not to endorse either of those associations. I should just add that although the term has been well established in Britain for some decades, it is fair to say that the discourse about 'the humanities' has had, and continues to have, a particularly intimate connection with the characteristically American conception of the 'liberal arts' education made up of elective courses, and I'll come back to this close identification with undergraduate teaching in a moment.

Thirdly, another way in which treating 'the humanities' as a single intellectual enterprise risks misleading us is that it almost always ends up focusing on 'the great books', and usually, therefore, reducing our diverse disciplines to the study of a few classics of literature and philosophy. But even in literature and philosophy, and still more in other fields, most scholars most of the time are not reading the great books but are engaging in some much more analytical or empirical enquiries concentrated on particular times and places, and our account of humanities disciplines should reflect this.

Even then, however, constantly emphasizing the category of 'the humanities' tends to operate at too high a level of abstraction, flattening out the distinctiveness of individual disciplines and losing what may be most impressive and persuasive about a good piece of work in ancient history or renaissance musicology or nineteenth-century Russian literature and so on. Individual disciplines, after all, are not merely accidents of institutional history: there are long and rich cultural traditions behind thinking about literature or religion or art and so on, and we need to harness the strength of those traditions to support the standing of the current forms of these enquiries. So, as a matter of tactics, it can often be more productive to try to illustrate what is valuable about work in, say, metaphysics in its terms, and in literary criticism in its terms, and in social history in its terms and so on. This should also help us to avoid making exaggerated claims for the moral benefits of studying these disciplines. So, instead of digging ourselves in behind a stockade of over-ambitious claims couched at too high a level of abstraction and delivered in a tone of defensiveness, it is usually better, when identifying the character and role of these enterprises, to start from some of the facts of our actual practice in our particular, diverse disciplines and work up from there.

Let me make two more positive points in this connection. First, as scholars, we do perhaps need to make a greater effort to try to provide politicians, officials, journalists, administrators and other public figures with a usable set of descriptions of what we do. In market democracies such as ours, politicians are acutely conscious of the kinds of justification for public expenditure which it believes the electorate will find acceptable. At present, the received wisdom in the policy-making world is that the only criterion with undisputed legitimacy across the board is that of contributing to economic prosperity. This situation is potentially unfavourable to the humanities in various ways, but one less obvious danger arises if we allow an external vocabulary of *justification* to come to provide an internal criterion of *quality*. Indeed, if research in the humanities *is* valuable to society, as I certainly believe it is, it makes its contribution by extending and deepening our understanding of human activities across times and cultures, and if we divert our energies from doing that to the highest possible standard in order to meet a perceived short-term requirement to contribute economic impact, then we shall in fact be *lessening* the social contribution of scholarly research. And the more we acquiesce in these crude measures of social and economic impact, the more such categories colonize our minds. One of the depressing features of the debate in Britain is how academics have internalized the language of contribution to economic growth as the defining purpose.

My second point is that alarmism, defensiveness and the alienation of public support are closely related. There are, as I've said, many publics, and we should not underestimate the level of interest in and enthusiasm for work in humanities disciplines in various quarters of society. Among several of these publics there is an instinctive recognition that unfettered intellectual enquiry is central to what universities are about, and that therefore there is, potentially, a much greater reservoir of interest in, and latent appreciation of, the work of universities than the narrow and instrumental official discourse about 'economic growth' ever succeeds in tapping into. Moreover, when so many people are already interested in questions about literature and history, philosophy and religion, art and music, it should not be impossible to persuade them of the value of developing more systematic understanding in these areas. The best work in the humanities disciplines does this brilliantly and we should not sell such work short by misrepresenting it as an indirect way of developing commercially useful skills.

II

Looking into my crystal ball, I'd say – first and very obviously – that we should recognize that the future of the humanities disciplines will be at least as much influenced by what goes on outside universities as by what goes on inside them. This is certainly true of the sometimes neglected question of the curriculum in schools: the recent sad history of modern languages in Britain is an obvious illustration of this point, though there are also longer-term cultural explanations for their shrinkage. A more specific worry that we might have in this connection is that students, and eventually scholars, in many of these disciplines are likely to be increasingly recruited from the offspring of the privileged classes. This is already true to a considerable extent of disciplines such as art history and classics, and is becoming true of modern languages. Funding patterns are another kind of external force, and they will surely encourage certain kinds of interdisciplinarity, so we can expect to hear much more in the humanities about connections with, for example, neuroscience or the environmental sciences. Finally, a further force that is at least partly external and that will do much to shape the future of all disciplines, especially as subjects for undergraduate education, is the development of digital technology, whose potential impact on our conception of what is involved in a university education, including in the humanities, we are only just beginning to explore.

Taking a wider perspective still, we shall of course hear more about the need for a global view, though it is important to recognize that the relation of many humanities disciplines to their native cultures will always remain more intimate than for other disciplines. Most work in the natural sciences, and even in many of the social sciences, can be pursued anywhere, and in a global economy it will, by and large, be pursued where funding dictates. But the study and teaching of, say, Swedish history is always likely to be particularly pursued in Sweden, or Italian literature in Italy and so on. This is a reminder from another angle that these enquiries are more continuous with interests and debates in the wider non-academic culture of which they are a part. The future of, for example, art history will be considerably affected by what happens to galleries and collections, the future of the study of English by what happens to literary publishing and literary journalism and so on. A narrow focus on funding policies for undergraduate education risks losing sight of some of the forces that give these subjects their vitality and wider appeal in particular cultures.

My guess is that in terms of numbers (both of students and staff) and in terms of their influence on decisions about processes and structures, the humanities disciplines are likely to be a still more reduced presence in the major research universities of 2050 and beyond, and will certainly not again have the centrality they had in the middle decades of the twentieth century. But nothing is forever. A hundred and fifty years ago many would have found it unthinkable that classics could ever lose its dominant place in education, and some would have regarded such a prospect as the end of civilization. I don't think we should encourage such apocalyptic or alarmist talk now. Outstanding scholarship in these disciplines will continue to be published (whatever 'published' comes to mean), and there will still be substantial demand for courses in them. We should not regard the mere fact that a smaller *proportion* of students may take courses in the humanities as spelling the end of civilization as we know it. The shifting proportions are, after all, reflective of deeper changes in the character of our societies and the humanities should certainly not be positioned as attempting to resist all such changes.

The contemporary political expression of some of these changes is another matter. At present, we may be witnessing the shift from the university as shaped by the social democratic era to the university as reflecting the era of the politics of market individualism. From the mid-nineteenth through to the late twentieth century one of the notable achievements of European and European-influenced societies was the way they managed to adapt the attenuated traditions of their few and rather marginal institutions of higher learning to turn them into powerhouses of culture, and the humanities disciplines prospered accordingly. Both aristocratic and social democratic values in turn contributed to this transformation. But from at least the 1980s onwards, other values have been more dominant and are in the process of reshaping universities in their own image. In these circumstances it would be unrealistic to expect the humanities disciplines to be able to continue to benefit from the older kind of deference to the ideals of 'culture'. Debates on the theme of the place (or nature or value or future) of 'the humanities' are one name we give to our anxieties about this transition. For these reasons, whatever we think may be the future of the humanities in practical or institutional terms, the future of debates *about* 'the future of the humanities' looks as bright as ever.

CHAPTER 11

Who Does the University Belong To?

I

It will be clear to everyone, contemplating the start of a new academic year, that the question of the role and future of universities is just at present a matter of unusually vigorous debate, not just in the Netherlands but across Europe as a whole and indeed in many other parts of the world.[1] These debates tend, I think, to take a particular form in those countries – such as the Netherlands and including my own country – where a system of publicly funded higher education has traditionally been combined with a considerable degree of academic autonomy for universities. Although there is much diversity both within and across national systems, there are certain family resemblances among what, simply as a piece of convenient shorthand, we may refer to as the European model of the university, and it is here that questions about public accountability have been posed most pressingly. But just as we should not let our shorthand deceive us into assuming uniformity where there is in fact great diversity, so we should not fall into that kind of temporal parochialism that presumes these questions are unique to the present day. The truth, I shall suggest, is that societies have always wanted their universities to fulfil diverse and not always compatible purposes, and that universities have always been partly responsive to, and partly resistant to, those wider social demands. But although the structure of this dynamic endures, the content changes: just as we no longer regard mastery of Latin and Greek verse-forms

---

1 An earlier version of this chapter was given as the Invited Address at the ceremony to mark the opening of the academic year at Leiden University in September 2015.

as the hallmark of a gentleman – and would, indeed, be uneasy with both the class and gender assumptions built into such a term – so societies no longer regard the principal purpose of universities as being to provide ministers for the church or officials for the state.

Nonetheless, it is hard not to feel that at present we face a particularly delicate and contested moment in this long relationship, as global finance remakes the world in its own image. Return upon capital is the shaping drive of contemporary societies, which leads to an assertion of the primacy of contributing to economic growth as the goal and the extension of market-driven competition as the means. Universities are suspected of being at best irrelevant, at worst obstructive, to this agenda, and there is strong pressure for them to reshape their own activities so as better to further these economic purposes. At the same time, the extension of ideas of democratic accountability leads societies to search for mechanisms by which to test and measure the performance of universities, along with all other industries and services, thereby generating another set of tensions as mechanical procedures are devised which attempt to provide some reliable quantitative indicator of forms of intellectual quality that, ultimately, can only be judged not measured.

The resulting tensions between such assertions of society's demands and universities' affirmation of their intellectual autonomy are what lie behind the current debates summed up by the question 'Who does the university belong to?' This is obviously not chiefly a question about legal status, but about who gets to say what universities should be doing, about whose conception of their purpose should have most weight. This is the question I have been invited to address, but I shall propose to you that we need to adopt a perspective which is less individualistic, less proprietorial, and less confined to the present generation.

Although, clearly, there is no timeless essence of 'the university', I would argue that there is a long history – with roots going back at least to the time of Wilhelm von Humboldt at the beginning of the nineteenth century – of seeing universities as *partly-protected* spaces in which the extension and deepening of understanding takes priority over any more immediate or instrumental purposes. This idea has been powerful and in some ways resilient. It is noticeable that many institutions that were initially founded upon some other model, such as being a technical training institute or a community college, have aspired to what is perceived to be the status and freedom of a university, but that no university has ever made the journey in the reverse direction. Part of the complexity of the history of universities in most European societies lies in the interaction of two patterns. On the one hand, long-established universities have frequently responded to pressures to accommodate new subjects or to educate students in new ways in response to changing social and economic demands. Yet on the other hand, institutions founded to further particular local or immediate aims have over time shown a tendency to devote themselves principally to more disinterested, long-term forms of intellectual enquiry. Critics have frequently claimed that universities need to be recalled to the socially valuable purposes of studying and teaching 'useful' subjects, rather than what are sometimes stigmatized as 'useless' academic disciplines.

But the truth is that the distinction between the 'useful' and the 'useless' is a rhetorical construction with no fixed or determinate content. Intellectual enquiry is in itself ungovernable: there is no predicting where thought and analysis may lead when allowed to play freely over almost any topic, as the history of science abundantly illustrates. It is sometimes said that in universities knowledge is pursued 'for its own sake', but that may misdescribe the variety of purposes for which different kinds of understanding may be sought. A better way to characterize the intellectual life of universities may be to say that the drive towards understanding can never accept an arbitrary stopping point, and critique may always in principle reveal that any currently accepted stopping point *is* ultimately arbitrary. Human understanding, when not chained to a particular instrumental task, is restless, always pushing onwards, though not in a single or fixed or entirely knowable direction, and there is no one moment along that journey where we can say in general or in the abstract that the degree of understanding being sought has passed from the useful to the useless.

In other words, it is not the subject matter itself that determines whether something is, at a particular moment, classed as 'useful' or 'useless'. Almost any subject can fall under either description: the study of classics was useful for the early modern statesman and administrator, just as theoretical physics may seem useless to the contemporary entrepreneur. Rather, it is a question of whether enquiry into a subject is being undertaken under the sign of limitlessness – that is to say, not just, as with the development of all knowledge, subject to the testing of hypotheses or the revision of errors, but where the open-ended quest for understanding has primacy over any application or intermediate outcome. This, we might say, is one mark of an academic discipline, and for this reason attempts to make universities into a type of institution where scholars and students study only what is 'useful' are bound, eventually, to end in a kind of failure. The attempt itself can do untold damage, of course, and I am not proposing we should take much comfort from this thought. But all endeavours after systematic understanding of some particular subject matter are prone to generate further reflections on the limitations or premises of that understanding which cannot themselves be entirely corralled or subordinated to present uses. Moreover, present uses soon become outdated, but the forms of enquiry they provoked do not, or at least they get absorbed into continuing larger enquiries. From time to time, efforts will be made by governments or other representatives of the presumed 'needs of society' to redirect these energies in some currently favoured practical direction, which partly accounts for the continuing gavotte danced by proponents of the 'useful' against the 'useless'.

Within what I am calling the partly-protected space of the university, various forms of useful preparation for life are undertaken in a setting and manner which encourages the students to understand the contingency of any particular packet of knowledge and its inter-relations with other different forms of knowledge. To do this, the teachers themselves need to be engaged in constantly going beyond the confines of the packets of knowledge that they teach, and there is no way to prescribe in advance what will and will not be fruitful ways to do that. Undergraduate education involves exposing students for a while to the experience of enquiry into something in particular, but enquiry which, in itself, has no external goal other than improving the understanding of that subject matter. One rough and ready distinction between university education and professional training is that education relativizes and constantly calls into question the information which training simply transmits. In this sense, education encourages the student to recognize the ways in which particular bits of knowledge are not fixed or eternal or universal or self-sufficient. That may be done in relation to almost any subject matter, though it can only be done through engagement with some *particular* subject matter, not simply by ingesting a set of abstract propositions about the contingency of knowledge; and the more there already exists an elaborated and sophisticated tradition of enquiry in a particular area, the more demanding and rigorous will be the process of acquiring and revising understanding. In other words, a university education has to be in large part an education *in* a discipline, though what is really happening is education *through* a discipline.

The dialectic between the push of immediate local pressures and the pull of long-term open-ended enquiry can be illustrated from the histories of universities in various countries, but let me take an example from the country I know best. From the mid–nineteenth century onwards, the business leaders in the great provincial cities that had grown up in Britain as a result of the Industrial Revolution – cities such as Birmingham, Manchester, Leeds and so on – supported the establishment of institutions that would both prepare young men (though not usually, in the early years, young women) for a career in commerce or industry and develop inventions and processes that would benefit local industries. The existing universities of Oxford and Cambridge were perceived as remote, conservative, clerical and irrelevant to the needs of these booming industrial centres. The new University of Birmingham, therefore, would have a 'Faculty of Commerce' – something that sounded like a contradiction in terms to the representatives of the traditional universities – and the University of Manchester, in the great capital of the cotton industry, would have a laboratory that conducted research into textile manufacturing.

But there was no evading the logic of what I call the 'Faustian pact' between universities and society. An institution that wanted to develop applied science had to have teachers who could master the underlying pure science, and that is necessarily an ever-moving frontier. An institution that wanted to teach commerce was quickly drawn into appointing those who understood the principles of economics or the development of recent and not-so-recent history and so on. And there was also what we could call either civic pride or a kind of cultural snobbery, whereby those who wanted their local universities to take their places among the world's great institutions of higher learning knew that they must also have departments of mathematics and astronomy and philosophy and classics. So powerful were these impulses that already by the early twentieth century the most influential school of medieval historians in Britain was to be found not in one of the ancient centres of learning but in Manchester.

I can illustrate my theme more concretely – indeed, with a lit-erally concrete example – by referring to the façade of the main building at the University of Birmingham, which finally received its charter as an independent university in 1901. When Josiah Mason, a successful local businessman, had founded a college in the city almost half a century earlier he had insisted that it was to be devoted to 'systematic education and instruction specially adapted to the practical, mechanical, and artistic requirements of the manufactures and industrial pursuits of the Midlands district … to the exclusion of mere literary education and instruction'. This represented the assertion of social purpose in its most imperious form. But by the time the new buildings were being erected in the first decade of the twentieth century, there was a strong feeling that the larger dignity of the university's purposes should be, literally, carved in stone. Accordingly, three of the four main friezes on the façade of the Great Hall represented several types of local industry, drawing on the applied sciences, but the fourth, over the central entrance, signalled something else, something intended to be emblematic of 'Learning', something that, as it was put at the time, 'refers to the function of the university at large'. This message was made even clearer by the placing of nine statues in niches over the main entrance. Initially, there was some tension between the desire to have figures with a connection to the Midlands district and the desire to choose representatives of, as it was put, 'great men of all time'. This led to some implausible claims: the composer Felix Mendelssohn, for example, was proposed on the rather shaky grounds that the first performance of his *Elijah* had taken place in Birmingham Town Hall. Special interest groups also had their say: the Faculty of Commerce proposed Adam Smith, the Law Faculty Francis Bacon. Eventually, the inevitable compromise and opportunism of the committee process issued in the agreed nine, who adorn the main entrance to this day.

Before I relieve your tension by announcing the lucky winners, let me just remark the presence of two nineteenth-century assumptions that operate less powerfully today. One was the veneration of an agreed canon that represented a wholly unrelativized notion of culture, and the other was the propensity to express important public convictions by means of statues. Modern sensibilities are both less prone to carve sermons in stone, and much less deferential to the idea of Great Men, and not just because of their maleness. But the first Principal of the new university, Oliver Lodge, insisted that in choosing the representative figures a broad view should be taken because, as he said, 'the University in the future will include all branches of learning, and not merely the more technical branches which are in special evidence today'.

The statues finally selected to represent this ideal were grouped in threes. On one side were Darwin, Faraday and Watt; on the other were Beethoven, Virgil and Michelangelo; while the central trio comprised Shakespeare flanked by Plato and Newton. It was a clever compromise; science and engineering were represented by Faraday and Watt, both of whom came from the Midlands; the biological sciences by the great Darwin, who came from the neighbouring county of Shropshire, and mathematics and physics by the immortal Newton. And, of course, Shakespeare himself, who came from just down the road at Stratford, was another local boy made good. The Midlands connections of Plato, Beethoven, Virgil and Michelangelo were, it's true, a little more elusive, but they nonetheless signalled the ambition of the university to be, in Lodge's words again, not just an institute of applied technology, but a 'school of general culture in the great European tradition'.

There is much more that could be said about this example, but I'm sure you recognize the general point. Universities respond to local needs, but they also partake of a wider inheritance and therefore, I would suggest, also of an open-ended future. No one, not even a wealthy local businessman who provides a large donation, can altogether determine their character, and that returns me to the theme of who owns the university. Although I am not addressing this question in legal terms, it may be helpful at this point to borrow a term from the legal framework governing many public and charitable institutions in the English-speaking world, such as museums and galleries as well as universities. Such bodies are often placed under the care of a board of trustees. A trustee is, of course, not an owner. Trustees have numerous duties and obligations, but no property rights. The very category of trustee raises the question of who they hold their institution in trust *for*, and this is one of the points at which we have to think beyond the present generation.

II

The fatal conceptual error involved in the new university funding system introduced in Britain in 2012 is that it treats the fee as a payment by an individual customer to a single institutional provider for a specific service in the present. By contrast, the proper basis for funding education is a form of social contract whereby each generation contributes to the education of future generations. It cannot be for a specific service because the 'customer', in the form of the student, is not in a position to know in advance exactly what benefit they may obtain from a university education. And it cannot really be to a single institutional provider because each university is only part of the world of learning: none of what they provide for their students would exist except for the work of many people over many generations in many other institutions. What we call a 'fee' is not really the price of a product: it is an undertaking to contribute to the costs of the system. In this respect it is more like a tax: just as a tax is the tithe which the citizen, as a member of society, pays towards the upkeep of that society, so a university fee is more like the National Insurance contribution in Britain, a recognition of human solidarity in facing the common perils and opportunities of life. All of this is even more emphatically the case when, as with the new system in Britain and elsewhere, such as Australia, the fee is actually paid by means of a government loan which the student then repays through an income-contingent scheme over the next thirty years. This should make it even clearer that the individual student is not actually paying for the libraries and laboratories in which they work or for the training and salaries of their current teachers, since that expenditure necessarily took place long ago. They are paying towards the maintenance of these things in the future, and it is a long future.

Moreover, universities do not fulfil their purposes merely by means of the formal instruction they offer, but by nurturing a broader atmosphere of open-ended enquiry. Although academic life has its hierarchies, it is in one sense irreducibly democratic, in that arguments and evidence are, in principle, sovereign, no matter who advances them. Let me illustrate several of these points with a small autobiographical story. I am shamelessly using it here as an idealized parable, and the only excuses I have for telling you a story about myself are, first, that it actually happened, and, second, that it has the merit of making me look ridiculous.

When I was an undergraduate I attended the annual dinner in which final-year students mixed with the academics who were fellows of their college. I was seated across from a much older man whom I had never met before, and in the course of the evening we fell into a discussion about such small topics as what the basis of law is and what the limits of the law's regulation of individual life should be. As it happened, I had just that week been set to read the classic works on the theory of Utilitarianism by Jeremy Bentham and John Stuart Mill for my course in the history of political thought, so, helped by the generous supply of college wine, I found I had many brilliant opinions to express on these topics. I started to argue with this older man, with all the assurance of a twenty-one-year-old who, a few weeks earlier, had never heard of Utilitarianism but who now knew exactly what was wrong with it and why no reasonable person could seriously entertain it for a moment. He argued back, thought-fully and tactfully but also with some vigour. We must have argued for quite some time because suddenly I was aware that most of the other diners had left and the staff were beginning to clear the tables. My interlocutor graciously said that he had found our discussion very interesting and we went our separate ways. I went to bed extremely pleased with myself for having so triumphantly set him straight about the obvious defects of the shallow theoretical position he had tried to uphold.

It was only the next day that I learned from one of my fellow students who my interlocutor at dinner had been: it turned out that he was none other than Professor Glanville Williams, at that time probably the most highly regarded modern exponent in the world of the legal and political theory of Utilitarianism. I was, of course, mortified that I had made such a complete fool of myself, but as the years have gone by I have come more and more to admire what Glanville Williams did that evening. He hadn't talked down to me or condescended to me or dismissed me: he had, or so it seemed, taken me seriously as someone to disagree with, and he had done so above all by meeting my half-baked arguments with better arguments. I think that evening he gave me an invaluable lesson not just in understanding Utilitarianism, but in understanding what universities are about, including the thought that the freedom to make mistakes may be crucial to the process of learning itself. Of course, in turning this selectively remembered experience into an illustrative anecdote I tacitly idealize it, but that may not be such a bad thing in the context of today's ceremony.

Glanville Williams is long dead and I suppose I am now in my turn likely to be perceived by the current generation of students as some old man across the table. But that sense of the obligation to hand on to others something precious that was in our time handed on to us should be both a chastening and a fortifying conviction – chastening because we are all too aware that we are pygmies standing on the shoulders of giants, and fortifying because there is something endlessly vigorous and self-sustaining in the enterprise of truly open-ended enquiry, an energy that is not easily suppressed or dammed-up no matter how foolish or dogmatic we may sometimes be. Just as the arguments for and against Utilitarianism didn't belong to Glanville Williams any more than they belonged to my opinionated twenty-one-year-old self, so the university, the indispensable setting in which all such arguments can be explored and developed without limit, does not belong to any one party in the present.

One of the most striking features of those accumulations of deepened understanding and exact knowledge that we call scholarship and science is how small a proportion of them were created by those who presently hold posts in universities. What a 'customer' 'buys' from an individual university is not a 'product' or 'service' that that university has created: it is access to a complex intellectual and cultural inheritance that is only maintained and passed on in the present by the combined efforts of scholars and scientists all over the world, a population that is frequently mobile and constantly being renewed. A single, isolated university is, strictly speaking, a mirage, just as inconceivable and unsustainable as Marx long ago pointed out was the Robinson Crusoe model of 'economic man'.

Ask yourselves what proportion of the books and articles students at Leiden are asked to read, or what proportion of the equipment they use and the experiments they replicate, were written or created by the present members of the academic staff of this university. If we cannot say who 'owns' an idea that was first thought fifty or a hundred years ago but is now discussed in seminars and laboratories across the world, so we cannot in any useful way say who 'owns' the universities in which such thinking is done. Of course, we have evolved such legal instruments as copyright, patents and intellectual property rights generally, but most of what happens, and really matters, in both teaching and research is very little constrained by such instruments. I may, quite properly, have to pay for the permission to reproduce a poem by a living or recently deceased poet, but everything that happens in the minds and imaginations of the readers of that poem, all the accumulated critical attention that is brought to bear on it, all the comparisons with countless other poems that are implicit in all characterizations and judgements of it, all the knowledge of the language or of verse-forms or of history that is presupposed by any probing discussion of it – we do not pay a fee to the 'owners' of the rights of these things each time we open our mouths or sit down at our keyboards.

Like all social institutions, universities have developed over time by a process that includes accident as well as design, a process that has taken different forms in different periods and different places, a process we don't altogether understand and are not wholly in control of. Perhaps we could imagine a world in which universities never existed; we could certainly imagine a world in which they are very different from how they are now – indeed, our descendants may well be living in such a world before too long. But they are what, as things have turned out, we now have, and we would surely be foolish not to recognize the immense value mankind has derived from having institutions in which pushing at the boundaries of present understanding is not a secondary or instrumental aim, directed just at a particular, local outcome, but is the very rationale of those institutions themselves.

Such a rationale is compatible with various forms of funding and governance, as the diverse history of higher education amply attests, and I am not suggesting that this perspective dictates one set of answers to the questions currently troubling this and other countries. But I would suggest that such a perspective should have a chastening effect on any attempt to treat universities entirely as businesses whose profits can be accurately quantified, or to treat academics as operatives whose output can be exactly measured, or to treat students as consumers the satisfaction of whose wants is the only relevant index of educational success. The premises of market individualism encourage us to think in terms of property rights – personal, exclusive, enforceable. Even by asking the question 'who does the university belong to?' we risk colluding with this language – language which is, as always, so much more than just language – and we risk losing our capacity to articulate the conception of a collective but intangible enterprise sustained across time, both past and future, which is not the property of any one individual or group or institution or even generation.

The university understood in this way certainly doesn't 'belong' to the government in the Hague, or to that nebulous entity called 'Dutch society', or to the good burghers of Leiden; it doesn't belong either to taxpayers or to donors, necessary though their contributions may be; it doesn't belong to the professors who sometimes think of themselves as the one indispensable element, and it doesn't belong to the students who are periodically tempted to stake a symbolic claim by repossessing an institution they feel is rightfully theirs; it doesn't belong, for all the magnificence of his title, to the Rector Magnificus, and nor does it belong to all those catering and support staff who might well say, in Brechtian vein, 'first there is lunch, then there is studying'. Universities belong as much to those figures represented on the façade at the University of Birmingham as they do to those whom Edmund Burke called 'the generations yet unborn', just as this particular university belongs as much to the first-year student who today begins one of the most exciting or most worrying, but anyway most intense, experiences of her life as it does to the shades of Hugo Grotius and Johan Huizinga. If there is any value in reflecting from time to time on the unanswerable question of who the university belongs to, perhaps it lies in this – in reminding us, amid difficult political and financial circumstances, that we are only the trustees for the present generation of a complex intellectual inheritance that we did not create, and which it is not ours to allow to be destroyed.

Acknowledgements

One of the central contentions of this book is that participation in public debate on a topical matter such as higher education policy requires that one be willing to repeat oneself. This goes against the grain in several ways, not least against the scholarly protocol that regards any repetition of a carefully worked piece of writing not just as unnecessary but as reprehensible. However, although I have emphasized that the different genres and occasions of public debate demand that one's message be tailored appropriately, it remains essential that the core of that message be hammered home in fundamentally similar terms. The pieces selected for inclusion in this book represent only a proportion of the 'speaking' I have done on the subject of universities in the past few years, and one result of that selection is to leave other venues and other audiences unacknowledged, though I remain grateful to all those who gave these ideas a hearing in one way or another. The enthusiastic and heartening responses of these readers and audiences has sustained me through the inevitable low moments, and my gratitude to them all is no less genuine for being expressed in this collective form.

In addition, I am particularly indebted to Ruth Abbott, Ruth Morse, Keith Thomas, Dorothy Thompson and John Thompson for their comments on earlier drafts of this book. Thanks are due also to my agent, Peter Robinson, who expertly guided the book to its natural home, and to my publisher at Verso, Leo Hollis, for his enthusiasm and his advice. I owe special thanks to Mary-Kay Wilmers and her colleagues at the *London Review of Books* who commissioned and published earlier versions of Chapters 4–6 and then gave me permission to re-use them.

The *LRB* has been notably staunch and outspoken in its criticism of the policies of successive British governments in recent years, not just in the area of higher education, and I feel lucky, as well as proud, in having been able to write for it on these and other topics.

I give here details of the originals on which these chapters are based.

1. Earlier versions of this chapter were delivered as public lectures at the universities of Melbourne, Sydney, Adelaide, Auckland and Otago in autumn 2014; I have incorporated some material from public lectures given in Lisbon, Amsterdam, Charlottesville (Va) and Manchester in 2013–14. It has not previously been published.

2. Earlier versions of this chapter were given as public lectures in the universities of Pittsburgh and St Andrews, to a conference at the European University Institute in Florence, and to the Manchester Literary and Philosophical society, all in 2014–15. It has not previously been published.

3. Earlier versions of parts of this chapter were delivered as the Ashby Lecture, Clare Hall, Cambridge, to mark the college's fiftieth anniversary, and also as a public lecture to honour the fiftieth anniversary of Wolfson College, Oxford, both in May 2016; a version was also given as part of a series of public lectures on the future of universities held at the University of Brighton in March 2016. It has not previously been published.

4. A shortened version of this chapter was published in the *London Review of Books* in August 2011, following the publication by the Department of Business, Innovation and Skills of the White Paper, *Higher Education: Students at the Heart of the System*. It also refers to 'Supporting analysis for the Higher Education White Paper' (BIS Economics Paper no. 14), and to

The Report of the Committee on Higher Education, the 'Robbins Report', of 1963.

5. This chapter was first published in the *London Review of Books* in October 2013. The two books under discussion are Roger Brown with Helen Carasso, *Everything for Sale? The Marketisation of UK Higher Education* (Routledge, 2013), and Andrew McGettigan, *The Great University Gamble: Money, Markets and the Future of Higher Education* (Pluto, 2013).

6. A slightly shortened version of this chapter was first published in the *London Review of Books* in January 2016, following the publication by the Department of Business, Innovation and Skills of the Green Paper, *Fulfilling Our Potential: Teaching Excellence, Social Mobility and Student Choice*, in November 2015.

7. This chapter was given as a lecture at a joint Universities and Colleges Union and Educational Institute Scotland/University Lecturers' Association Conference in Edinburgh in February 2011 on 'The Future of Higher Education in Scotland'; the Scottish Government Green Paper referred to is *Building a Smarter Future: Towards a Sustainable Scottish Solution for the Future of Higher Education* (December 2010). My lecture was then included in the submission made to the Cabinet Secretary for Education at Holyrood. It has not previously been published.

8. The opening section of this chapter was given as a presentation to a meeting of the All-Party Parliamentary Universities Group at the Houses of Parliament in February 2012; the later section was delivered as part of a paper to a conference on 'Shaping Higher Education Fifty Years After Robbins', held at the London School of Economics in October 2013, where speakers were invited to reflect on the bearing of the Robbins Report of 1963 on current debates. It has not previously been published.

9. This chapter was given as the first annual lecture of the Council for the Defence of British Universities at the inaugural AGM in London in October 2013. It has not previously been published.

10. An earlier version of this chapter was given as a paper at the President's Panel on 'The Humanities and the Fate of the University' at Harvard University in April 2013; a revised version was given at the Ax:son Johnson Foundation symposium held at the British Academy in March 2014 and subsequently made available in Sweden. (Some sentences from its opening paragraph were re-worked in my article 'Seeing a Specialist: The Humanities as Academic Disciplines', *Past and Present*, 229 (2015), pp. 271–81.) It has not previously been published.

11. This chapter was given as the Invited Address at the ceremony to mark the opening of the academic year at Leiden University in the Netherlands in September 2015. It has not previously been published.

Appendix: Short Work

Different genres of topical writing come, in time, to exhibit different degrees of datedness. Of all the forms of such writing, the short piece in a daily newspaper on a matter judged to be sufficiently 'in the news' to merit a few hundred words of analysis or opinion is usually the most ephemeral. In including several such pieces in this appendix, along with some cognate short forms, I do not, therefore, have any illusions about their durability. They were of the moment and their moment has passed. But since part of my purpose in this book is to illustrate some of the variety of forms of speaking or writing that may need to be undertaken if a more adequate case for universities is to be made, it seems right to represent this subset of the genre alongside the more extended varieties. Most of the themes these short pieces touch on remain, in some disguise or other, very much part of the current landscape of debate about higher education, and precisely because such discussion tends by its nature to be highly repetitive, the arguments sketched in these brief forays may retain a certain usability.

a) The London School of Economics and External Funding
This article was written for the Guardian *in March 2011. The LSE found itself at the centre of controversy when, having previously accepted a large donation from the Gaddafi family, questions were raised about the rigour of the process by which Saif Gaddafi, the son of Libya's ruler, was awarded a PhD. Sir Howard Davies, at the time the Director of the LSE, later felt obliged to resign over the issue.*

Commentators have been quick to seize on the revelations about the London School of Economics' Libyan connections to draw a moral. We are given recommendations about the length of spoon required for supping with the devil, and reminded that we should 'fear the x who come bearing gifts' (please insert name of dodgy foreign country as appropriate). There are, clearly, several overlapping problems here about the source of any such money or other deal, about the degree of control the donor hopes to exercise, about the maintenance (or otherwise) of academic standards, and about the effects of such tie-ups on an institution's reputation.

Simon Jenkins goes further and suggests that 'what happened at LSE is nothing more than an extreme version of the predicament facing all British universities', and he then tries to turn this into an argument for fundamental changes in higher education, calling on universities to have 'the guts to break the umbilical cord with government and the past, and … the guts to tell good private money from bad'. Along with some obviously irrelevant persiflage about 'the whole of higher education being stuck in a monastic time-warp' (which reveals that it is not universities whose ideas are stuck in a time-warp), there is a good and important general point here, yoked to a bad and unwarranted conclusion.

However, the general point needs to be widened to be properly illuminating. It is not just that universities are under pressure to accept money from businessmen and foreign governments. The wider problem is the fetishization in contemporary British universities of 'external funding'. This category embraces not only the kinds of donation and deal at issue in the LSE case, but all forms of income that are 'external' to the institution's own recurrent budget. All academics in British universities will immediately recognize that nothing they do as scholars and teachers wins anywhere near as much commendation and support from their university's 'senior management team' (older readers may still refer to them as 'administrators') as the securing of some kind of external funding. Such funding may range from a project grant from a research council or charity to the sponsorship of a post or studentship by a local business, and then on to the murkier regions of whole courses and centres being paid for by some overseas government or large corporation.

At first sight, it may seem absurd to bracket these disparate types of funding together, since the first and second kinds are not only innocent of any taint of corruption but are the bread-and-butter of most working scientists as well as of an increasing number of scholars in the humanities and social sciences. But that is precisely what is so insidious and why the LSE case raises systemic rather than merely local questions. Let me illustrate in two ways.

First, it is now axiomatic in British universities that a piece of research (and its resulting publication) that was financed by any of these forms of external funding is, *ipso facto*, superior to one that is, indirectly, financed out of the university's recurrent income. Such external funding is, in principle, supposed to cover the 'extra' costs of doing a piece of research, but this means that in practice academics are now under instructions to incur more expense. If a book or paper could be written either during the research time which universities still, just about, make available or during a period in which the scholar or scientist in question receives external funding for the notionally additional costs, academics are now obliged by their universities to opt for the latter. Indeed, being able to raise such outside money, from whatever source, is now being written into job advertisements as a *requirement* of the post.

Second, the internal accounting procedures of universities reward twice over those departments and research units that succeed in attracting such outside income. They are rewarded not just by having the grant or donation to dispose of, but their allocation from central university funds will often be in direct proportion to their success in attracting money from elsewhere. So, if you are the head of a department and you want to ensure that your university continues to support teaching and research in your discipline, you are strongly advised to find, over and above the normal departmental budget for posts and infrastructure and so on, some kind of outside deal. This might take the form of a 'partnership' with a foreign institution keen to have a guaranteed number of student places made available, or a 'contract' with a commercial company keen to have some of their research done for them, cheaply, by academics. If you succeed in generating such income, your internal university funding will in turn be assured and your university managers will smile upon your individual and collective efforts to expand your activities, gain promotion and so on.

Obviously these structural conditions within British universities do not entail that all money from 'outside' is tainted, and they do not absolve institutions from exercising due diligence in scrutinizing all arrangements very carefully. That, of course, is where the tricky questions about the origin of the money and the degree of outside control over it and so on come in. But these conditions certainly make it more likely that those within universities will be overwhelmingly eager to court *any* form of outside funding and be willing to take risks about the legitimacy or cleanness of any source.

The idea that these dangers could best be avoided by universities 'breaking the umbilical cord with government' is fanciful. If anything, the further universities move away from being properly funded by the state, the greater will become the risk of misjudgements such as seem to have happened at the LSE. It is the over-emphasis on 'external funding' that is at fault. We need not just to lengthen our spoons: we need to stop believing that money is more worth having if it comes from the devil we don't know than from the devil we do.

b) The AHRC and the Haldane Principle
This article was written for the Guardian *in March 2011. Critics had argued that the Arts and Humanities Research Council had shown itself improperly responsive to political pressure by including among its funding themes the topic of 'the Big Society', a term then closely associated with the policies promoted by the Tory Prime Minister, David Cameron.*

To judge by some of the responses to the story in the *Observer*, you might think that groups of cowering academics had been rounded up, formed into chain gangs, and forced to break rocks by hand to make way for nasty Mr Cameron's 'Big Society'. And to judge by the statement issued in response by the Arts and Humanities Research Council, you might think that this funding body was amazed to hear that the idea of the 'Big Society' was associated with the government, especially since the Council always decides on funding priorities in the light of academics' existing interests without giving a thought to what the government might favour. There is a very important issue here, but neither of these simplistic positions begins to address it.

It is, of course, disingenuous of the AHRC to claim that it has no case to answer in response to the *Observer* article, arguing that the 'Connected Communities' themes it has been prioritizing 'also *happen* to be relevant to debates about the "Big Society"' (my emphasis). The AHRC's own Delivery Plan states 'Connected Communities will enable the AHRC to contribute to the government's initiatives on localism and the "Big Society"', or again 'We will focus on issues such as the "Big Society", localism and cohesion.' These 'initiatives' are, without question, deeply controversial and highly party political. Should research in universities – institutions committed to the open-ended pursuit of disciplined understanding – be directed to 'contribute' to such initiatives, at the expense of intellectually more worthwhile topics?

The AHRC's response tries to scotch the story by going for an easy, but largely irrelevant, victory. It says, in effect, that no minister told them to fund research into the 'Big Society'. But that, of course, is not how these things work, and the AHRC's panicky declaration only underlines the impossible position which it has got into in recent years as it has desperately tried to justify the funding of research in the arts and humanities by directing energies towards areas it thinks Whitehall will approve of.

The real question here is not about a minister trying to turn research to party-political advantage. It is about the difficulty, in a consumerist democracy, of justifying the expenditure of public money on open-ended scholarly enquiry in the first place. This reflects the fact that politicians have lost the confidence to tell the electorate that universities best perform their distinctive and peculiar role when granted the intellectual autonomy to decide what areas of research will, in the long run, be most fruitful.

Thus, the key question is whether a funding council such as the AHRC is a mechanism for channelling public support to the best research being carried on in universities, or whether it is an agency of government, increasingly directing funds to themes which have been endorsed as 'national priorities'. If it is the latter, then no amount of talk about the 'Haldane' or 'arm's length' principle (named after R. B. Haldane, the early twentieth-century Liberal minister responsible for the earliest government funding of research) is going to make much difference: the funding council will, without having to be directly coerced, follow the lead of the government of the day as other indirectly dependent public agencies do.

The problem pre-dates the coalition. For some years now, governments have been insisting that research councils allocate less and less of their funding in 'responsive' mode – i.e. by choosing from among the strongest applications they receive from academics – and focus more and more of it on themes that can be made to seem to contribute to 'growth' or to 'competitiveness' or whatever other reductive aim currently enjoys political currency. From one point of view, the game is already given away by the inclusion of universities and research under the aegis of the Department for Business, Innovation and Skills (and its precursor), when their natural home would be somewhere between a Department of Education and a Department of Culture. The aim of BIS, as its mission statement announces, is to 'build a dynamic and competitive UK economy by creating the conditions for business success', so universities have to show that they are putting their shoulder to this utilitarian wheel.

This wider problem is illustrated elsewhere in the AHRC's Delivery Plan. For example, it announces that its major priority over the next spending period will be 'the creative economy'. 'Why the Creative Economy?' it asks rhetorically, and the first sentence of the answer is: 'It is an increasingly strong and forward-looking part of the national economy in the UK.' Perhaps so, but that does not mean, and should not mean, that it's a topic that historians and philosophers and literary critics have found to be intellectually fertile and significant in their own fields. It's obviously an attempt to make research in these fields seem 'relevant' to the narrowest and most reductive version of so-called 'national priorities'.

The officers of the AHRC claim that this is the necessary price to be paid for getting funds to support more traditional academic research. Rick Rylance, chief executive of the AHRC, emphasized in the autumn that the council now operates in a 'something for something' world: it has to be seen to be cooperating. He also insisted that 'scare-mongering and critique of the impact agenda are pointless'. But actually the impact agenda is at the root of the AHRC's current predicament, and so identifying the defects of this agenda is the very opposite of 'pointless'. By insisting that scholarly research must demonstrate a certain kind of economic and social impact, current funding policy effectively redirects researchers away from some topics and towards others. In these circumstances, no minister *needs* to micromanage the research agenda, and so David Willetts is, in a narrow sense, correct to say that the government is abiding by the Haldane principle.

However, he can only say this because the institutional framework and the prevailing ethos make it appear the merest common sense (and absolutely no threat to the intellectual freedom of researchers) if a certain amount of the council's funding is earmarked for topics that 'happen' to be on a current government's agenda. But in fact that is already a dangerous and potentially damaging basis on which to operate. It is dangerous because the language of 'national priorities' makes it seem as though the open-ended pursuit of deeper understanding, which it is the function of universities to cultivate and extend, is not itself a national priority. And it is damaging because it in effect asserts that contributing to economic competitiveness must automatically overrule contributing to enhanced understanding, and once that set of priorities is allowed to govern research, then quite soon we shall have third-rate universities. Specifying that a certain amount of the research budget must be spent on topics which are chosen for their electoral or party-political appeal is, especially in the area of the humanities and social sciences, the route to intellectual mediocrity.

This framework and this ethos are not likely to change any time soon, especially if academics don't make more strenuous efforts to bring a more adequate understanding of the value of universities to bear in public debate. Meanwhile, if the AHRC is to regain some of the credibility in the scholarly world that it has forfeited in recent years it needs to return to funding primarily in responsive mode, allocating money to projects that emerge from within the relevant disciplinary communities, rather than trying to steer researchers to work on topics that, today but quite likely not tomorrow, look as though they bear on themes that look as though they could count as 'national priorities'.

c) Conned by Degrees

This article was written for the Guardian *in August 2011 in the week that A-Level results were announced. There had been some tendentious commentary suggesting that, thanks to the coalition government's policy of replacing public funding with individual fees, those who secured the required results for university entry would henceforth be more demanding than their predecessors and would, therefore, 'drive up standards'.*

'Tis the season of whoops of joy and howls of despair. The arrival of A-level results triggers various forms of predictable, almost ritualistic, behaviour – and it's by no means confined to eighteen-year-olds. Each year, dyspeptic commentators line up to explain how the ever-rising scores reflect lowered standards and the decline of civilization (largely false), while pin-striped spokespersons solemnly intone that it is all down to hard work and good teaching (mostly, but not entirely, true).

But this year there is one major difference. This is the last year in which those English students lucky enough to get into English universities can think of themselves as being about to expand their minds and their horizons in ways that society believes to be valuable. Those who get their results at this time next year, by contrast, will – we are told – think of themselves as narrowly focused consumers, searching for 'value for money' among different forms of employment-directed training. They will – we are also told – scrutinize the goods on the shelves (aka university courses), calculate the investment yield in terms of the ratio of price to likely future earnings, and complain to a consumer tribunal if the provision of their chosen course deviates in the slightest detail from what was promised in the sales catalogue (sorry, university prospectus). As a result – we are told this *ad nauseam* – future students will be more demanding customers and universities will be more efficient 'providers'.

At least, that's how it will be if you believe the government's recent White Paper on higher education, *Students at the Heart of the System*. These are the terms in which the government justifies taking a largely very successful system of higher education, throwing it up in the air, and hoping that the pieces fall in a pattern that can be regarded as a 'market'. But there is, of course, no reason to believe any of these confident assertions. Other failings aside, they rest on a speculative and pretty unpersuasive view of human psychology, the root presumption being that people only care about anything if they are charged a lot of money for it. Well, it's only natural, isn't it – we'd all love our children more if we had had to pay a conception tax, a birth tax and an annual earnings-related birthday-party surcharge. Wouldn't we?

So let's start from somewhere else. If you think that those who will be celebrating their university entry this time next year are going to get a better education than this year's crop, then you have been conned. The one certain change is that most of them will be saddled with a special additional tax for the greater part of their working lives. A very probable change is that in most universities more of them will be taught by temporary or part-time staff. A highly likely change is that in many universities there will be a reduced range of courses on offer. A possible change is that more students will be attending a for-profit crammer entitled to call itself a university and to channel public money into its dividends.

It's true that if they go to the handful of 'top' universities that will do well out of the new system they may not notice much change, except that a higher proportion of their fellow students will come from comfortable backgrounds. But if they go to the majority of universities, especially those which in the past two decades have been the main vehicles for the great educational enfranchisement of people from social groups that did not previously go to university, then they will see signs of reduced resources all around them. In some cases, their 'student experience' may quite closely resemble their current social experience – boarded-up departments, dilapidated buildings, low morale, a resentful sense that the cards are stacked in favour of the few rather than the many.

Ah, but it's all because of 'the deficit', isn't it, the need to reduce public expenditure? No, it isn't. Whatever view you take of this government's macroeconomic policy, the truth is that the new higher education system will not reduce public expenditure in the short or even the medium term. Indeed, the reason why the White Paper now proposes a more centrally controlled system than obtains at present in terms of determining how many students with particular A-level results universities will be able to take is because the government has belatedly realized that the new fees will otherwise *increase* public expenditure in the short term. In fact, the independent Higher Education Policy Institute, which published its analysis of the proposals this week, thinks the government is still underestimating the cost to the public purse of the new system. The measures are clearly being introduced for political reasons, to install the simulacrum of a market and to make universities serve the economy more directly.

With a brazenness born of ideology, the government claims that charging future students for what they used (largely) to get as of right is 'empowering' them. It represents its proposals as 'putting students at the heart of the system'. But in reality the only system these changes will put students at the heart of is the tax system. (It is ironic that in the same week there is news of the proposal in Germany to take exactly the opposite course and to give students tax rebates for their years of study.) So, by all means rejoice in the success of those who have just learned that they will be going to one of England's (mostly high-quality) universities this autumn, but be aware that a new form of inter-generational injustice is about to take shape. Above all, be aware that if you believe 'competition will drive up quality' in the new system, then you really have been conned – and not just about higher education.

d) Student Protests Are Worthy of Respect
This article was written for the Guardian *in March 2012. Recent student protests against the new system of fees that was to take effect that year had attracted condescending comment from hostile observers, and this piece was a small attempt to get a hearing for a less dismissive view.*

The fact that there is a long tradition of student protest may encourage many commentators to assume that it is not something that needs to be taken too seriously. Far too often the mainstream media condescend to these events by treating them merely as a kind of *rite de passage*, more like Rag Week than serious political activity, suggesting this is just a phase, something the participants will 'grow out of'.

But this disdainful reaction is wrong on several counts. To begin with, the right to peaceful protest when other democratic means have been unavailing is a precious part of our political tradition. The effective replacement of public funding for higher education teaching by greatly increased individual fees was not signalled in any party's election manifesto, and indeed the *abolition* of existing fees was an explicit manifesto commitment of the Lib Dem partners to the coalition. It is hardly surprising, therefore, if many politically aware members of our society feel that they must, collectively, engage in some form of public protest if they are to get their arguments on this issue heard at all.

Secondly, participation in such protests can be a valuable form of political education in its own right, forcing people to examine their beliefs, to articulate and defend their convictions, and to encounter sometimes fierce criticism. When I have accepted invitations to talk to student groups involved in such events, I am always struck by the intellectual seriousness of the majority of those taking part, and by a level of engagement and sophistication that would grace any more conventional academic seminar. Many of those of student age really do want to understand why such a damaging policy is being imposed – and what can, even now, be done about it.

I am less optimistic than they are about effecting political change in the short term, and I do not endorse the tactics espoused by some of the groups who take advantage of these occasions. But I do believe in engaging in public debate with my fellow citizens in an attempt to alter the political weather in the longer term, and peaceful protests are one important and legitimate way of calling attention to matters which the government of the day would prefer to regard as closed.

To represent student protest as just the predictable whingeing of interested parties is a familiar, dismissive tactic, but this clearly misrepresents student (or other) protests against the marketization of higher education. Let's not forget that those taking to the streets today are not protesting on their own behalf: they are not the ones who will be saddled with the £40–50,000 debts, since this only applies to those entering universities from the autumn of this year. And in fact this is not a sectional interest on the part of those currently connected with higher education at all, but something in which our society as a whole has a stake.

However right some people may feel it is for graduates to make a contribution to the costs of higher education above that which they anyway make as taxpayers, the fatal flaw in the new arrangements is their attempt to treat education as a commercial transaction between an individual buyer (the applicant) and an individual seller (one particular university). What will be lost is the conception of a national *system* of higher education as a collective investment in a public good, where each generation bears part of the cost of educating its successor.

And don't be fooled by deficit-mongering. It has been conclusively demonstrated by independent financial analysts that the new fees regime will for the foreseeable future be more expensive than the present system. We can only conclude that, as with some of the parallel changes in the NHS, the government is principally actuated by an ideological belief in the desirability of making all areas of our common life subject to the market mechanism of competition by price (even when, as with the new regulations on university entrance, this actually involves an extension of dirigisme). The forcing through of these now muddled changes risks damaging a university system that has had a worldwide reputation for quality. Those who engage in peaceful protest to draw attention to this fact, even though they themselves have benefited from a more enlightened scheme, deserve our respect not our condescension.

e) BBC The World Tonight: *Higher Education Special*
This short piece was recorded as the introduction to a special edition of Radio 4's The World Tonight, *broadcast on 17 May 2012. (In accordance with BBC protocols, each segment had to be recorded in situ, with accompanying background noises.) The programme focused on the new funding arrangements for universities then coming into effect.*

The government tells us that the priority for universities must be to contribute to economic growth, that students should be treated as customers, and that competition from new for-profit enterprises will 'drive up quality'. But is there a reason to believe any of this? Do those who make such pronouncements really understand what universities do, what they're *for*?

I'm standing outside one of the biggest lecture halls in Anglia Ruskin University in Cambridge, as students mill around doing studenty things. Anglia Ruskin is a good example of Britain's newest universities: before 1992 it was a polytechnic and before that a local technical college. It now has over 30,000 students, two campuses, and courses that range from physics to film-making and from urban planning to English literature. We don't have to assume that, as they go by, these students' heads are only full of the ideas that have been discussed in their most recent lecture: a lot of the time they will also be thinking about the qualification they will get at the end of their course and the kind of job that might prepare them for, and quite right, too – universities have always, by one means or another, helped to prepare people for employment.

But beyond all that, they are experiencing something that people like them only a generation or two ago could not have dreamed of. They are experiencing a university education – something that can't be reduced simply to a direct training for a particular slot in the division of labour. They are being encouraged to question the received view about any given topic, to go beyond the immediate or local perspective, to see unobvious points of contact across ideas or across time or across cultures. The expansion of higher education, especially in the past twenty years, has been an enormous democratic gain in our society. We shouldn't knock it, with silly, ignorant jibes about 'so-called universities' and 'mickey-mouse courses'. These young – and in some cases not-so-young – people rushing past are getting something precious, something that the whole of society benefits from, and it's not something that any government should risk damaging or destroying.

I'm now standing in the main library of Cambridge University – the other university in Cambridge, the one that began a bit earlier. It is from here that one of the most remarkable scholarly projects of modern times is carried on, the edition of the collected letters of Charles Darwin. This project was launched in 1974 and the first volume came out in 1985. Volume 19 appeared this year and there are probably about eleven more to come.

The value of this majestic edition cannot be calculated in terms of contribution to the GDP any more than its so-called 'impact' can be measured by totting up the number of visitors to its excellent website or the number of television programmes made about Darwin. These carefully edited and annotated letters document in unparalleled detail the unfolding of an idea that revolutionized our understanding of the natural world and of our place in it, but they also provide an extraordinarily rich repository of information about the social, intellectual and scientific life of Darwin's time that may be of great value to scholarly enquiries whose existence we cannot even imagine at the moment.

Any adequate conception of universities and what they are for has to be able to embrace both the hurrying students outside the lecture halls of Anglia Ruskin and the patient editorial scholars here in Cambridge University Library.

Models of 'the market' only have limited application in these matters. We need, instead, to think about the benefits society as a whole derives from universities as a whole. These benefits are long-term, indirect and often hard to characterize briefly, but they go beyond employment and they go beyond profit. Needless to say, in practice Britain's universities are not perfect, but taken as a system they are one of the most successful and highly regarded in the world. Please, let's not do them irreparable damage in the name of short-term calculations about 'economic recovery' or ideological delusions about how 'competition always drives up quality'.

f) Two Models of Funding Research in the Humanities
This piece was written in January 2013. In recent years, academics have been under increasingly strong pressure to obtain 'external funding' to support research. Individuals and departments

are, as mentioned earlier, rewarded for obtaining grants from any source that is external to their own university. In the humanities, the research itself often does not require any such additional funds, and attempting to obtain them is always very time-consuming; nonetheless, scholars' lives are now ruled by the imperative to apply for them. This piece was an attempt to draw attention to some of the fallacies inherent in a system that is now virtually unquestioned. It has not previously been published.

Here are two hypothetical examples of mid-career academics, equally talented, equally committed, equally hard working, who are in the same field in the humanities but in different (though comparable) universities. Let's assume, merely for the sake of argument, that they each work forty-eight hours a week; let's also assume that they do this, allowing for holidays and closures, for forty-eight weeks a year; and finally, let's assume that during term time (thirty weeks a year) they have eight hours per week available for research and during vacations they have thirty-two hours per week available for research. That means that in a normal year they each have 816 hours available for research (let's call it 800; the accidents of life are much more likely to reduce the total than to increase it). The plausibility or otherwise of these exact figures is irrelevant for the purposes of this exercise; we simply need a set of numbers that enables comparison between two patterns of sustaining research to be made.

Scholar A's university is very committed to the pursuit of external funding. So in the first year of our exercise, A makes two grant applications. Each one requires approximately thirty hours to prepare and submit. Given the published statistics about the success rate of applicants, it is not altogether surprising, though disappointing, that A is unsuccessful in both applications (and was only able to spend 740 hours on research as a result). In the second year, A attends several seminars put on by her university's research services division about 'grantsmanship'. The research coordinator supported by her department then helps A put together a more 'innovative and ground-breaking' description of her project, and helps identify other possible sources of funding for three fresh applications. (Her department, responding to a directive from the pro-vice-chancellor [research], decided some time ago to convert the part of the departmental budget that used to underwrite sabbatical leave to a 'research fund', out of which come the salary of the research coordinator, a per capita contribution to the research services division, and a small amount to subsidize some teaching remission for someone preparing a big grant application.) The amount of time all this preparation of applications requires has crept up, and in the second year she spends 140 hours on it. (In her second year, therefore, she spent 660 hours on research.)

This time, however, A is successful with one of her applications, and the resulting grant pays for a part-time temporary junior person to do her teaching for one semester while she devotes herself to her research project. So, in her third year she is on grant-funded leave for one semester, calculated as fifteen weeks, with the result that in this year she spends 1,100 hours on research (it should have been slightly higher but the junior replacement needed some guidance about the teaching and anyway couldn't make any administrative contribution, so A's research time was eaten into a little).

During her fourth year, when she is teaching full-time, A is strongly encouraged by her head of department to make an ambitious inter-institutional grant application. She agrees, but then finds that even with the benefit of additional seminars from the research services division and considerable assistance and coaching from the department's research coordinator, the task of initiating, coordinating and submitting the large application across four institutions is very time-consuming indeed, and in this year A spends 180 hours of research time on the application. Again, the statistics are against her: very few of the first-time applications for these large but rare grants are successful. So, in her fourth year, she has spent 620 hours on research.

In her fifth year, her head of department decides that A should be given a 0.2 buyout for one semester to enable her to put more time into improving the big grant application. This means that in one semester two graduate students do a fifth of her teaching load, notionally freeing up ninety-six hours of extra research time. In practice, the graduate students turn out to need a good deal of help and monitoring, reducing the available extra time to seventy-five hours. And in fact the preparation of the new application, especially the coordination with colleagues and administrators in the two other universities and one non-academic institution who are partners in the application, still seems to consume a vast amount of time, in the region of 180 hours, so in the end A has 695 (let's call it 700) hours for research in her fifth year.

But this time she hits the jackpot, so that in her sixth and seventh years she is the Principal Investigator (PI) on a large inter-institutional research grant. The grant pays for her university's share (0.4) of a research associate to help organize and run the project and one PhD studentship; it also pays for A's teaching load to be reduced by half for one semester in the course of the two years of the grant. An enthusiastic paragraph, along with a bad photo of her, appears in the university's newsletter, a publication mostly devoted to congratulating those (nearly all scientists) who obtain substantial external funding. Her head of department also smiles on her and intimates that this will do her promotion prospects no harm at all.

But A discovers that being the PI on such an institutionally complex grant is not a bed of roses. Administratively it is a nightmare, and she also finds that she is in effect a small-scale manager of others' work. Moreover, the terms of the grant require the research to be genuinely collaborative ('the days of the lone scholar are over' her research coordinator tells her), and this turns out to hamper the book she has been trying to write at least as much as it helps it. Notionally, over the two years of the grant, she should have something like 1,840 hours of research time, but in the end she finds she has more like 1,500, making a total over the seven years of around 5,300 hours of research time in all. (At the same time, the department is facing complaints from students about the unsatisfactory nature of the part-time teaching it increasingly relies upon.) Nonetheless, at the end of her seventh year, A – nothing if not a determined, hard-working and resiliently adaptable scholar – has the draft of a new book, plus an edited volume of essays growing out of conferences hosted by the grant – or she will have once a few tardy contributors have submitted their essays. When added to the three articles she completed largely during summer vacations and the article she completed during her earlier semester of leave, this gives her a healthy submission for the next REF, which has been one of her main preoccupations throughout.

Scholar B works under a different regime. The number of hours available to her for research are, in the abstract, the same as for A, but B's university has decided that in the humanities a sabbatical system is a better use of money than endless grant-chasing, and it provides, for staff who have a plausible project and have otherwise pulled their weight in the department, one semester of leave for every three years worked. The ethos in the department is that sabbatical leave is so precious to scholars in the humanities that it is worth taking on a little extra teaching to help cover for a colleague who is on leave in order to benefit from the system in one's turn (this also keeps the quality of the teaching up). B therefore has on average 740 hours of research time in each of her first three years (800 minus the occasional extra seminar load), at which point she decides to save up her leave entitlement until she can take a whole year. She thus has 740 hours of research time per year for six years, and then in her seventh year she has 1,900 hours (it ought to have been 2,300, but despite her and her colleagues' best efforts, other professional and administrative tasks still eat up eight hours a week). This makes a total over the seven years of around 6,300 hours altogether. At the end of this she has the draft of a new book, plus the three articles she published over the previous six years (largely researched and written during the summer vacations), which qualifies her for inclusion in her department's REF submission. Student satisfaction in the department is high, since they are nearly always taught by an established full-time member of staff, but the non-humanities members of the university's central allocations committee are threatening to reduce the department's annual allocation unless it brings in more money from external sources.

A's book, her edited volume, and her four articles are the fruits of 5,300 hours of research time. B's book and three articles are the result of 6,300 hours of research time. It is hard not to believe that there may be some correlation between the quality of these publications and the time devoted to their completion. However, A's department is awarded a higher grade in the REF than B's, partly because it can show that it has a 'vibrant' research culture that encourages collaboration and partnerships with other institutions, a good record of 'grant-capture', and more evidence (as in the collaboration with the non-university institution in A's big grant) of the right kind of 'impact'. This means that A's department is looked upon favourably within the university and the funding available to support grant applications in future is increased. By contrast, powerful voices in the central administration of B's university argue that her department is clearly adhering to an outdated and ineffective model. When its head decides (or is encouraged) to take early retirement, the department loses his teaching post without any corresponding reduction in its student numbers, and the element in its allocation that used to support sabbatical leave is now to be used to put into effect 'robust procedures' for ensuring a record of successful external grant-capture. As B's department starts, over time, to become more like A's, the pro-vice-chancellor (research) congratulates its new head on the marked improvement in the department's record, and it can only be a matter of time before an enthusiastic paragraph, along with a bad photo of one of its members, appears in the university's newsletter.

g) *The University in Global Society*
This piece was written for a panel devoted to the above theme in June 2013. The panel was part of the 'Zamyn Global Forum'

which was held in London to coincide with the G8 summit meeting. The organizers' brief to the speakers emphasized that the audience would include leading political and administrative figures from developing countries in particular, though such figures did not seem to be noticeably present on the day. It has not previously been published.

From the many challenges and opportunities that will face all societies across the globe as higher education expands in both size and importance across the twenty-first century, I shall focus on just one: how are we to develop and maintain intellectual quality?

First and most obviously, you do need resources – I am certainly not denying that. It may be that you do not need to pay your top professors as much as some academic megastars are paid in some systems, and certainly that you do not need to pay your senior administrators as much as they are paid in many systems. It is also true that you do not need to lavish funds on amenities for students, in terms of accommodation, sports programmes, social facilities and so on, as some systems do at present. In these ways, some of the money might be better spent, but founding and running something that aims to be a good university still takes substantial resources. Money alone, however, will not build you a good university.

When establishing or expanding a higher education system, it is relatively easy to produce mediocre universities. You put in the resources, whether public or private, build buildings, appoint staff, recruit students, and you monitor and assess and report and so on. As a result you may get an institution that makes some contribution to the local economy and that helps some students into more remunerative forms of employment, and these are not negligible outcomes. But you will not get what is distinctive about universities, especially good universities: that extension and deepening of human understanding that comes from pursuing open-ended enquiry at the highest level. Instead, you will get what could be got more economically and directly from the laboratories of commercial corporations and from apprenticeship and other training schemes. If this happens on a wide scale, it will perpetuate a situation in which a very small number of so-called 'first world' universities will produce the work that ultimately determines the agenda of teaching, scholarship and research throughout the world. Genuinely flourishing local universities are one way to escape this undesirable cycle of cultural dependency.

The fact is that processes and institutions that will enable you to produce competent lab technicians will not serve to produce creatively original scientists. With relatively modest funds and sufficient political will you may be able to create effective community colleges, technical institutes, normal schools, and these are certainly worth having. But to create or maintain an institution that is more than a mediocre third-rate university, you need at least two other main things in addition to material resources, things that are more intangible and elusive.

First, you need a public discourse in your society that is conceptually adequate to the task of characterizing and justifying the core university mission of open-ended enquiry, and you need to find ways to make this discourse effective in public debate. At present, in many societies, such a discourse does not exist or is only weakly articulated. One reason I wrote my book, *What Are Universities For?*, is that in recent years the language used in policy-making circles and in media discussion of higher education has been increasingly impoverished by an exclusive concentration on promoting economic growth. I do not pretend it is an easy task to characterize accurately, and to give effective force to, the real long-term purposes of universities, but if you try to develop or expand universities without such a vocabulary being elaborated and made effective alongside them, then short-term instrumental social pressures will ensure that you simply end up with mediocre technical institutes.

The second thing you must have – even more nebulous but nonetheless vital – is a certain kind of ethos or morale among academic staff. The type of intellectual work required for good teaching, scholarship and research cannot be done by alienated labour. You cannot compel creativity or originality, no matter how thorough your system of surveillance. The lesson we should learn from activities as different as artistic creation or high-tech innovation is that you need the individuals concerned to have a high degree of autonomy. A sense of commitment to the values of scholarship and science and a sense of cooperation are far more valuable in encouraging the right kind of teaching, scholarship and research than is competition for financial rewards or fear of reprimand or dismissal. One of the challenges facing all societies in the twenty-first century is that the legitimate democratic concern with accountability constantly threatens to restrict and damage the necessary level of professional autonomy. It is a hard truth for legislators and administrators to accept that what, ultimately, determines the quality of a university is the quality of the thinking done by its academic staff, and that *that* is not something that legislators and administrators can control, though they can certainly constrain it.

It takes a long time to build up quality and to root it deeply in the ethos and processes of an institution. It takes a relatively short time to damage or even destroy it. The perspectives of politics are very short term: they are principally concerned with image-control and crisis-management, and they are largely shaped by immediate electoral objectives. The perspectives of universities are very long term: they are principally concerned with extending and deepening human understanding, and they are very little shaped by immediate practical purposes. In these terms, universities and their host societies are always on a potential collision course, and a society gets the greatest value from universities by maintaining this tension, not letting one perspective utterly eliminate the other.

Some of you may be in positions of power or influence in your own societies; all of you are in a position to influence those with the relevant power. I therefore urge you to reflect on the difficult and teasing question 'What are universities for?': to accept that only by leaving the academics in your universities free to determine the character of research and teaching will you get the kind of research and teaching that is not mechanical and second-rate; to acknowledge that the long-term value of universities to their host societies is not best served by trying to harness them directly to short-term economic impact; and to recognise, with appropriate humility, how much easier it is to damage or destroy good universities than it is to create or sustain them.

h) An Open Letter to Liam Byrne

This piece was written in December 2013. One of the frustrations of the years in which the Tory-led coalition held office from May 2010 was that the Labour opposition was practically silent on the question of higher education. Late in 2013, Liam Byrne MP became the opposition spokesman on universities and he soon made a speech in which he set out the beginnings of an alternative policy. This 'open letter' was written to encourage the formulation of such an alternative. It was, in the end, not sent and it has not previously been published.

Dear Mr Byrne

For the past three years the future of higher education in this country has been the subject of unprecedented discussion and controversy. We now have a funding system that many people consider damaging, unsustainable and unjust. The ill-thought-out policies hastily introduced by the coalition in 2010 are visibly unravelling as ministers desperately seek to limit the harm caused by their own market free-for-all. Yet the Labour Party has for the most part been oddly silent on the whole topic.

I was therefore pleased to see that in your first interview since taking up the post of shadow universities, science and skills minister you signalled Labour's intention to introduce a better system, saying 'our long-term goal must be to move towards a graduate tax'. And I was also pleased that in your first major speech in the role, given at the IPPR on Monday, you used the occasion of the fiftieth anniversary of Harold Wilson's famous 'white heat of technology' speech to emphasize the importance of a long-term framework for science and research funding, and the need for governments to respect the 'Haldane principle' of leaving universities free to determine the nature and direction of their research.

These are encouraging signs. But they don't yet look like a thought-through and coherent policy, even though this is a topic on which Labour could attract widespread public support. So let me make a few suggestions about what such a policy might involve. These can only be very sketchy at this stage: they all need to be argued for and many details need to be worked out, but here are a few principles on which a future government could base a better approach.

Universities are not businesses and students are not customers. If it is not possible to finance universities out of general taxation, then the funding must involve, and be seen to involve, a partnership between the public and the individual graduate. You should therefore restore an element of public funding for the teaching of those subjects from which it was removed in 2010. This is not expensive, but it is hugely important symbolically as well as practically. And you should change the nature of the individual's contribution, too. The principle of income-contingent loans is not a bad one: students do not pay, graduates do, and they only make an additional contribution to the costs of higher education when they are earning above a certain amount and then in proportion to their earnings.

But the crucial principle here is that this is a contribution to the costs of the higher education system from which they, like everyone else, have benefited. It is not a price paid to an individual university for being sold a product. Therefore, the loan repayment must be made to the system as a whole, as each generation helps meet the costs of educating its successors. There are various ways of doing this (a graduate tax, a graduate endowment and so on), but the key thing is to get away from the misleading fiction of seeing the loan as meeting the 'price' charged by a particular supplier to an individual customer.

It is right that any system of such loans should contain an

element of public subsidy, not least to cover the loans which can never be repaid in full. But it is not right that this subsidy should go to swell the profits of 'private providers'. The opening up of the so-called 'higher education market' to such for-profit companies since 2010, allowing them to access the loan system, has proved very expensive – and you should make clear that public funds are to be exclusively used to support a public system.

I realize that the issue of science and research may not seem like a vote-winner, but as you acknowledged in your speech yesterday it is in fact crucial to the kind of society we hope to have in the future. There are two key principles here. The first is stability of funding. Even if you don't feel able to increase the present allocation in real terms, it is very important to ring-fence the research budget to enable institutions and research teams to plan sensibly. The second is to maintain the dual-support system, whereby part of the funding is allocated as a grant to each university and part is allocated by research councils for individual projects. This system has served Britain well, and any move to distribute the research budget entirely through the research councils would risk undermining the human and physical infrastructure on which a flourishing research culture depends. I would hope that you would also want to scrap the Research Excellence Framework, the expensive and distorting system now used to determine the distribution of universities' share of the research funding. But a commitment at least to review it might, I recognize, be the more prudent course, and one that would be very welcome.

Finally, this year also sees the fiftieth anniversary of the Robbins Report, which gave such a vital push to the expansion and partial democratization of our higher education system in the 1960s and 1970s. One of that celebrated report's recommendations – in response to what it described as 'the most important and the most difficult of all the problems we have had to consider' – was not acted upon then, but perhaps the time has come to revive and update it. Considering 'what machinery of government is appropriate for a national system of higher education in this country', Robbins proposed that a new ministry of arts and sciences was needed.

At present, universities and science fall under the remit of the Department of Business, an awkward arrangement that suits no one. (The lumping of culture together with media and sport in another department is almost as unfortunate.) But there would be a natural affinity among the activities covered by a Department of Culture, Science and Universities. They are all activities that can only be properly supported on an 'arm's length' basis. They have a common interest in and suitability for external philanthropy. And they are all by their nature committed to long-term perspectives.

You yourself said in your *Times Higher Education* interview: 'There's a wider game here, and that's why I think universities will be an election issue.' I'm glad to hear you say that and I hope you're right. But, even more, I hope the Labour Party will set out principles that will enable Britain's universities to fulfil their proper purposes in the decades to come.

> With best wishes,
> Stefan Collini

i) Knowledge Institutions Under Pressure
A longer version of this article was delivered at a conference held at the Institut für die Wissenschaften vom Menschen in Vienna in April 2014. The conference brought together representatives from several different countries to discuss the various kinds of 'pressure' that 'knowledge institutions' are now seen to be experiencing. This shortened version of the paper was published in IWMpost, *the magazine of the Institut.*

Any attempt to understand the main ways in which the institution of the university may be said to be 'under pressure' throughout the developed world necessarily entails reflection on the long history of relations between universities and their host societies. We should not allow ourselves to be panicked into assuming that the pressures perceived to bear on universities now are entirely new or entirely bad. Many of the changes that have taken place in universities and their position in society in the past few decades have been expressions of a broader process of democratization and expansion which I believe we should welcome, and therefore we should not characterize all recent changes as loss or see the contemporary university as in sad decline from some presumed golden age. Nonetheless, there are some pressures that have taken particularly powerful forms in the present, and I shall focus on these as well as, briefly, on what might be done to mitigate some of the threatened damage.

One of the deep characteristics of individualist market democracies is that the combination of a reductive economism in public policy and an ostensible egalitarianism in public debate in effect cloaks a kind of practical relativism. Only those goals which follow from the aggregation of expressed wants then have legitimacy, something that necessarily favours the quantitative and the instrumental. The chief consequences of this as far as universities are concerned include a damaging short-termism, an emphasis on measurable forms of accountability, and a loss of both trust and autonomy. And these consequences shape, in their turn, the regimes of funding, assessment and governance under which universities increasingly labour.

This situation is not altogether new, but it is now underwritten by an increasingly aggressive form of economistic reasoning that is dominant in policy and media circles. This makes it ever more difficult to find effective ways to legitimate the values of education and scholarship in non-reductive terms in contemporary public debate. All I can do here is gesture towards some of the obvious ways of attempting to respond to this situation.

The first is to focus attention on the unexamined premises of the goal of economic 'growth' itself. What is it good for, how much do we need, who are 'we' in this case and so on? By raising questions about the human purposes economic prosperity is meant to serve, we open a small window through which discussion of other human values can be let in, including the values which the university exists to promote.

A second no less general response is to insist that many of the matters of greatest importance cannot be *measured* but must be *judged*. In making this case, it is important to be clear that judgement is not simply a matter of subjective opinion: if it were, we would immediately be back with the implicit relativism of aggregate expressed preferences. Judgements depend on reasons and some reasons can be better than others. In this respect, making an adequate case for universities will draw upon some of the very capacities that universities exist to develop.

A third, equally general, strategy is to identify and build upon the ways in which ordinary citizens, in their daily lives, do implicitly endorse values other than the prevailing economism. In a range of ways, from hopes for their children to concern for the environment, and from everyday curiosity to thwarted yearnings, most people do practically entertain values that are consonant with those which, ultimately, universities depend on and try to foster. It is important to keep trying to engage such values in addressing publics that go beyond policy and media circles.

Finally, let me suggest three more specific tactics which may be particularly relevant to debate *within* universities. The first is not to allow the running of these institutions to be entirely handed over to the cadre of professional managers that has grown so powerful in the last couple of decades in particular. This means that senior academics have to be willing to take their turn at these administrative tasks and to embody the self-governing ideals of collegiality rather than accepting the definition of a career purely in terms of so-called 'research achievement'.

The second is to try to make clear, in the face of much contemporary disparagement, that scholarly disciplines are the indispensable foundations of any broader or so-called 'interdisciplinary' enterprises, and that, institutionally speaking, academic departments are the units best placed to make sure these disciplines prosper from generation to generation. Disciplines are, of course, contingent and time-bound creations, not timeless essences, but in many cases they have taken their current forms for good intellectual as well as historical reasons. Thematic clusters and problem-focused programmes have their place, but by and large they have the effect of empowering managers, and the managers' control of funding, at the expense of the long-term support of disciplines and appointments sustained in the little republics that are university departments.

Third, we need constantly to make the case for scholarship and the scholarly career alongside 'research'. The latter is often construed on a scientific model as being limited to the discovery of 'new findings'; it is inherently project-focused and not intimately related to the accumulated intellectual capital that is a scholarly career. We need to emphasize the distorting effect which a regime of constant competition for external funding can have by comparison to the long-term benefits in terms of fruitful reading and thinking which the system of tenure and sabbatical leave encourages. A career is something built by a person, a scholar; it is not simply a sequence of funded projects, and a profession is not in good health when the main index of individual success comes to consist of the amount of time a scholar is away from their home institution.

I'm well aware that these are all ambitious and even idealistic prescriptions, and I'm not in fact such a wild optimist as to believe that they will always or mostly be successful. But if people like us don't try to make this case, then we shall bear some of the responsibility for diminishing the value of the academic institutions from which we have benefited and which we have a duty to hand on to future generations.

j) Dissidence and Persuasion: Arguing About Universities
This short text was the opening speech at a conference on 'Dissidence' organized by postgraduate students at University College, London, in June 2015. It has not previously been published.

Since the overall theme of today's event is 'dissidence', I want
to begin by dissenting, and I am going to dissent from some of
the established connotations of the term 'dissidence' itself. We
commonly understand 'dissidence' to indicate some departure
from, resistance to, or criticism of a set of prevailing norms or
discourses or practices, but in so doing it becomes fatally easy
to endow 'dissidence' with a kind of glamour. We come to feel
that there is something exciting about dissidence, something lib-
erating or at least independent-minded. There can be a glamour
attached to the fact of being 'oppositional' – another similarly
valorized term – of being against, or different from, whatever
are the established powers or the established practices. But we
also need to recognize that there is, potentially, a fatal circularity
and therefore emptiness about all this. You are against whatever
is currently dominant, and that's what makes you dissident, but
what happens when the current norms change? If you used to
be against A and therefore in favour of B, what is your position
when B triumphs? I say that this risks a fatal emptiness because
it suggests that what is really being valued here is some stance
of being anti – no matter what it is that one is opposed to. It
is rather like the self-described contrarian who congratulates
herself that she is never taken in by the dominant consensus but
always takes the contrary view. Ultimately, this entails having no
positive convictions because one always has to oppose whatever
positive convictions other people hold.

But we don't have to fall into these logical traps. We can think
of dissidence as a form of rational opposition to or critique of
a *particular* set of views or practices, a critique that is informed
by positive values of its own. What is then valued is not the
mere stance of being against things, no matter what they are,
but that of seeing a dominant discourse from outside it, challenging a powerful set of values in the name of other values.
Immediately, in relation to this more useful sense of 'dissidence',
the question arises as to what goal or purpose is served by the
expression of these alternative views. I am going to suggest that,
at some level, the expression of such views has to be seen as an

attempt at persuasion. Of course, we may sometimes feel that the dissident voice is not really trying to persuade but simply to bear witness, to signal the existence of another perspective. Or, we might hold some version of the purist position held by certain avant-garde poets and often attributed to critical theorists such as Adorno – namely, that to succeed in communicating with a corrupt society is to be collusive with that corruption. If what one says is easily intelligible to a public whose understanding has been corrupted by the power of bourgeois norms or other conventional ideas, then that, according to this position, is a sign that one's own thinking has been penetrated by the poison of the dominant discourse. Only by taking the extreme position of remaining unintelligible to that discourse can one proclaim one's real independence, one's real dissidence. On this model, the dissidence has to extend to the manner of expression as well: a certain rebarbativeness creates an obstacle or arrest in the process of comprehension, and thus enacts the critique of the norms that sustain easy everyday communication within that corrupt world.

One can see, of course, a kind of heroic intransigence in this position, a grand gesture of refusal, but actually I think even this purist approach is an attempt at a form of persuasion. Sometimes it is an appeal beyond the present generation to the future, on the model of the message put in a bottle and thrown overboard, but more often it is an appeal addressed to the select few, those who can hear the message and thus be led to share the critique. Persuasion is not a unitary or comprehensive activity, but at some level or other critique always involves an attempt to win assent from somebody or other. In so far as it succeeds, it involves that puzzling process of 'recognition' that will be familiar from the practice of literary criticism. Critics point to features of a literary work, inviting us to see them as they see them, and embedding them within a larger description of the context in question – the text it comes from, the habitual literary dispositions of its author, the resonances of the language at that particular time and so on, until we, too, recognize the feature in question in the same terms. And of course in doing so, critics make use of a vast, diverse and rich everyday vocabulary. That is, literary criticism of the traditional kind does not for the most part work with a specialized technical vocabulary, but deploys the almost infinite distinctions embedded in everyday language, in the course of which process other users of that language come not just to acknowledge the description, but actually to recognize a particular piece of writing in the terms the critic proposes, to *recognize* it as, say, ironic or moving or mannered.

Now, it seems to me that a similar logic is operative in certain forms of social or cultural criticism. When writing about a literary text, for example, critics rely on our having only half noticed certain features of it, or having partly registered some awareness of such features but without being fully cognizant that we have done so, and one of their prime techniques of persuasion is then quotation, in which we are confronted with a passage we have read but not fully understood or appreciated. The accompanying commentary then provides telling examples of what Wittgenstein called 'fictions', that is, those re-descriptions or contexts which enable us to see or read something as an example of this rather than that – what Wittgenstein famously called 'seeing as'.

But how does this work when the critic is writing about society more generally, when there is not a text to which critic and reader might have common recourse? Well, one part of the answer is that critics do treat societies as though they were, in the fashionable idiom, 'texts', meaningful arrangements of symbols that require to be interpreted. But here the 'fictions' with which the critic surrounds any contested episode or expression are inescapably historical: they are about the specificity of some feature of the present which is, explicitly or, more often, implicitly, set in a story of historical change involving assumptions about what things used to be like or the way they are going. And this is where the link between persuasiveness and recognition becomes particularly fraught or problematic. The experience of historical change is always in part an experience of the loss or destruction of the familiar. The activity of cultural criticism is always in part an appeal to the familiar, set within an implicit narrative of change, and it is *criticism* precisely because it is identifying something defective or inadequate in the present. A declinist logic is not, strictly speaking, entailed by this conjunction: in principle, we could always tell a historical story of how what is at fault in the present was even worse in the past. In my view, such narratives of improvement are often a good deal nearer the truth than the declinist alternative, but it is undeniable that it can be more difficult to give such progressive stories the same persuasive force as laments about how the world is going to hell in a hand-basket. And here is where the characteristic idiom or register of the literary critic can be particularly culpable. The critic is, after all, often figured as the guardian of intensity, of a fuller awareness, and so those who cannot see are convicted of superficiality or inattentiveness. The object of criticism appears to be a poor or inadequate example of the real thing, and in so far as we can recognize what the real thing is, its very familiarity tends to locate it in the past. The pitfalls here are obvious.

In the rest of the conference we shall try to explore how those of us who are critical of – and in that sense dissident from – the recent direction taken by higher education policy in this country and the arguments used to justify it might frame our criticisms. Objecting to misguided measures, even mocking or denouncing them, can certainly be a legitimate part of our response, but ultimately we have to try to bring others to 'see' the ways in which such measures are misguided. Dramatic gestures and glamorous despair, though they have their pleasures, are not adequate responses. In my view, we cannot escape the obligation to try to persuade.

k) Students Deserve Better Than This Consumerist Fallacy
This article was written for the Guardian *in August 2015. It was prompted by recent coverage of four news items: first, the announcement that tuition fees would rise in line with inflation; second, that maintenance grants for students would be abolished and replaced by loans; third, that the earnings threshold at which*

loans start to be repayable would be frozen at its present level; and fourth, the calculation that tuition fees alone would soon be reaching £10,000 a year.

The announcement by George Osborne that university fees are to be allowed to rise in line with inflation (at institutions that show evidence of 'good teaching') has been swiftly followed by reports that within a few years fee levels will have risen to £10,000. This comes on the back of plans to abolish maintenance grants and to freeze the earnings threshold at which loans start to become repayable. These stories then produce a flurry of predictable responses. The government says that its scheme drives up quality, ensuring students will get value for money. The organizations representing vice-chancellors emphasize that they must increase fees to stay competitive in the global market blah blah. Charities and think-tanks say that the changes will discourage those from disadvantaged backgrounds from applying to university blah blah.

All these responses miss the larger point. Once the current system was introduced (it was announced in 2010 and took effect from 2012), it ought to have been obvious, first, that fees would rise, and, second, that the terms of the loans would be changed. If you begin with the mistaken premise that it's a market, then prices will vary to reflect what, as economists say, the market will bear. The price of high-status positional goods will rise a lot; the price of low-status mass offerings will rise much less or may even fall somewhat (and so may their quality). At the same time, the government gave itself the power to vary the terms of the loans retrospectively, not just for future borrowers; the proposal not to uprate the earnings threshold at which repayments start to kick in is just one small step in this direction, with even more punitive changes likely to follow. There should be no mock outrage or astonishment at the calculation that a £10,000 fee will soon be the new normal, or that the level of individual debt will soon routinely exceed £50,000. Such developments were built in from the start. These relatively small fluctuations in the figures are not the story: it is the market dogma driving the fees system as a whole that is at fault.

When the Tories, with their coalition partners meekly in train, largely removed public funding for undergraduate education and replaced it with a system of fees supported by income-contingent loans, they were driven by two main aims. The first was that this move looked as though it could help to reduce public expenditure in the short term. Public support by way of direct grants to universities shows up in the accounts as an item of government expenditure. Loans to students, by contrast, figure as an asset. Even though future governments may in practice end up paying out as much (or even more) to provide the loans as they previously had for direct funding, the change registers, purely in accounting terms, as a reduction in public expenditure.

The other main aim was ideological. The Tories were determined to find a way to apply 'market discipline' to universities. They have tended to regard universities (quite mistakenly) as a kind of inefficient nationalized industry. Free market dogma says that if you make such institutions 'compete on price', this will lead to higher standards and lower costs, because that's what market competition always does – as in the case of, erm, the railways or energy suppliers. The policy explicitly encourages students to act as the executors of this new market discipline, demanding value for money and thus forcing sluggish or self-interested academics to raise their game. (I have to assume readers will hear the vacuity of these clichés without my putting inverted commas round every cant phrase.)

I have never taken the view that fees would, of themselves, significantly diminish the number of applications in the medium term: there are deep societal pressures driving ever-increasing numbers of school leavers (and others) towards higher education, and the pattern of growth in participation across the developed world is too strong and too uniform to be permanently derailed. The prospect of taking on what looks like a large debt may have some deterrent effect on students from poorer backgrounds, just as the current system seems already to have deterred many potential mature students. Even so, the issue here is not really about overall numbers but about the further entrenching of class privilege in education by driving the children of the less well-off into institutions that charge less (and perhaps provide less), while increasing the concentration of children from already advantaged backgrounds in those universities that then most augment their advantages in later life.

But even that, bad as it is, does not constitute, in my view, the main defect of the current system. The fundamental conceptual mistake of this system is to treat education as a 'product' that an individual 'consumer' purchases from an individual 'provider'. It is not hard to see how these assumptions can lead to lines of students standing at the tills arguing for their consumer right to a higher grade of degree ('I've paid good money, I'm entitled to a good degree'). And it is not hard to see how universities are thereby encouraged to market themselves and to prioritize getting good scores for student 'satisfaction' rather than providing a rigorous but exacting education.

Since 2012 it has looked as though the topic of higher education funding had fallen off the mainstream political agenda. The coalition had every reason to keep it out of the news, while Labour was sadly quiet on the issue – Ed Miliband's suggestion that he would reduce fees from £9,000 to £6,000 smacked of desperate electoral manoeuvring without really addressing the problem. Now, however, the current Labour leadership candidates are having to declare their hand, prompted perhaps by Jeremy Corbyn's announcement that he would abolish the current fees, so it is a particularly important moment at which to focus on the possibilities.

Ours is an enormously wealthy country, one of the richest history has ever seen. We can easily afford to support a high-quality system of public higher education if we choose to. The ideology of 'austerity', which obscures this truth, is a con-trick to bully us into replacing collective provision with commercial competition and thereby to shrink the state. But even if it is felt that there is not sufficient political will to return to a proper system of public funding, that does not mean that the present fee regime is the only conceivable possibility.

There are two essential truths to hold onto in thinking about an alternative. First, the provision of education is part of an intergenerational contract. Society as a whole benefits from the investment by previous generations, and society as a whole, represented by those who have the means, should contribute to maintaining such benefits for future generations. We need to recognize that it is a fiction to treat a tuition fee as though it paid the actual costs of that student's education; those costs have been incurred by the institution, indeed by the world of learning as a whole, long in the past.

Second, we have a national system of higher education: the aim must be to finance the system, not to pretend that universities are rival companies where one obtains a market advantage at the expense of its competitors. Vice-chancellors at the more prestigious universities may try to deny this truth, since they believe their institution will benefit from a free-for-all, just as they tend to be in favour of differential fees which the student pays directly to the university. But whether we are thinking of support for small subjects or of rewarding those institutions which provide more opportunities for students from the least-advantaged backgrounds, it is obvious that there needs to be some central academic oversight of the system as a whole. The funding arrangements should be designed to support such a cooperative endeavour, not to undermine it as the present system does.

Expecting graduates to make an enhanced contribution to the costs of educating their successors may have an intuitive appeal, and if it does, then there is every reason to make these contributions income-contingent. But because the present system treats the fee as the price an individual provider charges to an individual customer, the current loans compound the consumerist fallacy. If we have to fund higher education by some means other than a properly progressive form of general taxation, then some version of a graduate endowment or graduate tax or an equivalent of National Insurance contributions would be less damaging.

Of course, we shall be told that there are all sorts of practical drawbacks to any such proposals. Yes, there are, and the details would need to be worked out. But these can only be made to seem like devastating objections if we assume that the present system is working well and is itself proof against even more fundamental objections. But it's not. We now have a bad system that is unfair, distorting of educational priorities, and potentially very expensive. Above all, it is a system that threatens to replace the best features of long-term scholarship and willingness to learn with the worst features of profit-hungry companies pandering to the desires of value-for-money-seeking consumers. Our society benefited from having a better system in the past; we owe it to future generations not to saddle them with a worse system for the future.

Notes

1. What's Happening to Universities?

p. 15 'more like businesses'. Simon Marginson and Mark Considine, *The Enterprise University: Power, Governance and Reinvention in Australia* (Cambridge: Cambridge University Press, 2000), p. 61.

p. 16 'wealth or commodities'. Quoted in Nicholas Phillipson (ed.), *Universities, Society and the Future* (Edinburgh: Edinburgh University Press, 1983), pp. 125–6.

p. 16 'and commercial pursuits'. Quoted in E.W. Vincent and P. Hinton, *The University of Birmingham: Its History and Significance* (Birmingham: University of Birmingham, 1947), pp. 20–1.

p. 17 'bearing on industry'. Quoted in Michael Sanderson, *The Universities and British Industry 1850–1970* (London: Routledge, 1972), p. 307.

p. 19 'new map of learning'. David Daiches (ed.), *The Idea of a New University: An Experiment in Sussex* (London: André Deutsch, 1964), Ch. 4.

p. 26 'indirect and long term'. See, e.g., Stefan Collini, *What Are Universities For?* (London: Penguin, 2012), Ch. 9, 'Impact'.

p. 28 'other national systems'. Howard Hotson, 'Don't Look to the Ivy League', *London Review of Books*, 19 May 2011.

p. 28 'an implausible conclusion'. *Education at a Glance 2013: OECD Indicators* (OECD Publishing, 2014), p. 199, chart B3, 2b.

p. 29 '$450,000 per year.' Benjamin Kunkel, 'Paupers and Richlings', *London Review of Books*, 3 July 2014.

p. 29 'trustees in the second'. 'The Summers Also Sets', *The Economist*, 23 February 2006; 'Ousted Head of University is Reinstated in Virginia', *New York Times*, 26 June 2012.

p. 29 'core of scholarly quality.' Thomas Bender, 'Politics, Intellect, and the American University 1945–1995', *Daedalus*, 126 (1997).

p. 31 'others before that'. Richard Hofstadter, *Anti-Intellectualism in American Life* (New York: Knopf, 1962); Thorstein Veblen, *The Higher Learning in America: A Memorandum on the Conduct of Universities by Businessmen* (New York: Huebsch, 1918).

2. Measuring Up

p. 38 'with an opinion'. Peter Wilby, 'The OECD's Pisa Delivery Man: Andreas Schleicher', *Guardian*, 26 November 2013.

p. 38 'low social trust'. Jerry Z. Muller, 'The Costs of Accountability', *The American Interest*, 11 (3 August 2015).

p. 38 'intended to monitor'. Donald T. Campbell, 'Assessing the Impact of Planned Social Change', *Evaluation and Program Planning*, 2, issue 1 (1979), pp. 67–90 (p. 85).

p. 38 'a good measure'. Marilyn Strathern, '"Improving Ratings": Audit in the British University System', *European Review*, 5 (1997), p. 308.

p. 39 'reference to universities'. Helen Small, 'Fully Accountable', *New Literary History*, 44 (2013), pp. 539–60.

p. 41 'living by the world'. Michael Dobson, quoted in 'Impact Refreshes Parts Sector Ought to Reach', *Times Higher Education*, 22 March 2012.

p. 42 'some years ago'. Bill Readings, *The University in Ruins* (Cambridge, MA: Harvard University Press, 1997).

p. 44 'persons in the society'. Quoted in Phillipson (ed.), *Universities, Society and the Future*, p. 261.

p. 49 'themselves as problematic'. Marginson and Considine, *The Enterprise University*, p. 136.

p. 49 'this exercise before'. Collini, *What Are Universities For?*, Ch. 9, 'Impact'.

p. 55 '"top fifty" and so on'. See the readable summary by Malcolm Gladwell, 'The Order of Things: What College Rankings Really Tell Us', *The New Yorker*, 14 February 2011.

p. 58 'to worldly wisdom'. Veblen, *Higher Learning in America*, p. 157.

3. Reading the Ruins

p. 62 'and mechanical development'. F.R. Leavis, *Education and the University: A Sketch for an 'English School'* (London: Chatto, 1943), p. 16.

p. 63 'nineteenth-century Oxford'. The first edition of the book we have come to know as John Henry Newman's *The Idea of a University* was published in 1852; for full details, see Collini, *What Are Universities For?*, Ch. 3.

p. 64 '"Robbins Report" of 1963'. Full details of each of the books discussed here are as follows: Thorstein Veblen, *The Higher Learning in America: A Memorandum on the Conduct of Universities by Businessmen* (New York: Huebsch, 1918); Abraham Flexner, *Universities: American, English, German* (Oxford: Oxford University Press, 1930); 'Bruce Truscot' [E.A. Peers], *Redbrick University* (London: Faber, 1943); F.R. Leavis, *Education and the University: A Sketch for an 'English School'* (London: Chatto, 1943); Walter Moberly, *The Crisis in the University* (London: Macmillan, 1951); Jaroslav Pelikan, *The Idea of the University: A Re-examination* (New Haven: Yale University Press, 1992); Bill Readings, *The University in Ruins* (Cambridge, MA: Harvard University Press, 1997); Duke Maskell and Ian Robinson, *The New Idea of a University* (London: Haven Books, 2001); Gordon Graham, *Universities: The Recovery of an Idea* (Exeter: Imprint Academic, 2002); R.S. Crane, *The Idea of the Humanities and Other Essays, Critical and Historical* (Chicago: Chicago University Press, 1967); J.H. Plumb, *Crisis in the Humanities* (Harmondsworth: Penguin, 1964); Martha Nussbaum, *Not For Profit: Why Democracy Needs the Humanities* (Princeton: Princeton University Press, 2010); Helen Small, *The Value of the Humanities* (Oxford: Oxford University Press, 2013); *General Education: The Forgotten Goals* (The 'Harvard Red Book', 1945); *Report of the Committee appointed by the Prime Minister under the Chairmanship of Lord Robbins* ('The Robbins Report'; HMSO, 1963).

p. 65–6 'standard units of time' ... 'and good nature'. Veblen, *The Higher Learning in America*, pp. 18–19, 61, 187.

p. 66 'No scholar or scientist' ... 'in the academic body'. Ibid., pp. 63, 101–2, 176.

p. 67 'believed to serve'. Ibid., p. 112.

p. 67 'and "carry on"'. Flexner, *Universities: American, English, German*, p. 6.

p. 68 'The graduate school' ... 'entitled to enjoy'. Ibid., pp. 73, 124, 180, 208.

p. 69 'as simply "scandalous"' ... 'And this at Harvard!' Ibid., pp. 147, 150, 172.

p. 69 'Neither the faculty' ... 'has as yet created'. Ibid., pp. 318, 326.

p. 70 'a popular appeal'. Harold Silver, *Higher Education and Opinion-Making in Twentieth-Century England* (London: Frank Cass, 2003), p. 57.

p. 71 'the search after knowledge' ... 'putting research first'. Truscot, *Redbrick University*, pp. 47, 55.

p. 71 'remain to pray'. Ibid., p. 185.

p. 73 'In the fulfilment' ... 'or the MCC'. Moberly, *The Crisis in the University*, pp. 19, 230.

p. 73–4 'There is always the danger' ... 'treason of the intellectuals'. Ibid., pp. 239, 194, 93 and, e.g., 119, 269.

p. 74 'about university education'. Robert Anderson, in Phillipson (ed.), *Universities, Society, and the Future*, p. 164.

p. 80 'the early nineteenth century'. See Asa Briggs, 'Oxford and its Critics, 1800–1835', in M.G. Brock and M.C. Curthoys (eds.), *The History of the University of Oxford, Vol VI: Nineteenth-Century Oxford* (Oxford: Oxford University Press, 1997), part 1, pp. 134–45.

p. 81 'a people mirrors itself'. R.B. Haldane, *Universities and National Life: Four Addresses to Students* (London: John Murray, 1911), p. 29.

p. 83 'responsible for that policy'. See the discussion in Stefan Collini, *Matthew Arnold: A Critical Portrait* (Oxford: Oxford University Press: 1994), pp. 72–3.

4. From Robbins to McKinsey

p. 92 'and social mobility'. 'Supporting analysis for the Higher Education White Paper', BIS Economics Paper no. 14, June 2011, p. v; *Higher Education: Students at the Heart of the System*, White Paper, June 2011; both available at gov.uk.

p. 92 'to support delivery'. 'Supporting analysis', p. 115.

p. 93 'be socially optimal'. Ibid., p. 94.

p. 93 'all pulling together'. 'Tera Allas Takes up Post as Director General for Economics, Strategy and Better Regulation', BIS Announcement, 4 January 2011, at gov.uk.

p. 96 'learning and the arts'. 'The Robbins Report', p. 251.

p. 97 'its main recommendations'. See Collini, *What Are Universities For?*, Ch. 10: 'Browne's Gamble'.

p. 101 'universities and colleges'. *Higher Education: Students at the Heart of the System*, p. 67.

pp. 102–4 'wishes to take them' … 'healthy mix of subjects'. Ibid., pp. 50, 20, 21.

pp. 105 'student choice meaningful' … 'seamless customer experience'. Ibid., pp. 5, 6, 32.

pp. 106, 108 'education they want'… 'experience that they offer'. Ibid., pp. 45, 29.

pp. 109, 112 'student's university experience' … 'money to the taxpayer'. Ibid., pp. 25, 18, 23.

p. 112 'conform to their will'. Stuart Maclure, 'A Nudge Towards the Market-place', *Policy Studies*, 9 (1989), pp. 11–18.

p. 113 'protect students and taxpayers'. *Higher Education: Students at the Heart of the System*, p. 66.

p. 114 'change of status'. Ibid., p. 53.

p. 114 'fitted well with KPMG's'. Ibid., p. 63.

p. 115 'universities in England'. Ibid., p. 44.

p. 115 'who wish to do so'. Ibid., pp. 7 and 49.

p. 116 'handful of persons'. 'The Robbins Report', p. 182.

p. 116–7 'and advance knowledge'. Ibid., p. 170.

5. Sold Out

p. 121 'higher education institutions'. Paul Fain, 'The Results Are in: Harkin Releases Critical Report on For-profits', *Inside Higher Ed*, 30 July 2012.

p. 121 'unfamiliar with the product.' Andrew McGettigan, *The Great University Gamble: Money, Markets and the Future of Higher Education* (London: Pluto, 2013), p. 104.

p. 122 'solution to their struggles'. Ibid., p. 103.

p. 123 'degrees and other qualifications'. 'Ten Notable Transactions in the UK Education Industry in 2012', meissa-limited.com, 30 January 2013.

p. 125 'to staggeringly wealthy'. D.D. Guttenplan, 'London College Steps Up to University Level', *New York Times*, 20 January 2013.

p. 127 'private equity backers'. McGettigan, *The Great University Gamble*, p. 107.

p. 128 'application being received'. Ibid., p. 98.

p. 128 'degree-awarding powers'. Ibid., p. 135.

p. 128 'sector as "treasure island"'. Matt Robb, 'Here be Treasure', *Times Higher Education*, 12 May 2011.

p. 129 'into the new terrain'. McGettigan, *The Great University Gamble*, p. 97.

p. 129 'into the system'. David Willetts, speech to Universities UK, February 2011, quoted in McGettigan, *The Great University Gamble*, p. 97.

p. 131 'plans for the future'. Quoted in John Morgan, 'Company Policy: Where Uclan Restructure Plans Lead, Post-1992s May Follow', *Times Higher Education*, 22 November 2012.

p. 132 'the university will lose'. *Newham Recorder*, 23 June 2012; John Morgan, 'Mediterranean Retreat', *Times Higher Education*, 4 April 2013.

p. 133 'has certainly abrogated' ... 'commerce into universities'. McGettigan, *The Great University Gamble*, pp. 142, 114.

p. 133 'public funding per student' ... 'in higher education'. Roger Brown with Helen Carasso, *Everything for Sale? The Marketisation of UK Higher Education* (Abingdon: Routledge, 2013), pp. 81, 163.

p. 135 'and vice versa'. Ibid., p. 142.

p. 138 'national economic interest'. Ibid., p. 162.

p. 143 'by later regulations'. *Student Loans: A Guide to Terms and Conditions 2012–13* (Student Finance England).

p. 144 'one of the proposals'. Nicolas Watt and Patrick Wintour, 'Spending Review: How George Osborne Quelled Coalition Dissent', *Guardian*, 27 June 2013.

p. 146–7 'becomes a chimera'. McGettigan, *The Great University Gamble*, p. 176.

p. 147 'expose the majority'. Ibid., p. 185.

p. 147 'may also damage quality' ... 'every comparable system'. Brown, *Everything for Sale?*, pp. 125, 126.

p. 148 'the cost of joining'. Paul Jump, 'Quartet Pay Hefty Admission Fee to Join Elite Club', *Times Higher Education*, 30 May 2013.

p. 148 'we need to consider' ... 'higher education system'. Brown, *Everything for Sale?*, pp. 166, 168.

p. 149–50 'sector since 1992'. Ibid., p. 169.

p. 150 'annual grant letter'. Ibid., p. 57.

p. 150–1 'The changes to the RAE' ... 'actually counter-productive'. Ibid., pp. 53, 159.

p. 152–3 'most radical anywhere'. Ibid., p. 1.

p. 153 'higher education system'. Ibid., p. 179.

p. 153 'An experiment is being' ... 'value for money'. McGettigan, *The Great University Gamble*, pp. 2, 10.

p. 153 'system as a whole'. Quoted in Brown, *Everything for Sale?*, p. 129.

6. Higher Purchase

p. 155 'practical, of morality'. Alasdair MacIntyre, *After Virtue: A Study in Moral Theory* (London: Duckworth, 1981), pp. 1–2.

p. 159 'what employers want'. Robert-Jay Curry, 'Green Paper Blog: What is Going On?', 24 November 2015, at thestudentsunion.co.uk. The Green Paper, published November 2015, is available at gov.uk.

p. 160 'the job is not yet complete'. *Fulfilling Our Potential*, p. 8.

p. 161 'in line with inflation' ... 'the TEF level awarded'. Ibid., pp. 19, 30, 29.

p. 165 'how robust they are'. Ibid., p. 34.

p. 166 'employer/professional representatives'. Ibid., p. 28.

p. 167 'outcomes of graduates'. Ibid., p. 31.

p. 170 'This would be the first' ... 'employers and taxpayers'. Ibid., pp. 58, 62.

p. 170–1 'for BIS ministers' ... 'overarching body'. Ibid., pp. 59, 71.

p. 171 'the good of the UK'. Pallab Ghosh, 'Nurse Review Proposes Single Agency for UK Science Funding', bbc.co.uk, 19 November 2015.

p. 171 'would be George Osborne'. David Matthews, 'Nurse Review: Fears Over Greater Political Control of Research', *Times Higher Education*, 25 November 2015.

p. 172 'quality education providers'. *Fulfilling Our Potential*, p. 50.

p. 172 'innovation and diversity' ... 'wholly-owned subsidiary'. Ibid., pp. 13, 46, 51.

p. 173 'expense of other institutions'. Ibid., p. 54.

p. 174 'some in the sector'. Ibid., p. 72.

p. 175 'we must ... address' ... 'introduction of impact'. Ibid., pp. 73, 72.

7. The 'English Problem' and the Scottish Solution

p. 187 'for inhibiting innovation'. *Building a Smarter Future: Towards a Sustainable Scottish Solution for the Future of Higher Education* (2010), p. 40; available at gov.scot.

p. 188 'in the Green Paper'. Ibid., p. 42.

p. 188 'for determining excellence'. Ibid., p. 13.

p. 188–9 'for the real thing', Roger Brown, ed., *Higher Education and the Market* (London: Routledge, 2011).

p. 190 'to "national priorities"'. *Building a Smarter Future*, p. 18.

p. 190 'wake of the REF'. Ibid., p. 19.

p. 191 *'The Democratic Intellect'*. George Elder Davie, *The Democratic Intellect: Scotland and her Universities in the Nineteenth Century* (Edinburgh: Edinburgh University Press, 1961).

p. 192 'lie with the state'. *Building a Smarter Future*, p. 33.

8. Public Higher Education

p. 198 'public trust in science'. Philip Moriarty, 'Science as a Public Good', in John Holmwood, ed., *A Manifesto for the Public University* (London: Bloomsbury, 2011), p. 69.

p. 198 'are mutually compatible'. 'The *Lancet*'s Policy on Conflict of Interests', *The Lancet*, 363 (2004), quoted in Holmwood, *Manifesto*, p. 71.

p. 200 'powers of the mind'. 'The Robbins Report', pp. 6–7.

p. 201 'education in this country?'. Ibid., p. 228.

p. 201 'learning and the arts'. Ibid., p. 251.

p. 202 'particularly regretted'. Susan Howson, *Lionel Robbins* (Cambridge: Cambridge University Press, 2011), Ch. 23.

9. Speaking Out

p. 208 'analysis of the category'. Michael Warner, *Publics and Counter-publics* (New York: Zone Books, 2002).

p. 208–9 'rate of income tax'. Collini, *What Are Universities For?*, pp. 96–7.

p. 210 'something of that kind'. For an analysis of the difficulties with this kind of survey see Stefan Collini, *Common Writing: Essays on Literary Culture and Public Debate* (Oxford: Oxford University Press, 2016), Ch. 13.

p. 213 'repeat and repeat'. Howard Hotson, 'Don't Look to the Ivy League', *London Review of Books*, 19 May 2011; 'Short Cuts: For-Profit Universities', *London Review of Books*, 2 June 2011.

p. 217–20 'its principal direct purpose'. Although I nowhere identified the university or the report in question during the original lecture and I do not do so in the text of this chapter, the quoted passages are drawn from *Humanities Graduates and the British Economy: The Hidden Impact* (Humanities Division, Oxford University, July 2013).

11. Who Does the University Belong To?

p. 236–8 'university in 1901'. My interest in the façade of the Great Hall was initially stimulated by a visit to the University of Birmingham in 2010; my account of the relevant discussions is largely taken from Eric Ives et al., *The First Civic University: Birmingham, 1880–1980* (Birmingham: University of Birmingham, 2000), quotations at pp. 12–13, 118–20.

p. 244 'and Johan Huizinga'. The jurist Hugo Grotius (1583–1645) and the historian Johan Huizinga (1872–1945) are among the most distinguished figures to have taught at Leiden University.

Appendix: Short Work

p. 250 'and unwarranted conclusion'. Simon Jenkins, 'Universities Need the Guts to Break this Faustian Pact with Research', *Guardian*, 15 March 2012.

p. 253 'Mr Cameron's "Big Society"'. 'Academic Fury Over Order to Study the Big Society', *Observer*, 27 March 2011; 'Row Over Research Funding and David Cameron's Big Society', *Observer*, 3 April 2011.

p. 272 'towards a graduate tax'. *Times Higher Education*, 5 December 2013.

p. 272–3 'direction of their research'. Liam Byrne, 'Winning the Race to the Top: Labour and the Scientific Revolution 50 Years On', Institute for Public Policy Research speech, 9 December 2013.

p. 285 'really addressing the problem'. 'Tuition Fees: Labour Pledges Maximum Cap of £6,000', bbc.co.uk, 25 September 2011.

p. 285 'focus on the possibilities'. 'Jeremy Corbyn Announces £10bn Plan to Scrap University Tuition Fees', *Guardian*, 15 July 2015.